KAREEM

KAREEM

Kareem Abdul-Jabbar
with Mignon McCarthy

Random House
New York

Grateful acknowledgment is made to Fort Knox Music, Inc., for permission to reprint an
excerpt from "Maybe the Last Time" by Ted Wright. Copyright © 1965 by Fort Knox
Music, Inc., and Trio Music Co., Inc. All rights reserved. Used by permission.

Library of Congress Cataloging-in-Publication Data
Abdul-Jabbar, Kareem
Kareem / Kareem Abdul-Jabbar.
p.   cm.
ISBN 0-394-55927-4
1. Abdul-Jabbar, Kareem. 2. Basketball players—United
States—Biography. 3. National Basketball Association. I. Title.
GV884.A24A3 1990
796.323′092—dc20
[B]   89-28067

Manufactured in the United States of America
24689753
First Edition

Book design by Bernard Klein

In the name of Allah, the compassionate,
the merciful

Sic transit gloria mundi.

Athletes die twice.

—JACKIE ROBINSON

Bunbu itchi.
Pen and sword in accord.
—MIYAMOTO MUSASHI

Writin' is fightin'.
—ISHMAEL REED

Contents

Prologue:
Beginnings and
Endings

I'm on the red-eye to New York, after a game at home against Portland. It's two weeks into the season, and we won tonight's game by a point. I slipped out of the Forum early, up through the arena's truck tunnel and out onto Ninetieth Street, and took my private back-street route through the flats of Inglewood west to the airport, just a few miles away. The Forum lies directly underneath the flight path to LAX, so I watched one plane after another drop out of the sky ahead of me as I made my way on the streets below. It was a cool, moist fall night and there was a certain joy in making a deft getaway from the hot lights of the Forum into the anonymity of my car and the evening darkness. I made it to the gate just in time and the doors of the airplane closed some minutes after ten o'clock. An auspicious departure.

The cabin is quiet, but sleep doesn't come easily. Long ago, I trained myself to sleep on planes. It's a discipline like meditation is a discipline. You cover yourself in a blanket, head and all, and surrender. Three hours of airplane sleep may be worth only one hour of real sleep, but you can't exist in the NBA unless you master this skill. Napping, whenever possible, is an integral part of your job when you're a professional basketball player.

But tonight I'm fully awake. My mind continues to roam long after the adrenaline left over from the game has subsided and long after leaving Los Angeles behind. I won't see home again for ten days. This is the first long road trip of the season. It's rare, very rare, for me to be traveling alone without the team, who will follow on Monday, but I wanted a day to myself in New York before any obligations, before any press conferences, and before Tuesday night, when we play the Knicks in Madison Square Garden and when my farewell tour begins. There will be good-bye ceremonies in every city we play before the season ends. New York's will be the first, L.A.'s the last.

Ten years ago, the idea of a farewell tour would have been inconceivable. I probably would have slipped out the back door the way I slipped out of the locker room and out of Los Angeles tonight. For so long, all the attention, even the praise, was like a storm to get out of. I tried to win games, not trophies for myself. But I'm more comfortable taking center stage now, and it's a chance for the fans and me to communicate with each other for a few minutes. That's something we don't get to do as players; normally, our contact with the crowd is fleeting. We leave the court immediately after the game is over, however magnificent it may have been. As athletes, like actors on a stage, we are taught not to acknowledge the audience. It's ironic that I, a lone ranger of sorts, will make such a public exit from the game this year, such a public passage from one life to the next. I hope I make it gracefully. During the summer I looked ahead to this year of rituals and good-byes with fear and trepidation. Now I'm glad it's finally here.

New York will be emotional, an intense good-bye, because it was home. It's a fitting place for the farewells to begin because it's where my life began, and where I learned to play basketball. I learned to compete there. I learned about winning there. New York was the best school for basketball you could ever go to. I once dreamed of going back to play, but it didn't work out that way. Now this will be the last time I play in New York or in the Garden. I don't know what to expect from the fans. Through high school, I was a favorite son, but after leaving to play college basketball in Los Angeles and then professional basketball in Milwaukee, I became a villain in the Garden, for so many years the enfant terrible of the NBA as far as New York fans were concerned. The memories are passionate. My youth in New York is definitely long ago and far away, but it's still in me.

It's hard for me to comprehend that my last season is finally here. I have played organized basketball since I was eight years old. I was eight years old and five feet four and the pattern of my life was set. For thirty-three years, I have operated on the time clock and within the structure and order of the basketball season. It's a serious change coming up. It's as if I have survived the whole cycle, life and death, and here I still am. I never thought it would turn out this way. Every summer in college, I would tell myself that I'd play four or five years, make a million, and retire to the Caribbean.

I never thought when I started out that I would end up playing basketball longer than anyone has ever played the game before.

I have just stretched the records out so far now. I've been the oldest player for five years. I've held the scoring record for five years. I am out here in completely virgin territory.

All the guys who broke in with me are now gone. I can remember, very keenly, being a rookie and wondering what guys did after playing professional ball for ten years. Now, here I am, all lined up to go for my twentieth season.

On the Laker media guide this year, there's a color photograph of my locker in the team's dressing room. Hanging in the stall are my number 33 jersey, my warm-ups, goggles, laundry bag, and crowded up on the shelf a few old albums by Monk and Coltrane, a copy of *Giant Steps,* and even a book by Raymond Chandler, one of my favorite L.A. writers, whose hardened but virtuous hero never gets the girl, never has a private life, but tries to do some good in a corrupt world. They got everything in this picture except me. When they shot it at the end of last season, I had already left for my place in Hawaii. It seems a fitting absence now. Next summer, I will be in Hawaii again, my version of the Caribbean, and I really will be gone. I'll be turning the corner of the decade into the nineties without basketball and without the company of my teammates. This is the last season of the eighties. And this is the last season that we will all play together, James, Byron, Coop, Earvin, and me. This is the end of an era with this team.

I don't think it's too late. I don't think it's too early. This is the right time.

There are no more heights to scale, except for this final season. And we'll see what the season has in store. People around the game will make their predictions—they're already saying we won't make it out of the West. But the players know that each season is a new canvas, a new page to be written on. The real fans, the hard-core cognoscenti, know that too, and they will let the season unfold.

I will be under scrutiny this year as I make my final rounds. You're not supposed to play basketball when you're forty-two. I will be tested, and the team will be tested. You don't go for the triple crown in obscurity. Portland played us tough tonight, almost taking the game away from us, but we know to expect that. Last season, when we were the world champions going for two in a row, everybody was playing us tough. Against the champs, everybody's game goes up a notch. Opponents often play their best game of the season against us. You're out there playing against all that adrenaline every night, and contemplating a whole season of such nights can be daunting. So we know we'll be tested again this year, but the knowing is an advantage for us, and we'll go a game at a time.

I don't know how it's going to end, but it's going to end.

"We may not win, but let's make it worthy of us"—words from John Wooden.

Amir, my youngest son, came into the dressing room after the game tonight to say a quick good-bye. It was his birthday today. He turned eight. Another cycle—the cycle of generations.

We'll be away a hundred of two hundred nights this season.

Sunday, November 20

We got into New York at dawn yesterday. I took a cab to the Carlyle on the Upper East Side and slept most of the day. I like the Carlyle. It's quiet and has twenty-four-hour room service. Then, this morning, a limo picked me up at the hotel at ten o'clock and we headed uptown with a small film crew to shoot some footage for a retrospective I had been asked to do. This was our one day to shoot since I won't be back to New York again this season, but with the morning had come a downpour of heavy, persistent rain. This was no ordinary late-November eastern storm. Three inches of rain would cover Manhattan before nightfall. The film people seemed morose, but had to seize the time. For me, the dark sky provided a comfortable, evocative backdrop for returning to the places of my past, my old childhood haunts. I settled into the back of the limousine.

We headed up Madison Avenue and past 110th Street, the demarcation line for Harlem, which sprawls northward for about fifty blocks. I was born in Harlem and lived with my parents on 111th Street, just a block from Central Park, until I was three years old. Harlem wasn't paradise then, but neither was it the war zone it is today. Before my time, in the twenties, thirties, and early forties, Harlem *had* been a kind of paradise, an exuberant and flourishing black metropolis. I thought about that and about Harlem's three hundred years of complex history as we crossed over to the West Side and continued upward on Amsterdam Avenue through Harlem.

Our first stop was the Battlegrounds in Sugar Hill. The sign on the corner of 152nd Street says "Carmansville Playground," but to us it was always called the Battlegrounds, where, during all the time I was growing up, playground players waged some serious on-court warfare. Once I got mobile, from the seventh grade on, I came down to the Battlegrounds on the IRT and honed my game here. With the guys in the neighborhood, this is where I first really started playing competitive basketball. A lot of people would come by and watch us play, and it was very important to look good out there in front of the folks. You learned the importance of face. On weekends and in the summers, we would spend a good part of the day here—me, Sonny Johnson, Gay Brown, Busby, Tyrone—and then we'd walk about six blocks uptown to see who was at Roy's, a little coffee shop with a hip jukebox. It used to be on St. Nick just around the corner from P.S. 28, another asphalt playground where we liked to go. We all traveled with our own basketballs. We went everywhere. Tyrone (whom we used to call Spareribs because he was so skinny) and I used to baby-sit sometimes for Monk's drummer, Ben Riley, who lived in Tyrone's building. Then, when Ben's wife came home from work, we'd go down to one of the clubs and catch Monk, Thelonious Sphere Monk. Jazz and basketball began to lace themselves inextricably together in my life during this early period. My passion for music came first because of my father's passion for music. He was studying at Juilliard on the G.I. Bill when I was still in my mother's womb, from where I have no doubt I heard him practice his classical and jazz trombone. I have never not been surrounded by such sounds. They were taken for granted in our home, and also in the city, especially Harlem, where you could take your pick of what you wanted to hear. It was a luxurious time for a boy, all that creative improvisational genius around, in the jazz clubs and in the city playgrounds, where the elite worked on their manhood and immortality playing the highest caliber of competitive playground basketball.

I first saw Wilt Chamberlain on the playground when I was fifteen and he was twenty-five. I was a freshman in high school, six feet ten inches tall, and he was seven feet. I never would have had the nerve to go up and introduce myself, but my friend Wesley Carpenter initiated a meeting. That was when he had the Bentley and the racehorses and every beautiful woman in Manhattan, and we became friends for a while. I used to borrow his jazz records. He was a brilliant soloist on the asphalt and as a pro used to play in the Rucker Tournament in Harlem, which was a summer-long meeting ground for professional players and uptown playground types. Thousands would turn up to watch, lining the court ten deep and climbing the trees to get a look. I always had a spot.

Earl Monroe was another demigod who used to show up at Rucker. They called him Black Jesus back then, and I remember the first time I saw him play he wore one white low-cut and one black high-top. In the first play of the game, he got a rebound on the defensive end of the court and started spinning. Man, he spun four times and was ninety feet from the hoop! On the fourth spin he threw the ball in a hook motion, and it bounced at midcourt and then just rose and fell into the hands of another guy, who was running full speed at the other end, and caught it in stride and laid it in. A full-court bounce pass! After I saw that I understood all the Black Jesus stuff. I didn't find out the dude's real name until way later. After I joined the pros, Earl and I reminisced and laughed about those days.

Then there was Hawk, Connie Hawkins, a legend in New York, who took on Wilt in a titanic battle at Rucker. He was the greatest I ever saw on the playground, like Doctor J before Doctor J. He did things on the court that no one had even thought of doing before. He showed me what great athletic talent applied to the game of basketball could do. He was one of the first with huge hands who could glide and swoop and dunk and stuff all kinds of ways. He'd tantalize you. I watched his moves, his bursts of inspired improvisation, and received revelations about the game. Hawk represented an entire subculture of competition and playground excellence that was part of my adolescence in New York.

Because of the rain, the Battlegrounds was empty. It had an abandoned look, the wire fence, the wet blacktop, the bare rims on the backboards, no nets. There are never any nets in inner-city playgrounds. I got out and walked into the courtyard. The driver had handed me a big black umbrella and I was wearing my long black overcoat. It must have cut a moody scene. I had been back about ten years ago with Tyrone, but this time it was more shocking somehow. Just that extra decade in there—as you pull away in time, the place gets smaller. It hasn't changed that much, and neither has the neighborhood—but it's gone further and further away from what I remember. I spent hundreds of hours here under the hoops, sometimes even in winter. The serious ballplayers played fifty-two weeks a year, which would be true for me later in the pros. Playing pickup or playing alone, many older players now say that when younger they imagined themselves into the skin of one of their heroes. I had my heroes then, but for some reason I never made believe I was anybody else when I played. I was always just me.

We drove through the rest of Sugar Hill, passing the cemetery at Trinity Church, the largest cemetery in Manhattan. My friends and I used to go in there and read the tombstones of the Astors and Van Burens and other historic New York families who used to live the sweet life in Sugar Hill brownstones. John James Audubon, the naturalist, had had a huge estate along the Hudson River, and he was buried in that cemetery too. My friends used to drink wine and smoke reefer in there, but I was 100 percent clean. My parents had really done a good job. I managed to cop a smooch or two in that cemetery, but that was about it.

From inside the car I kept wiping the moisture that was fogging up the window, looking out as we traveled block after block of these streets that I had traveled so well and so long ago. I knew all this real estate.

I remember going uptown a few years ago to a black bookstore to replace some of the books I had lost in the fire. From midtown, I took the subway up and back and nobody recognized me. You know how you can fit in sometimes? It was comfortable. I fell into an old rhythm.

We passed the movie theater where, because of my height, I had to bring my birth certificate to prove I was only eleven. And then we hit Inwood on the northernmost tip of the island, where I lived from age three until I left for college at eighteen.

Inwood is a strange little place, insulated, with water on three sides, the Hudson River to the west, the Harlem River to the east, and a ship canal above. It has the wildest acres in Manhattan, lots of green wooded parkland and rocky hills. We used to find arrowheads and musket balls in Fort Washington and Fort Tryon parks. It is still the only part of virgin forest left in New York.

We drove to Nagle Avenue, where I lived in Building Five of the Dyckman Street projects. It was a two-bedroom apartment up on the fifth floor, and my parents had one bedroom and I had the other. This was middle-income housing, city-owned, which had issued from the massive public-housing scheme of the late and debatably great Robert Moses. You used to be fined $2 for walking on the grass. The subway, which was elevated in Inwood, ran right down Nagle Avenue, right by our building. I remember its sounds, at all times of day or night, and I also remember the sounds of Pontiacs wrapping themselves around the support poles for the tracks in the middle of the street. When my mother's Boston relatives came for a visit once, it took eight or nine days before they could sleep with the trains going by. To me, it was never a problem. Having the El out the door was good because it meant transportation was good. You could just hop on the train. You could really get around. As I grew older, I made full use of that mobility, down to Harlem, to high school, to the Village—to anywhere, it seemed.

The Dyckman projects have been devasted by the same crack epidemic that has devasted New York, but in my time it was a great environment to grow up in. We had the whole world in that project. We had immigrants from China, Russia, England, Scandinavia, Cuba. There were gypsies, Jews, West Indians, and American blacks. It was a cosmopolitan, multiethnic enclave. I got to play with kids of every description. It gave me an enduring tolerance and appreciation of differences, and an early awareness of how big the world was and how wide the range of human experience. Our world view was a very broad one. It wasn't until I was about eight, Amir's age now, that the first stings of racism began to penetrate my young consciousness. All during the years I was progressing through grade school, my parents talked openly in our home about what was going on with blacks in the South. My best friend from the projects, Johnny Harrison, who was white, eventually hung out only with his white friends, and the racism that separated us, a prejudice bigger than both of us, culminated in an incident in the seventh grade in which one day after school he screamed at me, "Hey, nigger, you big jungle nigger!" Turning my prideful ice on him, something I'd had to learn how to do, I sloughed him off with, "Fuck you, milk bottle," the only white thing I could think of to say. We never spoke again.

After Dyckman, we made two final stops in the limo, at P.S. 52 and at St. Jude's, the two elementary schools in my neighborhood around which revolve my earliest basketball memories. We were a few hours into our tour, and the rain continued to fall.

P.S. 52, a five-story red-brick public school, looked from the outside as I remembered it, with the two large doors leading right off the street at ground level straight into the gym. It was in this gym that I first picked up a basketball and first started putting it in the hoop. That was the summer between first and second grade. The gym would open up early in the morning and I'd sneak in before the big kids arrived. Nobody would be in there but me. I was deeply intrigued with getting the ball in the basket. My whole young concept was to see if I could get the ball up to the rim. I had no upper-body strength and the ball was bigger around than my chest. I was only a little taller than average then, and a lot skinnier. But I would try morning in and morning out to get one through, and every now and then, miraculously, I'd bang one up against the backboard and it would go in, somehow.

It was Sunday, so the school was all locked up, and we expected the same at St. Jude's, another red-brick building, though smaller and with a cross above the entrance. But as we stood outside on the sidewalk in the rain, one of our group, an Irish Catholic, went idly poking around and found that the main door was open. I went to school there up through the eighth grade, with one year's interruption halfway through to attend an all-black boarding school outside of Philadelphia for reasons my parents never made clear to me. It was the best of times at St. Jude's—St. Jude, the patron saint of hopeless cases, the patron saint of the impossible. I had been past the school a number of times over the years, but hadn't been inside the building since I graduated more than twenty-five years ago. It was an unexpected emotional experience.

I walked into the small front lobby, the chapel to my left, the doors to the gym straight ahead. I stepped inside. It was exactly the same. I remembered *all* of it. The baskets at either end of the court, the wooden backboards, the letters sj in the circle at center court. I looked down to the basket where I first leapt toward the hoop and dunked a basketball.

I was thirteen. It was during a game early in the eighth grade and our guard Patrick Dourish flipped me a real nice pass on the fast break. The ball came into my hands and I was able to jam it. I think I was as shocked as everybody else. A moment of elation on the court I have never forgotten.

A lot of sports in the neighborhood revolved around this gym. We used to watch the Golden Gloves fights from the inside second-story windows up above the floor, where the nuns, a semicloistered order, used to watch our games. The gym was also used for mass, so for practices after school and for games at night we'd have to tear down and set up six hundred chairs, along with kneelers eight feet long. The custodian, Mr. Kelly, used to let me come in at odd hours and practice because he knew I'd be conscientious about putting the chairs back and not screwing up the arrangement for mass. Sometimes a benediction or novena would be going on in the little chapel on the other side of the gym wall during a tight game with a team like Good Shepherd, which was the rival parish next door, and Father Burns would send out an altar boy to somehow quell the din, requesting that the cheerleaders cheer more softly or the refs blow their whistles more lightly. I used to serve mass occasionally with Cardinal Cooke back when he was Father Cooke and helping out St. Jude's on weekends. Father Tubridy, who was six feet three, would lend me his cassock, but I still looked as if someone had chopped the skirt off the bottom. I was six-eight by the time I left St. Jude's at age fourteen.

As I stepped out onto the court, feeling as if I were stepping back in time, a nun I'd never seen before came up to me and warmly introduced herself as Sister Kathleen, the school's principal now. She invited me to take a look around and offered to open up the upstairs if I'd like to see any of my old classrooms. After a moment's hesitation, I said yes. We went up the stairs together to the corridor of classrooms on the second floor, a statue at either end of the long hall. This was serious memory lane. On the classroom doors were the same saints' names that were there when I was there, Saint Bernadette, Saint Dominic, Saint John. Saint Bernadette had been sixth grade, taught to us by Sister Mary Sebastian, and I remembered the famous incident when Michael Farrell got real snotty with her and she had to punch him out. I got real good grades in conduct that year. There was no way I was going to cross her up.

From the upstairs classroom windows you could see the El going by, and also the red-tile roof of the Cloisters, the medieval-period stone monastery and museum in one of the parks overlooking the Hudson nearby. Like the neighborhood, St. Jude's was surrounded by the mundane and the sublime. The sublime out my window in second grade, a room halfway down the hall, was my glimpse one spring day of the top of Willie Mays's head as he played stickball down below in the street in front of the school. My desk was next to the open window and the noise from outside had caught my attention. I clamored to be let out, but Miss Doyle failed to understand. It was the only time he ever showed up. It was the closest to him I ever got.

Sister Alacoque's room was at the end of the hall. She taught me in seventh and eighth grade and had that rare inner light that you never forget. My chair, in the last row along the wall, looked like it had never been moved. The same long pole that opened and closed the windows was hanging in the usual spot, as was the cross above the blackboard in the front of the room.

We retraced our steps, and at the bottom of the stairs, in the shadows of the smaller school lobby, I spied the display case that in my last year at St. Jude's held that first trophy. Eddie Clark, Joe Heffernan, and I played in a three-man city tournament in Central Park and we won it for all of upper Manhattan. We brought the trophy back to St. Jude's. It was the first for the school and the first for me, the most special and pure moment that I can remember from my career. After that first thrill, that flush of pride at having had something to do with putting a trophy behind glass, after that you lose a little each time. At the sight of the display case now, I smiled. It was empty except for a vase of flowers.

St. Jude's was the perfect training ground for the realities of competition. Except for our one laurel, we didn't win anything in the first eight years of the school's history. Later, in high school and in college, I experienced the romance of dramatic winning—in my last six years of amateur varsity basketball, my teams lost only three games! That was unreality. When I finally entered the pros and we'd lose two, three, or four games in a row, it was like coming back to normal, like returning to my humble beginnings in grammar school. You won't win until you learn how to lose. I don't like to do it, to lose, but I can stand it. Along with everything else, you have to acquire the ability to accept defeat. No one makes it without stumbling.

I wore number 5 on my jersey until our coach, Mr. Hopkins, managed to get us new uniforms in the seventh grade. After that and ever since, I have worn number 33. That was the number then of one of my favorite football players, Mel Triplett, of the New York Giants. I had consulted my mother, who gave a measure of mystical credence to numerology. She said she figured that thirty-three would be a good number for me to wear. Was it prophetic? By the end of this, my last season, I will have played thirty-three years of organized hoops.

I started playing team basketball in the fourth grade, during that one year when I was away at Holy Providence in the outskirts of Philadelphia. Holy Providence didn't even have a gym and they probably wouldn't even have had a basketball program if it hadn't been for one of the local Catholic laymen, Mr. Duke, who would come and take us in his car to the gym of a seminary nearby. Everyone, it seems, was aware of my potential except me. I took part in the sport mostly as a means of getting off the school grounds for a couple of hours. When I returned to New York in the fifth grade, Mr. Hopkins encouraged me to try out for St. Jude's team.

Farrell Hopkins was my first coach. He has told me since that when I came in to say hello to him in September of eighth grade and had to duck under the door to his office because I'd grown two or three inches over the summer, he said privately to himself, "Oh, shit, every team is going to be trying to kill us now. We'll *have* to be great. I won't have time to go to the bathroom. They're going to crucify me. They're going to beat my brains in, and his too. Now I've got to work with him." At St. Jude's, it was one of those situations where Farrell coached everything, not just basketball, and then I came along with all my difference. We would have talks and he'd tell me, "They're going to make fun of you. They're going to call you names. Practice your foul shots, because they're going to foul you constantly!"

Farrell had an old beat-up car, a two-door 210 Chevy with a two-by-four holding up the front seat. We used to get the whole team—and we're talking about eleven kids—in Farrell's car, and that's how we'd show up at games. We'd all fit somehow, eight in the backseat and five with Farrell up front, just feeling so proud riding with our coach.

One night we were coming back from the Kennedy Center in Harlem when Farrell mistakenly went the wrong way up a one-way street.

We got stopped by a cop, who looked in the window and saw that Farrell had too many kids in the car. Farrell said, in his New York Irish voice, "Officer, we just came out of the gym there. We won the game and we want to get home."

"Okay, all right, back up," the cop said.

But the brakes on Farrell's car were stripped. "I don't know how to tell you this, officer, but I don't have no reverse."

As far as safety and having a million kids in the car and going the wrong way, there was too much the policeman would have had to write Farrell up for. It was like a death trap. "Mac, just go straight ahead," he said, defeated by all our earnestness.

I was at an age when my awkwardness could have been a trademark, but Farrell gave me a confidence well beyond my abilities then just by letting me know he was going to care about me no matter what. He was in a position to have a positive influence on a lot of kids, and he did. Farrell loved sports and he loved kids; he had four of his own and at one time he had ten when he took in his brother's kids for a while. In his twenties, Farrell's great ambition had been to be Athletic Director of Notre Dame. Now in his fifties, after a career of being sidelined by a vocation of working with hard-core adolescents in the city, troubled, abused, poor, and even middle-class kids because they too can be forgotten, he says that in his mind he's still Athletic Director of Notre Dame, only back here, where he always wanted to be.

A few summers ago, I had the occasion to see Farrell and also Father Tubridy. We had a good chuckle about Father Tubridy's having mentioned to Farrell those many years ago that he was glad I was a good student since, being so skinny, I probably wouldn't make it as a basketball player.

The tour was over. Sister Kathleen asked me if I'd sign one of the backboards in the gym before I left. Sister Kathleen was a class lady. She didn't seem to care that I was an excommunicant. I stood up on a milk crate that somebody grabbed from the school cafeteria and wrote in big black letters under the hoop, "Go, St. Jude's! Best wishes, Abdul-Jabbar, St. Jude '61."

We headed back down to midtown on Harlem River Drive, which was wet and slick from the rain.

The site of the old Polo Grounds, where the baseball Giants used to have their stadium, came into view, the crest of Coogan's Bluff climbing west above it from where you can see across the Harlem River to the Bronx. I can remember walking down to the Polo Grounds when

I was a boy. But the ballpark isn't there anymore and hasn't been for years. It was torn down shortly after they tore down Ebbets Field in the late fifties, using the same wrecking ball. I was ten when the Giants and the Dodgers left New York.

Before basketball, baseball was my first and most passionate love. And it was something that I pursued all the time, never missing an opportunity to play stickball or hardball, or to listen to Red Barber on Dodger radio. I started listening to the games on radio in 1950 with my mother and sometimes my father if he didn't have to work. I remember Bobby Thomson hitting that home run off Ralph Branca in 1951. That snatched everybody's heart out of their chest. It gave the Giants the pennant that year, and Dodger fans were crushed. Everybody was calling it "the tragedy at Coogan's Bluff."

Baseball in New York was glorious then, with Willie, Mickey, and the Duke. The Duke batted left-handed for the Dodgers, Willie Mays right-handed for the Giants, and Mickey Mantle switch-hit for the Yankees. It was some kind of perfection. Three center fielders who everyone knew were future Hall of Famers on three big-league teams in the Bronx, Harlem, and Brooklyn. The rivalries were intense. Who you rooted for was part of your identity, like your religion or your nationality.

My father had been raised in Brooklyn, so, in spite of the Giants being in our backyard and the Yankees not much farther away, we were serious Dodger fans. That made living in my neighborhood tough at times, taking a whole lot of crap from a whole lot of people. I endured it, though. I had a Dodger cap that I wore everywhere through maybe second grade, and when the "B" fell off I cried. When he could, my father would take me to games at Ebbets Field, the Dodgers' tiny wooden stadium on Bedford and Flatbush in Brooklyn. We didn't go a lot, but enough that I remember what seemed like a million trolley tracks crossing each other on Flatbush. The ballpark was old, odd-shaped, and idiosyncratic, even back then, but it seemed like a green cathedral to me. I saw the Duke, Edwin "Duke" Snider, and Jackie Robinson play there. The summer of '56, after the team won their first World Series championship ever and the only one they would ever win in Brooklyn, I took some pictures, including one of the Duke. About ten years ago, shortly after he was inducted into the Hall of Fame, I saw him at an old-timers' game at Dodger Stadium. I showed him that picture and told him I had taken it, and that I had been nine then. He was stunned. He didn't realize how far back it went with me.

I used to dream about playing on the Dodgers, even in my first few

years of playing basketball. My size hadn't become a major factor in
my life yet, and I had my eyes on the pitching mound or first base.
Pitching was the one thing in baseball at which I had a serious talent.
There was only one problem, a problem all pitchers must master—
control. I had a nasty curve and a very fast fastball, but getting it over
the plate was many times an iffy situation. I can remember seeing some
parents cringing as their sons in the batter's box ducked and leaped
away from some of the heat I was throwing.

In the seventh grade I was no longer eligible for Little League, so
I played for St. Jude's team. I pitched a game that we won 8–6. It was
a no-hitter; the other team scored its runs on walks and passed balls—a
very unstable life for a pitcher.

It was that summer that I grew so many inches and started at least
to *look* like a basketball player. I started to be able to do things like
palm a basketball and touch the rim, and it was soon obvious that the
long frame could be put to use in places other than the baseball
diamond. Around this same time, one event changed my view of
basketball and how to play it dramatically. I went to see a high school
all-star game at the Brownsville Boys Club in Brooklyn. Guys like
Connie Hawkins, Roger Brown, Billy Burwell, and other All-City players were on the court doing their thing, and I was awestruck. I had
never seen people dunk and soar and change direction in midstride the
way these guys did. This was before I saw the Hawk on the Harlem
playgrounds. The warm-up was awe-inspiring, and I feel that evening
in Brooklyn changed my concept forever of what is possible on the
court. Baseball would remain close to my heart, but here was a game
that was best played by individuals with *my* physical attributes. The
possibilities seemed endless.

I still miss Willie and the Duke.

Monday, November 21

By this morning the rain had stopped, but the temperature had
dropped, and it was cold. The team was arriving later in the day so I
had to pack my bag and switch over to the Hyatt, the team's hotel on
East Forty-second Street, next door to Grand Central Station. It used
to be the old Commodore Hotel. A car picked me up at the Carlyle
at ten and took me first to a one-hour press conference. Was I ready

for the forest of microphones and questions that I knew were waiting? I had to be. A whole season of them stretched out before me.

The press conference was scheduled down at the Garden, and as I entered through the players' entrance on Thirty-third Street, I noticed the street people. Madison Square Garden is built over Pennsylvania Station, the train tracks and also subway tracks running three levels down from the street. The homeless are living in Penn Station now, and in Grand Central too, New York's indoor Calcuttas. Everything is central and compact in New York. There's a lot of activity to live off of.

The press conference went easier than I expected. There's more press in New York, more powerful press, than in any other city in the league, and the room was full. I explained that L.A. is home now, New York no longer, but that there still is and always will be a lot of emotion associated with my hometown. Sam Goldaper of *The New York Times* was there. He has covered me since eighth grade at St. Jude's, back when he was writing for the *Herald Tribune*. He and I think Phil Pepe, now with the *Daily News*, wrote the first articles that introduced me to New York's sports pages. I was Lew Alcindor then.

When those first pieces were written, I was fourteen, living in the nation's largest city, the citadel then of both basketball and the media. That circumstance of fate forced me to grow up real fast. It feels sometimes like I went straight from being a kid to where I am now, and that I have been living under the glare of public scrutiny forever. The early notoriety pushed me inside myself. Vastly outgrowing my peers physically pushed me inside too. And I was put into the position of having attention focused on me, attention mainly unwanted, by the press, by strangers. I have always enjoyed my height—I view it as a gift—but there is a price you pay.

The first to put into words for me how the world alienates tall people was Joe Lapchick, a great coach and a great person, who left his stamp on New York basketball in his three decades with St. John's and with the Knicks. He's in the Hall of Fame now. Until I learned that he was going to retire the same year I graduated from high school, I had been giving serious thought to staying in New York to go to college at St. John's. Lapchick himself was tall, over six feet five. He had played center for the original Celtics. The world expects more from a giant, he told me. People scale up their demands. And since you are larger than life, you must somehow be less affected by it, as if it takes more noise to get your attention or more pain to hurt you.

I had gotten to know Coach Lapchick in high school. Jack Donahue, my high school coach, and he were close. Donahue admired him. We used to watch films of the St. John's games that Lapchick would send to Donahue. I became a fan. One summer, Coach Lapchick came to Donahue's camp on the Hudson up in Saugerties, New York. His son Richard was there. Then in his sixties, Lapchick talked to me about when he was a kid growing up in New York City, the son of Eastern European immigrants, and unusually tall. With his excessive height, people in the neighborhood who didn't know him would stop and stare, point and yell, "Look! A gypsy!" I could identify.

Early on, when I was the most impressionable, it was Jack Donahue and Joe Lapchick who made the important impression on me in basketball. Lapchick believed in basketball as a means to advance yourself and to forge some type of character as a human being. And Donahue expected your best and didn't let anyone get discouraged. That inspired combination is what keeps your pride alive and moving forward. Day in and day out for four years, I was in his coaching hands. If you didn't put out your maximum, no matter how badly or even how well you played, Donahue would needle you through benign but scalpel-precision humiliation. He needled you to total concentration. He was a great motivator. I had one bad experience with Donahue during a game one winter afternoon my junior year, when his generally well-intentioned humiliation turned racially misguided. Outwardly, not a lot changed in our relationship after that. But inwardly, it was never the same for me. A shard of distrust had entered in, and it is a wound that kind of sits there among the many other memories of those years. But as far as what Coach Donahue meant to my career in basketball, I learned the most about winning and about the game in high school with him.

High school basketball in New York was serious.

From my freshman year on, I was the starting varsity center for Power Memorial Academy, an all-boys Catholic high school downtown in the heart of Manhattan. It was about 150 blocks from Inwood, one subway ride. The school's building looked like a nineteenth-century sweatshop, a high-rise dungeon in the shadows of Lincoln Center; in fact, out my classroom windows I watched them build Lincoln Center. But it was a good atmosphere academically, which I liked because I was ambitious about my education. And Power had a great new gym, full court with six other baskets. I remember it well. I knew the gym even before I went to school there because during the winter it was open on Saturdays, and Art Kenney and I used to pack a lunch, take the IRT down from the projects, and stay there all day playing basketball. Kenney had been a year ahead of me at St. Jude's and preceded me to Power. I was still in eighth grade and he had already stepped up to ninth and onto Donahue's team.

When I got there myself the next year, I didn't know at the start if I had what it took to make it in high school basketball. I had the size but not the skills, and no clue that I would end up being any good at the game. Donahue threw me in with the varsity, and I guess that's how it began. Our first game of the year, my first ever in high school, we lost to Erasmus. It was a nightmare for me. This kid Charlie Donovan, an All-City guard, had killed me, making shots from out at half court and from under my armpits. In the locker room afterward, I cried with abandon, the child inside me coming out with all that emotion in the agony of defeat. I haven't taken a loss like that since.

I believe that I grew as a basketball player then by having no choice but to compete hard against the older, better varsity athletes. By sophomore year, I had grown to seven feet and had developed into an agile, fluid, fast ballplayer. I had found my rhythm and stride. I was like all the other black players you read about, putting all my waking energy into basketball and learning the moves. Power hadn't won a city championship since 1939, so there was no legacy of victory to inherit, but our team went undefeated all that year, all of the next, and almost went undefeated in my senior year until DeMatha broke our streak down at the University of Maryland field house. In my last three years at Power, we lost only that one game, a long time to go between losses.

One of the benefits of going to Power was that many of the pro teams that came into town to play the Knicks would practice in our gym. Donahue knew a lot of the pro coaches, and our gym was only eleven blocks from the old Madison Square Garden. He'd be given free tickets to games at the Garden, which he then liberally passed on to me and my teammates. All of that, known by me in advance of my arrival at the school, had made Power irresistible. In fact, Donahue had given me passes back in eighth grade. I was in the Garden the night Elgin Baylor had the seventy-one points against the Knicks. I was in awe. I wanted to play like Elgin then, even though I was a center. I remember signing my first autograph that same year at Madison Square Garden. Somebody thought I was a Knick because of my size. When I explained otherwise, that I was in grade school playing for St. Jude's, the man told me to sign anyway. I signed "Lew Alcindor" compliantly and the guy said, "What kind of a name is that? Is this some stupid name you thought up?" That sort of sealed my attitude as far as autographs went.

The Knicks were terrible then. They were my team just because they were in New York, but they were terrible and those years were pretty

bleak. They should have been the elite of New York basketball, the
epitome of all the city's basketball excellence, but it took them twenty-
four years to win their first championship. Wilt scored one hundred
against the Knicks, still the record for the most points scored by a player
in a game. That's the kind of team they were then. I liked to watch
Willie Naulls and Johnny Green, an incredible athlete, but that was
about it.

Donahue liked to take us down to watch the Celtics, who were as
sublime then as the Knicks were terrible. Donahue's whole emphasis
was the team game, and the Celtics were the best at winning within
a team concept. He wanted me to pay particular attention to their
center, number 6, Bill Russell. I learned a lot about how to win from
watching Bill play. He played for his teammates. He passed the ball,
he rebounded and started the fast break, he was always there plugging
up the middle on defense—and he was content to do that, to forgo the
pleasure of the individual statistics. Nobody had really blocked shots
until he came along. He turned defense into an offensive weapon. In
the Celtic game plan, he was the perfect man in his position. Boston
won eleven world championships in the thirteen years he played with
them. Bill Russell's era in the sixties was the Celtics' era, their decade
of dominance in the NBA. When he retired, exactly twenty seasons
ago, the team's hegemony retired with him. He was a great ballplayer,
a dazzling competitor with supreme athletic ability who defined the
modern basketball player. And he was a master of the mental aspect
of his sport. I think Bill Russell understood how to bring all the forces
to bear, at key times, in key games. He knew how to rise to the occasion,
as though he had studied Eastern philosophy or achieved the mastery
that one sees in Zen masters. He understood the dynamics of the game
and applied himself wisely, doing the right things that needed to be
done for the win at the right time, putting his ability in tune with the
four other guys who were doing the same thing. I think that was the
secret to the Celtics' success.

My nights of watching Bill Russell in the Garden those many years
ago have helped me throughout all the nights of my own career. The
unselfish player wrapped in all that talent, more hungry for the win
than for glory—I hooked on to that inspiration. Coach Donahue tried
to introduce me to Bill one afternoon when the Celtics were working
out at Power's gym. I had had the opportunity to meet a number of
professional basketball players in our gym back then. As a freshman,
I remember once turning a corner outside and coming upon Nate
Thurmond and Wayne Hightower leaning languidly up against the

wall by the gym door. I knew immediately who they were. They played for San Francisco and I was in awe of them, of Nate in particular, who played center. It was a shock to realize that I was as tall as they were. They seemed so distantly mature, something I could never develop into. Al Attles, who played for the Warriors then too, used to ask me all the time about my grades, until somebody told him how tough a school Power was and that my grades were good. I always got the feeling he took a genuine interest. We're friends today. Nate too.

But Bill Russell was stand-offish, gruff, not easily approachable then. When I went over to shake his hand, he said something to Donahue like "I'm not standing up for no kid." I didn't know if he was hostile or not, but I didn't take it personally, and it never affected my admiration. Russell had some brains and intellect, I thought, and a pride that was never arrogance. I liked the way he handled himself, as a dominant player in what was then a sport dominated by whites. Russell was the only black player on the Celtics in his rookie year. He said he was excluded from mostly everything but practices and games. He was a proud black man at a time of great prejudice against blacks. I remember reading an article he wrote for *The Saturday Evening Post* when the civil rights struggle was going full blast. I admired what he had to say, and I noticed that it didn't have anything to do with sport. I see Bill from time to time now when we play up in Sacramento, where he is the general manager. We never exchange many words, but when we pass each other he always says, "Hi, kid."

The old high school gym isn't there anymore. There's now a residential tower at Sixty-first and Amsterdam. They closed the school about five years ago and tore it down after the Christian Brothers of Ireland, the Catholic brothers who used to run the school, sold the land. I got involved with trying to save it, but it didn't work out.

The school mascot was the panther. Now I am the last panther, the last one still playing from those days. The high school's gone. The gym's gone. Everything's gone. I'm the last one left. I'm a dying breed here.

Tonight my friend Richard Rubinstein, a filmmaker and fellow New Yorker, threw a party for me in a rented loft down in Chelsea, which is between the Village and the bottom of midtown. It brought back memories of some sweet episodes down there at Kenny Kelly's place. Kelly was one of the dudes from high school that I used to hang out and go to jazz clubs with. He graduated before me in January and got himself his own place in Chelsea. For a little money toward rent, he gave me my own key, and new worlds opened up. The place wasn't exactly sophisticated, but it was freedom, freedom and privacy.

Kelly turned up at the party, which was a surprise because he doesn't live in New York anymore and I can't remember the last time I saw him. I knew Barbara Nielson would come, though. Barbara lived in another building in the project and I'd had a serious crush on her back when we were both fifteen and I was a pencil-necked geek to be avoided. (That was a few years before my amorous nights in Kelly's apartment.) Barbara's aunt thought I was all right, and she was four years older and *mature*, but I only had eyes for Barbara. She and I were born on the same day, in the same year, in the same hospital in Harlem, Sydenham, another building that is no longer there. She was born at 7:30 in the morning and I was born at 6:30 that night—and we ended up in the same housing project. She must have been in the next nursery, though, and gotten tuned out to my vibe. Maybe I made too much noise and she said, "I'm going to avoid this dude in the future." But we're friends now.

I had heard that Mayor Koch wanted to crash my party. But he knows I had problems with the inflammatory racial remarks he made in regard to Jesse Jackson, saying that any Jew would be crazy to vote for Jesse. Opposing a candidate for legitimate reasons is one thing, but appealing to emotion based on race is another, and one I find repugnant in an elected official. As it turned out, the mayor never showed up.

Many of the people in the room were strangers, associates of Richard's, so even though the party was top of the line, it was a little stiff for me, and I was glad that friends were there. Kamaal came by himself. We've been tight since we were three years old. Some things endure. Kamaal moved into the projects the same year I did and lived in Building Seven. He was "the Dab" in my first book, the guy I wrote about who went into the army during the Vietnam War and got himself out smartly, early, and honorably. We called him the Dab, after the Brylcreem ad "a little dab'll do ya," because he was so slick with the one-liners. Kamaal always had a certain intelligence. We didn't go to school together except for a very short time at P.S. 52, where he was in one first-grade classroom with Henry Lemon and I was in the other with a girl named Tempie Beaman; we were the only four black kids in the whole class. After that, we took separate tracks, his public, mine Catholic, but we always saw each other at the projects. Kamaal was like a lone wolf. He was an independent thinker, which I liked. We used to go see James Brown together at the Apollo. At that time, as far as we were concerned, James Brown wasn't the godfather of rock 'n' roll, he was the king. I can remember James Brown and wicked Wilson Pickett on the same bill.

No matter where I am, I usually talk to Kamaal in New York at least every other week. We stayed close after I left New York for UCLA. As Kamaal says, we've been through the ups, the downs, and the in betweens together, the good, the bad, *and* the ugly in each other's lives, in our careers, in our romances. There's been a natural simpático between us. And we have both been students of history, especially African and Caribbean history, roots we share in common. Our grandfathers were both immigrants from the West Indies, Kamaal's from Barbados and my own from Trinidad. The summer after I graduated from UCLA, I took my first trip down there and Kamaal came with me. We visited his people in Barbados and mine in Trinidad. My great aunt was still living there then.

I never knew my grandfather, my father's father. He was six feet three and a bobby in Trinidad—my father ended up being a cop too, in New York. Early in the century, before World War I, my grandfather and grandmother immigrated to America, winding up in Brooklyn, where my father was born. My grandfather died when my father was only nine, but my grandmother had a long life there in the Brownsville section of Brooklyn. I remember her well, especially the rhythms of her language. She spoke French and Spanish fluently. Everybody in her neighborhood and building was West Indian, and if I spent two weeks with her my own speech would start to lilt. The traditions of folklore and storytelling are strong in the West Indies, and in her musical patois my grandmother used to tell me vivid stories about vampires and other zombie stuff straight out of West Africa. She used to scare the shit out of me too. "Vampire," she'd say. "You put salt on him and he won't be able to get back into his skin." *Jumbies* is the West Indian word for the West African zombies, and when Kamaal and I went to the islands, there was a *jumbie* scare in one of the towns; the windows in a local house had broken seemingly spontaneously. All the word was *jumbie* terror in San Fernando.

On Trinidad, I visited Alcindor Trace, my family's property on the eastern coast of the island, land originally bought by my grandfather Alcindor. The name Alcindor comes from the French planter Alcindor, who brought my ancestors to the islands from the Gold Coast of West Africa, and whose name I inherited. My father's people were Yoruba, from Nigeria. Archives documenting this still exist in Trinidad. But I first learned about my heritage from my father and my grandmother

when I was a kid. They educated me about all this. They talked about
our background with great pride. I was always taught that behind me
was something real and authentic and dignified, and this helped give
me, as a child, some self-worth. I always had that feeling of pride in
where I came from. This probably saved me, especially in the neighborhood, and no doubt buoyed me up during wrenching times like the civil
rights struggles in the sixties. The Alcindors are not meek or recessive
people. We are not ashamed of ourselves.

My father came to the party with my mother, and I know he was
wishing he had his horn. Freddie Hubbard was there, playing with his
band, and his music was wonderful. I can remember listening to Freddie my first year in the pros during the play-offs with the Knicks; I used
it to "get myself in harmony with the universe." I have known Freddie
Hubbard since I was fourteen and he was one of the young members
of the musical elite in New York. Most of the bebop musicians knew
my dad. In the autumn of my freshman year, he took me down to
Birdland to see Art Blakey. That's when I met Freddie, along with
Wayne Shorter and Cedar Walton. Art Blakey has known me since I
was less than a year old, when my father would bring me along to jam
sessions. He remembers me from then and I remember images, like the
first time I saw a baritone saxophone. I thought it was the biggest, most
tremendous instrument ever. It was taller than me. I must have been
two or three. I remember it vividly, and the dude playing it, at the Elks
Club at 126th Street and Fifth Avenue, where they jammed.

As a teenager, I roamed the jazz clubs, able to get into places like
the Five Spot and the Village Vanguard because my size made me look
eighteen. I was a dutiful Catholic boy at that time, but at heart I was
Dizzy Gillespie.

As much as my mother loved music and jazz herself—Count Basie,
Sarah Vaughan, and Duke Ellington were all common sounds around
the house—I think she was bothered by that private artistic part of me
that roamed free. I think it still bothers her. I am a child of the bebop
era. It became a fixed part of the rhythm of my life. The music was
something to be passionate about. And the musicians in whose midst
I was fortunate enough to find myself were not a meek generation of
musicians. They were renegades who considered themselves artists. I
studied their conscious cool, the way they let nothing leak through
gesture or expression. To me that was presence. Dizzy would understand. You go all the way back to the great black kings of West Africa.
Esteem came from presence. That's in me.

Tuesday, November 22

Shootaround was scheduled for late morning today at the Garden. This was the last day in New York, the day of the game, and it was the first I had seen the team since the Portland game at home four days ago. The morning papers were full of two things, me on the front pages of every sports section in town, and JFK, in remembrance of his assassination twenty-five years ago today. I was in my eleventh-grade social studies class at Power. It was a Friday, I remember, because the scrimmage we were supposed to have out on Long Island that night was canceled. It felt strange to see black-and-white stills from Dallas in the same paper with photographs of me, then and now, with GOOD-BYE printed in giant letters above a picture of me shooting the hook.

Everybody was on the team bus that took us down to the Garden from the hotel: the three coaches; Gary Vitti, our trainer; and all the players except Coop, who had strained his back and had to stay behind in L.A. for treatment. Spirits were easy. Riles is strict about no civilians being on the team bus, but he made an exception for my friend Julian, who showed up at the hotel this morning. Julian does that, just shows up. I have known him since I was around Amir's age, seven or eight, when Julian lived across the street from my mother's cousin in the Dunbar projects on 150th Street. I don't remember when we actually started being friends, but it was long ago and it was in Harlem.

The time he showed up that was the most memorable was in Boston four seasons ago. This was during the world-championship finals in 1985, a series that was haunted by twenty-five years of epic rivalry between the Lakers and the Celtics and also by our having lost the year before to Boston *in* Boston, in Game 7, by one point—one of our worst moments. In '85, it was between games and I was sitting up in my hotel room when Julian called to tell me he was in town. He had taken off work and come up from New York to see the series through. Over the phone, he went on a tirade. "The Celtics ain't shit! They've been talking too much! Shut 'em up!" It was just like we were back in high school and getting ready to play. "Shut 'em up!" It got me ready for the whole scenario. We went out and kicked the Celtics in the butt.

At the Garden, we took the players' back elevator up to the basketball court on the fifth floor. The Garden is the only arena in the league

that is eight stories high. It's like a set piece out of *Blade Runner.* As
we walked out onto the floor it was quiet, the stands empty, nothing
like it would be later, a big November basketball night in the Garden.
I noticed the two banners hanging from the ceiling above, the badge
of two world championships won by the Knicks in 1970 and 1973.
Those are what you play for.

Memories of the Garden seemed to float by me all day. The Garden
of my childhood and adolescence was the old Garden, not the very first
structure on fancy Madison Square that was long before my time, but
the plainer red-brick building at Eighth Avenue between Forty-ninth
and Fiftieth streets where my father took me to see the rodeo when
I was five and where I saw my first pro-basketball game and later
watched Bill Russell play. It was one of the temples of the game, and
I remember the awe it inspired, and the intimidation. I played my own
first game there the winter of my freshman year, January 1962. We
didn't even know we were going to play there until the day before the
game. It was supposed to be a home game at Power. We were playing
St. Helena's, a Catholic high school from the Bronx. But at the eleventh hour the game got switched to the Garden.

The first thing I noticed was that the court seemed so big. Our court
at Power was only about eighty-eight feet. The Garden, of course, was
ninety-four. Minutes before the game, I told Coach Donahue I didn't
feel too well and didn't know if I could play. He said, "None of us feel
too good, but we're all going out there. Look at it this way. Every time
you do something, every time you *fall down,* you'll be setting a Garden
record for fourteen-year-olds."

I definitely had stars in my eyes. And I did all right in that game.
We beat St. Helena's by six and, according to the papers, our game
drew more attention than the one played afterward by the Knicks and
the Syracuse Nationals. It was a thrill.

The old Garden survived in New York until about the time I entered
the pros and they tore down Penn Station and put up the present
Garden. The tracks remained underground. Penn Station had been a
rare architectural masterpiece, one of the beautifully ornate buildings
designed by Stanford White, the city's most famous architect during
the renaissance at the turn of the century. I always loved the late-
nineteenth-century buildings in New York. But they demolished this
one, the one building in the Tenderloin, the one work of art that made
the neighborhood attractive. I thought it was crazy.

The new Garden inherited none of the beauty of the late, great Penn
Station but all of the long tradition of the old Garden. I might have

ended up playing there if the Knicks had won the right to bid for me as I was coming out of college. But as things turned out, it was Milwaukee that earned the draft pick. After that, the Garden was no Eden for me to play in. My first year in the pros we made it into the play-offs and came up against New York in the conference finals. I was twenty-three then, and that was the very tough Knicks team, with Walt Frazier, Willis Reed, Dave DeBusschere, Bill Bradley, Dick Barnett, and Cazzie Russell, who were on their way to winning New York's first NBA title. (With Earl Monroe, they would win the second one three years later.) As the final game slipped out of our reach that April in the Garden, the crowd began to sing derisively to me, "Good-bye, Lewie, we hate to see you go." My father still lived in New York then and told me that football fans had written a song, "Good-bye, Allie," aimed at Giants head coach Allie Sherman, and that the Knicks fans had seemingly and somehow spontaneously appropriated the tune for me. Years later, after the Knicks stopped being contenders, the fans eased up on me. But I had a long stretch of boos and little charity here in my hometown. Bill Russell and Wilt used to be rancorously booed in Madison Square Garden too, and the Knicks' own center, Patrick Ewing, when he was still in college. I can remember as a kid seeing a picture in the New York *Daily News* of Wilt with four teeth knocked out after a game at the Garden. I felt sorry for him, and I bet I was the only person in New York City who did. I think sportswriter Dave Anderson put it best: "We don't easily give the big men our hearts."

Shootaround wasn't tough. Our game-day practices rarely are, and also it's early in the season. We were back at the hotel by early afternoon. I said good-bye to Julian, went up to my room, and drew the drapes in order to sleep for tonight's game.

It was dark by the time we left the hotel again at six. The team bus inched its way through the snarl of night traffic down Eighth Avenue to the arena. The game was at eight and the word was that it had been sold out for months. A throng of people surrounded the bus as we pulled up to the players' entrance at the Garden.

Once dressed in the locker room, I read, as usual, before it was time to go out on the floor. Reading has been a long-standing pregame ritual with me. It is a way to clear my mind so I can focus on the game at hand. Tonight's game was the beginning of a four-city road trip, so starting out with a win was important. Wins on the road, even for the best of teams, don't come easy and are worth double the wins at home. These Knicks are a young team on the rise. The oldest player is twenty-

nine-year-old Trent Tucker, and the coach, Rick Pitino, is thirty-six, in
his second year with the team. Last season, they made it to the play-offs
for the first time in four years, and this season has seen their best start
since 1980. The excitement is back for the Knicks. With both of our
teams sitting at the top of our divisions, the intensity level was high
on both sides tonight, and the Knicks didn't want to lose one at home.

This is my fourth season matched up with Patrick Ewing, the
Knicks' twenty-six-year-old, seven-foot center who came from Jamaica
when he was twelve—another West Indian connection. His first few
seasons were tough. The Knicks were in the middle of a three-year run
with the worst record in the league when Patrick came out of college,
and the expectations were enormous for him to turn the franchise
around. The fans wanted immediate play-off contention, and I think
Patrick was criticized unfairly in the New York press. The media didn't
give him a chance. Patrick has both the talent and the desire to do very
well, but he has had injuries that hampered his play and he suffered
without the presence of a true point guard until Mark Jackson filled
that spot nicely as a rookie last season. Jackson gives the team continu-
ity and that center–point-guard combination gave Patrick his best
season so far. He's a fine player and he is going to get even better. I
like the fact he works hard.

At last the moment arrived to leave the locker room and walk out
through the tunnel to the court and the capacity crowd of twenty
thousand. During warm-ups, I spotted my friends Lou Gossett and
Spike Lee and, sitting courtside across and down from the Laker bench,
my parents, who came to take part in the festivities at halftime. I knew
Julian and Kamaal were up in the stands somewhere, and also Taaj, a
beautiful woman and one of my best friends since the Milwaukee days;
sometimes she just shows up too.

I looked upward around the arena and saw hand-printed signs big
enough for me to read from the floor like "Thanks for the memories,
Kareem," and I realized there were a lot of people in the building
tonight who had seen me play as a kid and had come to say good-bye.
I could feel the Garden fans begin to pour out their message in an
ovation of applause during the player introductions at the start of the
game. It was going to be an emotional evening.

We jumped to an early 11–2 lead. I hit my first two hooks over
Patrick, and feeling them drop was gratifying. The Knicks emphasize
a running game like we do, and I felt no fatigue running tonight.
Sometimes there are games when every possession is painful, but for
us this wasn't one of those nights. Nothing was painful. The Knicks

made twenty turnovers in the first two quarters and the half ended with us up eleven points. The score was 55–44.

I felt Earvin's arm go around my shoulders at the start of the farewell ceremony. Farrell Hopkins was introduced first and walked out to midcourt, then, one by one, seven of my high school teammates from Power, Joe Straining, Ed Klimkowski, Jack Bettridge, Paul Houghton, Oscar Sanchez, Jack Bonner, and Art Kenney, with whom I used to spend those long Saturdays in the gym. Riley and Larry Costello, my first pro coach, were introduced and then, last, my father and my mother. The crowd showered my parents with affection. I noticed there were tears in their eyes and that they had that quiet glow of pride. The only other time I ever remember seeing tears in my father's eyes was at my grandmother's funeral.

"And now, tonight's guest of honor," I heard the emcee, Marv Albert, say over the microphone, "in his unprecedented twentieth and final NBA season, six-time NBA most valuable player, six-time member of NBA championship teams, the greatest scorer in the history of the NBA, let's say thanks for all his contributions to the game, with one last Madison Square Garden salute, to the master of the skyhook, future Hall of Famer Kareem Abdul-Jabbar." As I was half hearing these words, I walked through the high-fiving tunnel my teammates had set up for me, touching each of their hands as I made my way out by myself to center court. The Garden exploded. The roar of applause was deafening. Just as the boos used to begin high up in the balcony and rain downward to the floor, the appreciation came down in waves tonight, and every time it seemed as if it were ebbing, it would renew itself. I don't know how long I stood there. There was nothing I could do but let it wash through me. I *knew* this crowd, so I knew this was real. A New York crowd doesn't give you anything they are not ready to give. You don't get any grace. They give you exactly what they feel is appropriate, no holds barred. They pride themselves on their knowledge of the game, its tempo and its subtleties. You have to earn their cheers. I guess I'd earned some. Some in the crowd were chanting "Kareem," some "Lew."

When it quieted enough for me say a few words, I just had to trust the right ones would come out. "What can I say? I have been dealing with this good-bye since last season ended. I have been trying to think of something appropriate, something that would work. And what can you say at a moment like this?

"Some of you old-timers probably know that I've had some tough moments here and you were the cause of that. But tonight you are responsible for something very wonderful. This equaled it out.

"I've enjoyed coming here. I've enjoyed the challenge of playing the very tough Knick teams, and it looks like this year there will be another very tough Knick team that will be in the play-offs.

"I'm going to steal a few words from a song by James Brown called 'Maybe the Last Time.'

" 'It may be the last time we shake hands, it may be the last time we make plans,' but whatever happens, thank you from the bottom of my heart."

Mark Jackson presented me with a silver apple with the inscription "Kareem Abdul-Jabbar night, November 22, 1988, Madison Square Garden, to one of New York City's own from New York's team, thanks for the memories." Patrick then presented me with a large framed set of my four road jerseys from Power, UCLA, Milwaukee, and Los Angeles, all jerseys that I wore playing in Madison Square Garden. This carried the inscription "To Kareem, always a champion."

The apple will go on the mantelpiece and the jerseys in my gym at home.

We won the game by twelve. It almost got by us in the third quarter, though, when New York tied us 77–77 and took the lead by as much as five. The crowd's chants of "Lew, Lew, Lew" modulated smoothly into "Beat L.A., beat L.A., beat L.A." Having been up by eleven at the start of the second half, we were down by one at the start of the fourth quarter. But it was as if Earvin had decided, as he has so many times before, that this wasn't one we were going to lose. The Knicks collapsed in the final quarter and Earvin earned his first triple-double of the season. The team is 7-2 in nine games.

It was a gratifying win.

After the game, in the hallway outside the Lakers' locker room, Sister Alacoque came by with my parents to say hello. She goes by Sister Hannah now, since Vatican II. She was one of the guiding lights of my childhood and she has the same inner glow now that she had then. She showed me an old shapshot of us that had been taken at the time of my eighth-grade graduation from St. Jude's. The gown was too short and I towered above her. It wasn't long after that that I had played in the Garden for the first time, at age fourteen. Now here I am, twenty-seven years later, at age forty-one, having just played my last game here.

. . .

Around eleven, the bus took us back out into the Manhattan night.
Kamaal and Taaj came over to the hotel and we just hung out together
for a few hours.

It was a warm night filled with nostalgia.

It was a nostalgic four days.

11

Preseason: It's That Time

Klum Gym was steamy, a sweatbox. At ten in the morning, the temperature outside had already hit the nineties, so inside the gym, at the start
of practice, the sun already high, it must have been a hundred. Today
was day one of training camp, and for the next six days this will be our
workplace, the University of Hawaii's gym in the foothills of the Koolau
Range on Oahu. We flew into Honolulu yesterday, arriving in the
midst of one of Hawaii's occasional tropical doldrums, when the trade
winds that normally cool the islands year-round lie completely still.
We're staying in a hotel down by the water at the other end of the
beach from Diamond Head. But this is no vacation. Once inside the
gym, it's all work, and you get so tired you can't do anything afterward
except recover for the next day's practice. Gary Vitti has exhorted us
to keep hydrated by drinking lots of water and eating plenty of fruit.

There are few changes in the team from last year. Kurt Rambis and
Billy Thompson got picked up in the expansion draft by Charlotte and
Miami, the league's two new franchises this season, and Wes Matthews
is gone. But the first seven players remain, the core of the Laker team
that has been put together over the last ten years—me, Earvin "Magic"
Johnson, James Worthy, Byron Scott, A.C. Green, Michael Cooper,
and Mychal Thompson. We're a serious veteran team. We've been
through so much together. We've shared the agonies and ecstasies of
competition. We enjoy the cohesiveness of a team that has been
together for some time, so we don't have to establish that. It's all about
what a group can do together, continually. Last year, in our seventh trip
to the finals in this decade, we went as far as our collective abilities
could permit, winning the second consecutive world-championship
title, the back-to-back, at the end of the longest season in the history
of the NBA. Nobody, it was agreed, had ever played harder to win a
championship. No team had ever had to go the full seven games in the
last three rounds of the play-offs before, extending the length of the
season for the first time to the day of the summer solstice, the longest
day of the calendar year. We survived the longest test any champion
had ever faced, and won after being closer to defeat than any champion. We repeated in an era when no one repeats and when even to
reach the finals two years in a row is rare. We're the only team, in any
professional sport, to have repeated in the eighties. And in basketball,

no team had repeated since 1969, the year Bill Russell retired and the
year I entered professional basketball. It was a euphoric moment, and
it sweetened our shortened summer.

Between then and now, it's been a quick three months, and this is
the first time we have all been back together since June. Everybody has
come into camp in good shape and Earvin is in great shape, the best
of his career. Two players who joined the team last season are here,
Tony Campbell and Jeff Lamp, and also two new team members,
six-foot guard David Rivers, just out of Notre Dame, who will be the
only rookie on the team this year, and six-foot-nine-inch forward Orlando Woolridge, a seven-year veteran who we hope might be our
eighth man. Everything is pretty set except for the eleventh and
twelfth spots, but that will be up to the coaches. We are starting camp
with sixteen players, including Mike Smrek and Milt Wagner, who
both played with us last year also, and new faces Scott Meents, Kannard
Johnson, and Mark McNamara. One of these five will be on the team's
final twelve-man roster before the start of the regular season a month
from now.

This will be the tenth time I have prepared for the season in training
camp with Earvin and Cooper, the seventh year with James, the sixth
with Byron, the fourth with A.C., and the third with Mychal Thompson. We have come together from such separate routes, me from New
York City, Cooper and Byron from Los Angeles, Magic from Lansing,
Michigan, A.C. from Portland, Oregon, James from North Carolina,
Orlando from rural Louisiana, and Mychal Thompson from the Bahamas. But what we share in common is that most of us have had the
formative experience of winning in the playgrounds and in our school
gyms reaching as far back as grade school. With that much winning
in the collective background of a team, you have a heightened will to
compete and a severe dislike of losing. That experience unites us no
matter how diverse our origins and backgrounds.

I remember well the first training camp with Earvin, in the fall of
the 1979–80 season. During the time he was a star at Michigan State,
I had only seen him play in a few games on television, and from those
I couldn't judge what he could do exactly. That fall, after my first day
in practice with him, I was sure that with Earvin at point guard we
could go a long way, maybe all the way. His abilities were immediately
evident. He could run the ball all day and he saw everything on the
court. It was obvious that he was capable of playing intense winning
basketball. He was an unselfish player and a joyful passer, highly skilled
at "passing out the sugar," in the words of Bob Cousy, the first great

assist man. Earvin was twenty then, and I was thirty-two. It was the beginning of a great and fruitful partnership on the court; the first of five championships came our way that year. In those days Earvin was into George Clinton's music and P-Funk. That first training camp, I can remember him playing "Knee Deep" on his box. He kind of wore me out with that one.

Earvin has a lot of nicknames: Magic, a name he's had since he was fifteen; Junior, Junie, and June Bug, all family terms of endearment; and that fall the team gave him another one—Buck, as in young buck.

"Listen up," Riley said, and his chalk talk began. The players were all seated around a blackboard set up in a far corner of the gym, intentionally out of earshot of the press, whom Riley restricts to the other end of the court during practice. Only members of the Laker organization and selected members of the press are permitted in practices during training camp. Sitting along the sidelines this morning were Chick Hearn and Jerry West. The Lakers' general manager, Jerry was one of the greatest guards to have ever played the game of basketball. Chick Hearn is the Lakers' radio and television voice, who broadcasts every home game from high above the western sidelines of the Forum, who travels with the team on the same grueling road schedule we do so that he can send his eyewitness accounts of the away games back to L.A., and who has been with the Los Angeles Lakers from the start, the only play-by-play announcer the Lakers have ever had, respected thoughout the league as an elder in his domain. Sharp-tongued, colorful, irascible at times, ardent, Irish, Chick found his own voice in basketball early on and imprinted it in the minds of Laker fans, some of whom even bring radios with them into the Forum so they won't miss Chick's descriptions of the action. Chick was here when I got here, and since he's missed no game after that time I guess that means he's called every skyhook and shot I've made since I've been in Los Angeles.

The fourth estate was sitting down at the far baseline, just a few reporters from the local media and then the five beat writers who cover the team for L.A.'s five major metropolitan-area newspapers and who will be in lockstep with us from today onward through the full seven months of the season, and longer if we elude an early play-off exit.

For me and the sportswriters, it has been a long, slow getting-to-know and -understand each other over the course of my professional career. In the beginning, I tended to see them all as wild beasts of misrepresentation who would hurt me, and we became locked in dubious battle for a number of years. Questions were interrogations. But for the most part, time has taken care of my problems with the press. I still believe the writers often throw off more heat than light, but basically the players and the press are working the same event, so we have to learn to get along and appreciate each other. Talking to the press is part of the working conditions. What's hardest is knowing what to share with them and what to keep to yourself. They all are hungry for something unique from you.

Riles scratched on the blackboard and talked for half an hour. All the vets know this stuff, but the new guys need to be shown around the court. Gary led us in a long stretching session afterward and then we hit the floor, all the old familiar court noises filling the gym, the stampede of bodies on the hardwood, sneakers squeaking, grunts of effort, the shouts of instruction from Riles and Bertka and Pfund, the assistant coaches. We broke into a sweat immediately, our shirts soaked, the intense humidity preventing the water from evaporating off. This wet heat will help us in our conditioning.

Basketball is a game of supreme conditioning, and Riley always runs us extra hard, full tilt, full court, baseline to baseline. All of the running and ball-handing drills we do revolve around the accelerated, fast-break, ninety-four-foot game we like to play. I learned long ago that I can't hold back on the running, the most important part of practice and also the hardest. That's where you can lose your game. It is doubtful whether any other game is as demanding athletically as basketball, and physical conditioning is an absolute necessity. By the end of training camp, your timing, wind, and strength become so finely tuned that from that point on you feel a noticeable difference if even three days elapse between workouts.

I spent the summer getting into condition, or thinking I was. In college the summers were luxurious, but in the pros you spend much of your time getting ready for the next season. You have to come into camp in good shape. For the players, the season is really twelve months.

Last season, after winning the final championship game, I remember getting to Hawaii and being completely exhausted. You can be so spent after the play-offs that it can take a month just to recover to the point of functioning normally. And last year's play-offs were the toughest I had ever been in, an ordeal for the team and for me. We had to give everything and we were tested every kind of way. The ordeal began with Utah. I had three hundred pounds of Mark Eaton draped over me for seven games, and then James Donaldson for another seven with Dallas. Eaton and Donaldson made Bill Laimbeer seem like a midget by the time we got to the final seven with Detroit. The days following that last game are a blur.

Four days after Sugar Ray Leonard came out of a five-year retirement to beat Marvin Hagler, one of the most remorseless, murderous middle-weight punchers in the history of the fight game, he said that he was still in a kind of trance: "I didn't feel nothing and I didn't hear nothing." That's the kind of numbness after battle you can feel after winning a hard-fought championship title. For the first few weeks, I just let Hawaii take me in and let the season roll off.

I have had my land in Hawaii for ten years, but it was only three years ago that I had a house built for me on the property. Listening as a kid from the city to the lilting tongue of my grandmother and her West Indian stories, I'd dream of living in Trinidad, which I thought was paradise, but I discovered Hawaii in the summer of 1975 after I got traded by Milwaukee to the Lakers, and that's where I go now when I want to get away. I have traveled through all of Asia, the Middle East, and large parts of Africa, so much of my wanderlust has been satisfied. Hawaii is a refuge for me now. I have lived here for the past three summers, in between seasons, and that's where I'll be returning when this one ends.

My land is on a bluff about two hundred feet above the beach, and I have planted mango, citrus, avocado, and banana trees on my mini-plantation there. The house is tiny but I had it tailor-made to fit me, and the sound system I put in transforms it. I have my music, and I can go to sleep and wake up to the natural sounds around me, the rain, the seabirds on the cliff, the surf below. I windsurf off the beach down below the house, but with caution always. You could get beaten to death by those waves. It's beautiful and quiet on the island, the moon and stars the only light at night out where I am. I don't keep track in hours when I'm there. I just train and relax, soaking in the sun and the climate and the company of friends when they come.

This summer, I ran, lifted weights, swam, and toward the end, in September, did a long stretch of intensive yoga with my teacher back in L.A. Still, I have come into training camp over 270, about eight pounds above my midseason form. I am running the floor better than I did last year at this time, but my conditioning is suspect, and I want to get to 100 percent physically.

The practice goal in training camp is to reach fatigue stage. You usually hit it mentally before you do physically. Today it got mental about two hours in. Riley let us go after three and a half. We were back to the hotel at two o'clock. Quality sleep will be important from this point on. The first day of practice is over and Hawaii almost isn't here, a distant memory.

· · ·

Last night, after we flew in from Los Angeles, we had our traditional team dinner in a private room at the hotel. It was the usual start-of-season team meeting except that when Jerry West stood up to give his customary state-of-the-union message on behalf of management, his voice cracked and he got tears in his eyes when he opened with words about my retirement. "This is Cap's last year," he began, and emotion seemed to crowd his throat. (Cap, as in Captain, is my name within the family of the team.) He went on to talk about my years with the Lakers and how we have become a part of history, and then he turned to Magic and Cooper, who after me have been with the team the longest, and said, "When you guys retire, it's going to be like this for me too."

Sitting there listening, I was touched by Jerry and also struck by the fact that in the big-pressure, bottom-line atmosphere of the NBA today, there can exist some real loyalty and friendship. I always knew that Jerry cared, but never how deeply until last night. I think his words really hit everybody between the eyes because at the start of recent seasons the matter of my retirement has been an open question. Jerry brought home the reality that this, decisively, will be my last time around.

I came close to retiring a number of times over the last five years. Like false starts, I had some false leave-takings. At some point, I began to look for a logical place in my career where I could say, "All right, I'll end it here." Often athletes quit because they think they are supposed to, and I had people like those from the press trying to make up my mind for me as far back as ten years ago. But I wasn't going to give up my sport until I had taken it all the way, as far as I could go. Physically, my conditioning remained solid, and I knew that management would not let me stay too long. Management will let a player know when it's time to go; otherwise, it's up to you. I had somewhat arbitrarily decided to make the 1984–85 season my last. That marked the first of several interventions by Jerry, who has played a key role in my staying on longer. In his easy manner, he let me know that the organization needed me, and he told me then that if I stayed around we would continue to win more championships. He presented me with a no-lose situation, as he's done a number of times since, and the financial reward, rather than diminishing, only got better during that time. The carrot got to be the size of the Chrysler Building. Hearing Jerry speak as he did last night, I know for sure now that staying has been worth the risk of quitting too late. And he proved right about the championships. Three more lay ahead of us, including the coveted back-to-back.

. . .

I knew about Jerry long before I met him. He was nine years ahead of me as a player. He and Oscar Robertson were the stars coming out of college basketball as the first two draft picks in 1960. Both guards, Jerry and Oscar Robertson ended up in the Hall of Fame, two of the greatest players in the history of the NBA, still in the record books, and I had the privilege of a close association with both of them—with Oscar in Milwaukee, with Jerry in Los Angeles. Jerry came from a small town of five hundred in the hills of West Virginia, one of six children in a hardworking family. He says he still misses the rural softness of his boyhood there. He started playing basketball when he was eleven.

As a player, Jerry did everything. He was known as a great shooter, but he was a big defensive player too. He always could affect the game with his steals, and his passing was on a level with his dazzling ability to score. People never gave him credit for that. At six feet three he was the perfect guard size-wise. He wasn't real big and he wasn't real small, quick enough to stay with the little guys he was guarding, but big enough to get off his shots consistently as a strong offensive player. With great range, Jerry could shoot from anywhere on the court. Our playing careers overlapped when I joined the league, and I remember one time getting a little crazy on the court thinking I was going to have to fight one of Jerry's teammates. Jerry came over to me on the floor and said quietly, "Hey, man, he's not worth fighting. Don't get hurt over him."

In the sixties, Jerry and Elgin Baylor were the nucleus of the first generation of Lakers in Los Angeles, and Wilt joined them in 1968. I think it is probably impossible to overstate the frustration of that team in those years. Six times they faced the Boston Celtics in the finals, and six times they came up short, going all the way to the brink in the seventh game on three of those occasions. The rivalry between those two great teams dominated the NBA, but for the Lakers each championship defeat sank like a sword into the body of the team. That was Bill Russell's era. I went through high school and college during those years, and I can remember from New York feeling sorry for the Lakers in those early battles, coming so close and being turned away, time after time. After a while, the win seemed foreordained each springtime for Boston. It was a tragic play and Jerry was the tragic hero, like Hamlet, the fair prince of Denmark. Elgin was Falstaff. Wilt was Calaban. It was *Lakers Agonistes.*

Jerry may have taken the losses harder than anybody. He felt responsible; that was the kind of player and young man he was. It got to the point where he thought he was being divinely punished. The times that hurt the most, he says now, were the first and last meetings with Boston, in 1962 and in 1969, both seventh-game encounters. He has thought to himself since that maybe if the Lakers had won the first one, the team's second year in L.A., the history for that decade would have been different. That first series was the one in which Laker guard Frank Selvy, in Game 7, the score tied 100–100, missed the last-second shot that would have won the game and the title. From fifteen feet out, his jumper was straight on target but hit the rim, falling maybe no more than an inch too short. The game went into overtime and Boston won it by three points. Bill Bertka says that Selvy is still upset today about that shot. He has done a quarter century of penance. Nobody talks about the fact that, before missing, Frank had just made a shot in that game, says Jerry.

In 1969, the last try with Boston and Bill Russell's last championship series, the Celtics won in Game 7 by two points. Jerry was named MVP of those finals, the only time in the history of that award, before or since, that it has gone to a player on the losing team. But Jerry was disconsolate and had one of the toughest summers of his career. The next season, he was right back in the finals again, only this time against the ascendant New York Knicks team. New York hadn't been in the finals since Lapchick's Knicks of the fifties. This was to be their year to win it. It was my rookie year with the Bucks, and I was there in L.A. when Jerry made his memorable sixty-three-foot shot to tie Game 3 at the end of regulation. With three seconds left on the clock, from under the Knicks' basket at the baseline, Wilt inbounded the ball to Jerry, who took three dribbles and heaved it one-handed from far behind midcourt, from the New York side of the line, and it went through. The Knicks' forward Dave DeBusschere was so stunned, he toppled backward onto the floor. The shot made it 102–102 and sent the game into overtime, but the Knicks won it by three. For a year or so afterward, the spot was marked on the Forum floor where Jerry had made his shot.

Twice more in the early seventies the L.A. Lakers faced the Knicks in the finals, finally winning their first championship title in 1972, in five games. That Laker team of '72 set a record of sixty-nine wins, thirty-three of them consecutive wins, which is still the best regular-season mark in league history and one that may never be duplicated. It was my team then, the Milwaukee Bucks, with the nation watching on television, that put an end to the odds-defying streak that winter in Milwaukee. We beat L.A. by sixteen.

By chance, both the Bucks and the Lakers had held training camp in Honolulu at the beginning of that year. Jerry and I, here now together after so many years, were both there then, on separate teams. I can remember Elgin being in Hawaii with the Lakers that fall and then his retiring nine games into the season, so the championship went to Wilt and Jerry in the spring. Wilt retired the next year, and then Jerry the year after that.

As a player, there had always been a quality of the impassioned about Jerry. His hands would drip water before every game and then he would go out on the court and be stupendous night after night, year after year. He brought that same impassioned nature with him when he returned to the Lakers as a coach a few years after he retired. It was 1976. I had made the move from Milwaukee to Los Angeles and was just beginning my second season with the Lakers. We were together, side by side as player and coach, for three years before he moved into the front office, where he has worked behind the scenes ever since. A coach who has been a great player runs the risk of high impatience with younger players who can't execute on the floor the way he once did. I always thought, for instance, that if Oscar had become a coach he would have yelled at everybody all the time. But Jerry was patient as a coach. Everybody wanted to feel about the team the way he did. With a certain solitariness, though, he took losses and imperfections hard. Coaching can make you old in about five years, and Jerry had the wisdom to see that. He gave it up, the year before we got Earvin, and joined Bill Sharman at the helm.

Sharman, twelve years older than Jerry, was one of the first stars in the league. He perfected the jump shot. Together, he and John Wooden defined fast-break, racehorse basketball, Sharman in the pros and Wooden in college basketball. They wrote a book about it together. For basketball in the West, they were our tradition out here. By the time Sharman came to the Lakers as a coach he was considered among the best. He arrived in Jerry's twelfth year as a player, 1972, the season they took it all the way to the title. It was then that Sharman innovated "the morning meeting," the day-of-game practice that we call shootaround now. Sharman was a master at pregame preparation, and the purpose of shootaround was to get the team loose and familiar with the arena before the night's game. He also believed in a kind of muscle memory, that moves made earlier in the day would imprint themselves so as to be effortlessly unerring later. Because the Lakers won the championship the year Sharman invented shootaround, within the following two years every other team in the league had instituted it, and now it's a routine practice.

Sharman was still coach during my first season with the Lakers in
1975–76. If we had to travel for a game, his favorite thing was to leave
town as early in the morning as possible and, before checking into our
hotel, go straight to shootaround practice. I hated that. I remember I
overslept one time. That was a wonderful day. We were in Chicago on
a road trip and had played the night before in Chicago Stadium. The
next morning, I knew when I woke up that something was wrong
because I felt relaxed and refreshed and well rested. I looked at the
clock. It was eleven. The team had left for Atlanta at eight. I promptly
made my own arrangements to get down to Atlanta, and the flight felt
leisurely. As it turned out, because of my absence, the team hadn't yet
gone to practice by the time I arrived at the hotel. They were just then
getting ready to leave for the arena. I checked in unnoticed, I thought,
and slipped up to my room, where the phone began to ring. I knew it
was about practice. When I didn't answer, knocks came to the door.
I stayed quiet inside. Shortly afterward, I heard a key turning in the
lock and immediately got into the closet. They had sent for a bellman.
Convinced I wasn't there, they left me in peace. My taste of freedom
had felt too good for me to consider rejoining the team at that point,
and after all, I'm paying for it, I thought to myself. There are always
team fines for missing planes and practices.

Later, when Sharman asked me to explain my mysterious whereabouts, I told him that I had arrived at the hotel after they had gone
to practice. He said, "But you checked in." Gratefully, another lie
sprung to mind. "No, I called the hotel from the airport and let them
know I was on my way," I said.

In twenty years, that was the only time I ever intentionally missed
practice.

My year with Sharman was his last as Laker coach, and then Jerry
took over. Sharman had suffered an uncommon injury in his first year,
the year of the championship, straining his larynx and vocal cords so
severely in practices and games that by the end of that season, by the
time they got to the finals, he could barely speak. And his voice never
recovered fully after that. This was not one of the ordinary wounds of
NBA life. His voice faded gradually, irreversibly, over his remaining
seasons as coach, and then deserted him almost entirely as general
manager. By the time he retired as president of the organization last
year, his voice was a whisper.

It was Sharman's astute basketball mind during his tenure as general
manager that began to lay the foundation for the Laker team of the
eighties. Then, following in Sharman's footsteps once again, Jerry took

over as team architect, instinctive, shrewd, far-seeing, and over his last six years as general manager, making all the right moves at the right times. Jerry has had to be especially smart in his position because, each season since 1980, we have been finishing at or near the top, and that means we were placed, due to rules of parity, in the lowest or near-lowest draft position. Coming into the pros, the best college players in the country go to those teams with the season's worst records, which is the NBA's way of keeping the talent level even and ensuring some measure of competitiveness. But Jerry, subtle and soft-spoken, has maneuvered deftly around this obstacle, and also around the reluctance of other teams to negotiate creative deals that could make the Lakers even better. It was Jerry who signed Orlando, who engineered the trades for Byron and Mychal Thompson, who got us A.C., and who drafted James based on a transaction made years before by Bill Sharman. With Jerry in the front office, blending talent and character like Bill Sharman before him, we have been able to endure as a solid contending team. And the Lakers' owner, Jerry Buss, has had the wisdom to give him the reins.

Jerry was twenty-two when he started with the Lakers. He's fifty now. Because his own first year was the team's first year in Los Angeles, he's the unifying human thread over the three decades since then. He is the only one who was here from the beginning. The past and the future of the team are alive in Jerry. He prowls the Forum halls during games, he is the unknown player on the NBA logo, and if you ask him about the star-crossed years with the Celtics in the sixties, he still has trouble shaking off the solemnity of those times. Jerry wears a championship ring on his left hand. It isn't the '72 ring that his team won against the Knicks. It is the '85 ring that our team won against the Celtics. It was our generation of Lakers that finally took it from Boston.

Wednesday, October 12

The temperature has stayed high all week and the practices long, but I have found out that my conditioning is all right and I just might make it. I sustained myself through every drill, and the conditioning drills were brutal. The eight pounds are gone. So far, my daily notes say the same thing: Practice is tough.

Since the night of the team dinner, Riley has been talking to us about

the pressures that lie ahead. He wrote his usual personal letter to us at
the end of the summer and reiterated its key points at the meeting. We
have an opportunity to go for three. We start out the season with the
toughest schedule ever, seventeen of our first twenty-four games on the
road. And the year's theme song is "Dedicated to the One I Love,"
by the Shirelles, for Kareem Abdul-Jabbar; Riles is a child of the
doo-wop. Before camp, he had also written that if we showed up in peak
condition, the normal two-a-day workouts would be cut to one. He has
kept his word on that.

Defending champs are expected to come into the season mentally
soft. We've been here before, though. We have been through all the
traps and mental potholes of returning champs. Some of the glory of
last year's triumph lingers, you get caught up in the relief of having won
it all, and then the next season is on you immediately. You kind of
resent the hassle of having to gear up again, and something slips by you.
As the season starts, every opponent is playing you like it's the NBA
championship, you remember the effort it took, and you say to yourself,
"Oh, man, this is what we did last year." And you get a little drop-off
in desire. You're contemplating epic weariness.

Every team is hungry to take it away from you, and if you lose your
own hunger, they jump on it. That's what the rest of the league is
waiting for. And you're not supposed to lose two or three in a row, even
though it's hard for any team in the NBA to win a lot of games in a
row. You are eligible to lose at any time, as Riley says, and no one has
it made in the NBA, ever. The world chips away at the base of a
champion the moment you become one. You have to fight the mentality that you *were* the champs. That's what makes it so hard to repeat.

All of this was talked about in our meetings during the week.

There's a tremendous work ethic and seriousness on the team, and
we know how to stay hungry and to keep the complacency of success
from getting a grip on us. We instinctively know how to pace ourselves
so we are ready to go when the play-offs come around in the spring.
It is tough, three months after athletic combat, to return with any
degree of intensity or concentration, but we seem to have done it this
season. Everybody seems to have come in with the motivation to go
on and win it again. The title is ours until somebody takes it away. And
there's another one out there to be had.

No one else expects us to be contenders. It was the same thing last
year and the year before. No one expected us to win in '87 and no one
expected us to win last year, in '88. At the beginning of that season,
we were the defending world champs, but the analysts buried us:

"Kareem is too old, Magic complacent, the Lakers too tired to hold off a field of improved opponents."

Last April, on a Sunday afternoon before the play-offs, CBS televised a roundtable discussion with Hubie Brown, Tommy Heinsohn, Billy Cunningham, and Billy Packer. They didn't pick us to do well; the panel was unanimous in projecting that we would not repeat. They even raised concerns about our ability to get out of the West, to advance past the second and third rounds of the play-offs into the fourth round of the finals with the opponent from the East.

This preseason, the national prognosticators have foretold that we will fall early to either Seattle, Portland, Dallas, or Utah. No one has picked us to win the Western Conference. "If winning two in a row is so hard, isn't it crazy to think about three for the Lakers? After two mentally draining championship campaigns, hasn't the effort left them too depleted to try it all over again, and aren't the Lakers entitled to a rest?"

The press has adopted a little more of a wait-and-see attitude this year, but basically they don't stick with us. There's still an element of new-kid-on-the-block about the Lakers, even though we have dominated the league this decade. It is the consequence of eastern media myopia, which sees the world on the other side of the Hudson River indistinctly. The three major television networks are based in New York, as well as the major wire services, magazine publishers, and the most influential daily newspaper. As a result of this New York media bias, there is a certain denigration of events that happen in L.A. as less serious or nonserious, as bizarre coastal exotica. In world-championship play, the Lakers have taken two out of three from the Celtics, who are supposed to be the gritty blue-collar boys. But we are portrayed as dreamers from lotusland, flash without substance, talented but spoiled, on location rather than on the job. And they always end up talking about Los Angeles weather ultimately weakening our style of play. That one always gets to me. But I think Los Angeles as a city has finally come a long way out of the shadow of New York. And I think in winning the back-to-back the Lakers obliterated a lot of the stereotypes. We finally impressed a few people last year.

Around six o'clock this evening, the sun low in the sky, there was a sudden downpour of rain that started to cool things off some. A few people stayed in the water, but the beach below my hotel balcony was mostly deserted. I went out for Thai food, as I have done most nights since we've been here, and then back in my room watched the tape delay of the Dodgers winning the pennant against the Mets today in L.A. Though I'd already heard the news that they'd won, I wanted to see how they scored the runs. The Dodgers are long shots, but this offers some hope.

Yesterday, the Warriors came in from Oakland to play two exhibition games with us, tomorrow night and the night after, before we return to the mainland. As of today, our six days of training camp are over, and, in spite of the intensity of the workouts, there were no injuries this year. Physically, I think we're ready. Everybody is in great shape, and I believe Orlando is going to help us. He looked strong in practices. He's a tremendous athlete, and we're in need of backup help in the forward position for James and A.C. I believe Orlando will fit in on the floor, and socially he fit in right away.

Orlando is coming to our team under tough circumstances. He was a starter with the Chicago Bulls for five years and with the New Jersey Nets for the last two, an explosive, quick, acrobatic player and a big scorer. He had developed into one of the best all-around forwards in the league and, like many forwards in basketball, has the powerful frame and outline of a great boxer, only he's taller. Orlando is six feet nine, the same height as James and A.C. and also Magic. He said that in his rookie year he started using cocaine, and the using became progressive until last year, when it ran him off a New Jersey highway.

Orlando is from a small rural town in Louisiana, south of Shreveport. His father taught high school down there, and Orlando is seriously educated. He didn't go to college at Notre Dame just to play basketball—he got some education while he was there, and his sister now is studying to become a doctor. I always like that in a family, a high value placed on education, because it means they understand what life in America is about, especially for blacks. For Asians and Jews and other immigrant cultures, education has been a constant. But it's not something that most American blacks have focused on. We have only been here three hundred years, and it's about time we figured that out. Personally, I was fortunate that my own family passed on to me a legacy of using education as a means to better ourselves. The West Indian blacks had that tradition, and both of my parents felt strongly about learning as a key to a future.

I knew something was wrong with Orlando last year when I heard that he hadn't shown up for a game, an event that made the national news. I first got to know him when he approached me at the '84 All-Star game and said, "Hey, man, I read your book and loved it. My wife read it too. Will you sign it for me?" He was twenty-five then, playing for

Chicago, and he had married his high school sweetheart. They have a two-year-old son named Zachary now. Whenever I would see Orlando after that, we'd talk a little. He was a nice young man and anybody who reads is always a find for me.

So I *knew* Orlando. And when I heard that he said he had gotten into a car accident, became woozy, and checked into a hotel so he wouldn't be out on dangerous rainy roads, I thought to myself, "He's messing around with drugs." I recognized his account as the kind of lie that people tell when they have given themselves over to that shit, when they don't want to have anything to do with anything but their drug, the Peruvian marching powder. I have known other athletes who have wound up with a cocaine addiction and, beyond athletes, too many other people.

Orlando actually had been in an accident, but it was drug-related. He had missed the Nets' team bus to Philadelphia and tried to rush, loaded, to the game in his own car. It was a rainy night in February and he ran his car off the New Jersey Turnpike and into a ditch, striking his head on the steering wheel and blacking out. After he came to, he didn't tell anyone of his whereabouts for twenty-eight hours.

It was that incident, fortunately, that woke Orlando up. He checked himself into the league's drug-treatment center in Van Nuys, a town in the San Fernando Valley just north across the hills from Los Angeles. Making recovery his first priority, he sidelined himself for the rest of the season and then, in August, just two months ago, signed with Jerry to play with the Lakers for the next four years. Jerry had been a boyhood idol of Orlando's. And Orlando said that last spring he had followed the play-offs on television and that while watching James drag his chronically tender left knee through each series he thought to himself, without imagining it would ever happen, "I bet I could fit in with them. I bet I could be their third forward."

Under salary-cap restrictions, the maximum Jerry could offer Orlando for the first year was half of the $1 million he had been making with the Nets. But Orlando took the drastic cut in pay and came with us. Both Washington and Philadelphia offered him more, but the Bullets and the Sixers are teams in transition, a lot like the team he left, and they are also three thousand miles away from the home base of his recovery program. Over money, Orlando chose Los Angeles and the stability and success of the Laker team. After having been a starter for New Jersey, he'll be coming off the bench for us, along with Cooper and Mychal Thompson, but he has come in an unselfish player and that should help him make the adjustment.

Orlando's excitement to be playing with us has been obvious all week in the gym. He says he has "an attitude of gratitude" and that it's like a dream come true after seven long, cold, losing seasons. Neither Chicago nor New Jersey has ever won a championship. His battle with drug and alcohol abuse will be an ongoing thing and he will be under a national microscope, but he doesn't have to prove anything to the Lakers. He may have to prove something to himself, but the team is going to accept him because we respect his talent and the courage and discipline he exhibits in recovering after stumbling along the path. There isn't one of us who hasn't stumbled in some way.

I told Orlando where he could get some good soft-shell crabs in L.A. and he thanked me for that.

Friday, October 14

Shootaround for the first exhibition game with Golden State was at nine-thirty in the morning yesterday and when the team got to Honolulu's Blaisdell Arena where the games were to be played, Jerry was out there alone on the court shooting baskets. He does that sometimes. He still has his touch. Everybody was feeling good. We won both sold-out games with the Warriors, the first by nineteen and the one tonight by twenty points. They were straightforward wins.

I noticed that Ralph Sampson has gained some needed weight and Manute Bol has improved. They both play center for Golden State. At seven feet, seven inches, Manute is the tallest player in NBA history. And Ralph Sampson and he together, Sampson being seven-four, are the tallest teammates in NBA history. I remember being in Paris in the off-season three or four years ago and hearing from a friend about Manute for the first time. I said to my friend, "Come on, seven-seven and a hundred and ninety pounds?" I remember laughing and saying, "No, that's impossible. People don't come in that shape." But then there he is, narrow, vertical, long-limbed, like some rare exotic elongated plant, his arms reaching nearly eight feet outstretched, the length of a long picnic table. Manute can merely lean on the court and cover distance. Taking a shot, you can be far enough away from him that were it anyone else you could shoot completely unmolested, but then Manute's arm just extends and he taps it away. He's disconcerting.

Manute comes from a family of farmers and cowherds in Africa, where he was born a member of the Dinka tribe, the largest and tallest tribe in the Sudan. His physical outline is the same as his people's, spearlike. This leaves him vulnerable on the court in a way he would never be in the African grasslands. Without weight proportionate to his height, Manute collapses when you bump him on the floor, and when he collapses he can't shoot. So against him, I get to be a bully. It's hard for him to deal with the crunch inside. But I can see that Don Nelson's coaching has really helped him work on shooting the ball, including a shot from three-point range. With Manute on the court, I am constantly made to understand how others who are smaller must feel around me. He is not the first guy taller than me to have come along, though—that was Tom Burleson, who started with Seattle in my last year with Milwaukee. He was seven-four, two inches taller than me and three inches shorter than Manute.

Within our team, we call Manute the Dinka dunker.

We leave Hawaii with high hopes.

The season starts for us with a tough road schedule—in two months we will be home only for ten games—but I think it's good we get it out of the way early this year. The coaches have given us a 19-10 goal, nineteen wins, ten losses, by the end of December. For now we are not looking past that.

Last year, the team began the season with the mantle of Riley's guarantee, however loosely some of us may have worn it. Minutes after we had won the championship the year before, to the press and to the fans, Riley had "guaranteed" that we would repeat the following season, a feat no team had accomplished in nineteen years. This year, we don't have to deal with that, with either a raw guarantee or with our own private unsatisfied passions to repeat. I think we took a big burden off by winning two in a row. During the regular season this year, the extraordinary still will be expected, losses will be seen as signs of weakness, victories will be passed over, and game to game we still will be the team to beat—all familiar pressures. The fierce instinct to defeat the champs will remain undiminished. But it's not like the competition can take anything from us now. We did what we wanted to do, when we wanted to do it. Psychologically, the competitive chemistry has been altered in our favor.

I can't predict whether we will win it all again this year, or even whether we will make it into the finals. But if it's supposed to happen, it will happen. Muslims call that kismet, *qismah* in Arabic. Fortunately, for the most part I have been able to take this attitude with me into every professional season. Musashi says that to win in battle, you must prepare yourself for everything, but without attachment to outcome. Do not have preferences, he says. Do not let the enemy see your spirit. Do not let one success be the final success. Miyamoto Musashi was the most renowned samurai warrior in Japan, the "sword-saint," who was inspired by the teachings of Zen and who transformed the military arts into the highest form of spiritual study. His swordsmanship was his art and his spiritual discipline. He left behind a guide, which, toward the end of his long life, he wrote on sheafs of paper from within a solitary cave in Japan's mountain country. His few thousand words from the seventeenth century became *A Book of Five Rings*. I read from it constantly.

Monday, October 17

Over the weekend, I started reading Hunter Thompson's *Generation of Swine*. I read his earlier collection of essays *The Great Shark Hunt* and think he is a great essayist. I see Hunter Thompson as our late-twentieth-century answer to Mark Twain. He's got that insightful, outlaw view. Mark Twain's essays jabbed at people's bullshit and hypocrisy, and Hunter Thompson's do the same. He is still on Nixon's case. And now he's got Ferdinand and Imelda to work on. Three thousand pairs of shoes! And she tried to say they were for the maids, all of her maids wearing size eight and a half.

I am back in L.A. We got back on Saturday, two days ago. I slept most of the day except to watch the opening game of the World Series on television. I dozed off in the ninth inning, though, right when Kirk Gibson hit the game-winning homer that sent everybody reeling. The Dodgers were one out away from a 4–3 loss to the Oakland A's. Dennis Eckersley had just come in at the start of the ninth to pitch the last inning for the A's, getting the first two batters out. The Dodgers sent up pinch hitter Mike Davis, who walked, and then there was that long wait for Gibson. Somewhere during all of that I fell asleep. With two bad legs—a hamstring strain in one, a sprained knee ligament in the other—Gibson had hobbled out of the dugout and limped up to the plate to face Eckersley. Seven suspenseful pitches later, with a full count of two strikes and three balls and having fouled off twice, Gibson hit one over the right-field wall of Dodger Stadium, one of the most dramatic home runs in the history of baseball, and the Dodgers won the first game of the Series 5–4. Gibson could hardly make it around the bases. I snapped awake about thirty seconds after he did it. I console myself that I caught the first replay.

Sunday we had off and then practice was scheduled for eleven o'clock this morning at Loyola. On top of a bluff overlooking the wetlands of Ballona Creek, which joins the ocean within eyesight, Loyola Marymount is the Catholic university just north of Los Angeles Airport. Loyola's gym is our regular practice facility during the year, and this was the first time we had been inside it since the end of last season. From now until the end of this season, I will be driving, on a daily basis, either to Loyola, to the Forum, or to the airport. Grooves have been worn in my routes to these three places. Each only minutes from the other, they constitute a small three-cornered piece of geography that is the center of the Laker team's work life. The Forum is several miles to the east of the airport, which is several miles to the south of Loyola. I live about fifteen miles above this triangle, directly north, up in the hills that stretch across the city of Los Angeles. I have lived on the same lot in the same canyon for all of the years I have been here. I wanted my home to be as far away from the arena as possible without having to move into the flat plain of the Valley, on the other side of the hills.

The hills here are semiwild and semidesert. In the canyon where I live the road is narrow, and the houses have landscaped gardens and flowering trees that coexist with impenetrable scrub brush and chaparral on the steep hillsides where deer, coyotes, raccoons, lizards, and rattlesnakes also live. Before I built a fence around my house, the deer used to come into the shade of my backyard and eat my roses when the heat would drive them down into the cooler parts of the canyon. At the top of the road is an earthen dam and reservoir that has been there since the twenties. In the movie *Chinatown,* this is the reservoir where they found Hollis Mulwray dead and where Roman Polanski's character knife-slit the nose of Jack Nicholson's character, Jake Gittes. So there's a *film noir* quality here too. Raymond Chandler was a master at capturing the night darkness prowling slowly upon these hills. The hills run to the east all the way to Dodger Stadium in Chavez Ravine, just yards from downtown, and to the west all the way to the ocean. Sometimes the sea fog is here all day.

This place is my urban retreat. I enjoy the abruptness of transition from basketball and the city streets of L.A. to the relative wilderness and quiet of my home here. One of the things that sold me on the property when I first saw it so many years ago was the tall grove of sycamores standing on either side of the road by the house. There had been sycamores back in my neighborhood in upper Manhattan and I used to climb in them all the time. As it turns out, there are also sycamores native to the canyons of Southern California, massive ornamental trees, deep-rooted, and found growing in stream bottoms and ravines, like in the ravine that borders the road here. The sycamore tree has a beautiful light-gray bark that makes the black gash on the trunk of the large one on the side of the house stand out all the more. That particular tree bears the charred scar of the fire that burned my original house to the ground nearly six years ago. It is the fire's only remaining visible mark.

I was on the road in Boston when it happened. It was the last day in January during the 1982–83 season. During the night, a fire had started in some wiring behind one of the walls in the house. The call to the fire department went out quickly enough to have saved it but, ironically, the house's fireproof roof had turned the house into a raging furnace. In the canyons, explosive brush fires are an ever-present danger, especially during fire weather in the summer, or any time of year when a Santa Ana wind comes blowing hot and dry into Los Angeles from across the Mojave Desert. Cinders and ash falling onto a roof of wood shakes could ignite easily. So I had put a new fireproof roof on my then one-story house, and it had acted like a sealed lid, escalating the fire inside into a conflagration. The fire annihilated my material existence.

I had gotten a call about the fire at seven in the morning, Boston time. I flew home, and I remember riding up the street to the house, expecting to see maybe a corner of it burnt up. But as I came to the bend in the road where normally I could see the roof of the house up ahead, it was gone. When I pulled up front, media and onlookers all around, there was nothing left but the black remains of some of the walls. It looked like somebody had dropped a bomb on it. Slowly, I got out of the car and walked through the rubble. The house and everything in it, everything I owned, a lifetime of possessions, my book and music libraries, priceless Korans, the jazz collection I'd started in high school, my Asian and Middle Eastern rugs, old photographs, my wardrobe, every sock, every dish, all had been incinerated. In an instant, my material world had been reduced to a carry-on bag, the few things that I had brought with me on the road. It was a neat statement on life.

I had never thought of myself as a materialist, but when you lose it all, you discover quickly and exactly where you stand in that respect.

It was a test for me, a kind of invoice from the universe. Flash fires come through and clean the earth for fresh growth, and that's basically what happened to me. I learned a lot about myself and also about the things we all strive to own, including shelter. They are nice, but they aren't what make life wonderful. No matter what their quality of beauty or comfort, they are still only things, and transitory—you can't take them with you. That was a hard lesson to learn. There was some pain involved, but the lesson was timely for me, and probably necessary. Step by step, I got my priorities straightened out, and my life since then has only gotten better.

The fire happened just around the time that I was finishing up my first book. I had been at work on it for a few years, excavating the past and trying to put down the main lines of my story up to that point in my life. Writing it had been cathartic and cleansing. It represented a kind of opening up for me. Ever since childhood, I have had an ability to draw into myself and be perfectly contented. I *had* to hone that ability. I had been a minority of one, the only child, singularly tall, black, and Catholic. I learned the essential lesson early on that there's a place inside oneself that no one else can violate, that no one else can enter, and that we have a right to protect that place. But in regard to other areas of my personal development, as far as relationships with others were concerned and as far as making decisions on my own about my life, I was late in getting started. For a long time, I didn't let too many people in, and also it was a long time before I was able to take my own life in my own hands.

Only in the last ten years do I feel I have made some serious breakthroughs in that direction. I had been taught obedience by the masters, by my parents, my coaches, my religious teachers. As a basketball star, beginning back in high school, it was just so easy to let the elders insulate me from everything, including the fans and the press. I liked it that way then, and there were immediate rewards, like winning basketball games. At the same time, at home, I had picked up a quietness and a certain formal demeanor from my father that, without my understanding it fully, created another kind of distance between myself and other people.

Only with time and after feeling often misunderstood was I able eventually to realize my part in any misunderstandings and the ability I have to close the distances. Writing my book was really the final act of getting that all out. And looking back on it now, the fire and its aftermath were like the final punctuation marks.

As word got out about the fire, albums and books began finding their

way into my hands from every part of the country. Friends and strangers, fans, people I never knew were there before, tried to help replace
my collections and my loss. It was like Frank Capra's classic film *It's
a Wonderful Life*. James Stewart is in financial trouble and in need of
help and doesn't realize how much he has coming back to him in life.
Then everyone in town shows up and brings him things and, in the end,
overwhelmed, he has more of everything than he needed. I felt something like that in those first disorienting months.

The day after the house burned down, I remember Quincy Jones
came up here with his wife. They lived just down the street from me
then, and Quincy and I had become friends. Knowing that all my jazz
recordings were gone, he had brought with him some Clifford Brown
tapes to give to me. Clifford Brown had been a genius trumpeter, like
Quincy himself, and had overshadowed Miles Davis. In the fifties, he
had died at a young age on the Pennsylvania Turnpike, along with Bud
Powell's brother. Those Clifford Brown tapes from Quincy were the
start of my new music collection.

At the end of that year, my book came out. I called it *Giant Steps*,
inspired by a Coltrane title. At the final hour, though, I had terrible
second thoughts about publishing it, afraid my private revelations
would wipe me out with the public. I called New York a few weeks
before the release date and told them to forget it. They said to me, in
essence, "Sorry, son. You should have said something sooner. The
books are printed, bound, and ready to be shipped. It's too late to stop
it now." Fortunately, the book was well received. After telling everybody all my sins and indiscretions, my angers and fears and dreams, I
still had some fans out there, maybe more. That let me know that
people can accept me with all the bumps and blemishes. I started
looking up at faces in the crowd and realizing there could be many
friends up there.

It was almost three years before there was another house on this lot,
the house I live in now. For a while, I rented a place at the end of the
street, and then I moved to another house a few miles west of here.
At the time of the fire, I was living with my two-year-old-son, Amir,
and his mother. They had been there that night and had awoken in
time to escape unharmed.

At that point, I had been involved with Amir's mother for more than
five years. But long before the fire I had begun to see that our relationship was not going to last forever. There were some basic incompatibili-
ties that we ultimately couldn't overcome. After the house was
destroyed and we were uprooted, and also after a tough season in my

basketball life—Philadelphia swept us 4–0 in the finals that May, a horrible and haunting experience—things started to come apart. I was gone by the next April.

I moved out of the place we were renting and into one of the high-rises on Wilshire Boulevard in Westwood. Right away I established that Amir would be spending time with me there; I didn't leave until that was straight. By that time, construction had started on the new house. I was putting my life back together and knew it was best that Amir's mother not be a part of that, but I was adamant that my son would be. I was determined not to be separated from him, that he and I would have substantial time together. Amir was three and a half then, and the first of my four children with whom I'd had any stretch of time to function as the father I should be and wanted to be. At my place on Wilshire, Amir had his own bedroom. I went out and got him a bed, toys, everything, for when he came and stayed with me.

A year and a half later, I finally made it back to my spot in the canyon. I live now in a large two-story house, spacious enough for my size, and with enough bedrooms for Amir and my other three children when they visit: Habiba, Sultana, and Kareem. I've also got my own gym, a little workout space separate from the house, on the side in back. Slowly, I have replaced my rugs and art and furniture. Many weekends, when I am not on the road, Amir is here with me. And Lourdes, my housekeeper, stays here when I'm here; she is part of the trusted infrastructure of my life. Otherwise, I live alone. It's peaceful, and I find a lot of freedom in my privacy. In the past six years of my life, I think I have finally grown up.

Last summer, I had the idea to level off a spot of the rough hillside up behind my house that is open to the morning and afternoon sun. Steep, there wasn't much room for a perch, but what there was I had paved with flagstones and had about a hundred steps cut into the side of the hill. Now I can read up there, listen to music, and catch the sun, with no shadows to chase me around. From my aerie, I watch the hawks circling the canyons.

Thursday, October 20

I watched the Dodgers win the World Series tonight. They beat the A's in Game 5 up in the Oakland Coliseum to win their first world championship since 1981. They were seeded low this year and weren't supposed to go anywhere. But the way they played and were winning over the last week, beginning with Kirk Gibson's heartstopper in Game 1, they captured everybody's imagination.

Wednesday, November 2

At practice this morning, we found out that Mike Smrek had been traded to San Antonio, so as of today our team for the season is set. Smrek was the last player to go, and taking the twelfth spot is Mark McNamara, a five-year veteran, six feet eleven, who will be the second backup center behind Mychal Thompson.

The first game of the regular season is Friday in Dallas, two days from now. After the game we'll take a midnight flight to San Antonio, where we play the Spurs the following night. So we start off on the road. We leave for Dallas tomorrow. We practice at Loyola at ten o'clock and then go directly from there to the airport, where we have a two o'clock plane.

Our first game at home, in the Forum, will be a week from today.

Now we begin the long walk through eighty-two games, and my last climb up Everest.

From now until the play-offs begin at the end of April, my job and that of my teammates will be to stay consistent and to stay healthy. Championships aren't won in the regular season—they're not won until June—but you can't get to them without giving your best each night when it comes time to play. You want to do well. That's what it's *all* about.

Basketball is a game of the long season. And once the season starts, daily life revolves around practices, naps, and games, hotels and airport terminals. There are no regular weekends as most people know them. Under arena lights, we're out there running on a hardwood court most Friday and Saturday nights, either away or at home. Time isn't broken up in the usual ways for us. It's not punctuated into weeks. It's punctuated more by places. Days run into days. Games run into games. And when one game is over, the most important thing is the next game and keeping your state of preparation constant. From the beginning of October until the end of the season, which could come as late as June, there is usually no longer than a day at a time without basketball.

So, it's that time.

Time to go to work.

III

The Season: Life in the Salt Mines

The Forum is located on the Los Angeles basin's coastal flatlands in the town of Inglewood. Manchester Boulevard borders it to the north, Prairie Avenue to the west, a small arena-created street called Forum Road to the east, and then Ninetieth Street to the south. Below Ninetieth Street is Hollywood Park, which stretches farther south, three hundred acres of stables and racetrack built back in the thirties. The Forum was built on a parcel of thirty acres during a building frenzy of sports arenas across the country in the late sixties. It opened just three months after the Spectrum in Philadelphia and two months before the present incarnation of Madison Square Garden. In fact, the same architect who designed the Garden designed the Forum, except that trains run directly underneath the Garden, which stands all above ground, and planes fly directly over the Forum, which stands both above *and* below ground, right on the flight pattern for jets coming into L.A. Airport.

The Forum occupies a large square block, the major portion of it a vast parking lot, and in the center is the arena, a massive circular building supported by eighty white sixty-foot-high arched concrete columns. The design is a modern, roofed version of the ancient open-air Colosseum in Rome, civilization's oldest stadium in the round. The building itself occupies about four acres, and the arena floor is a couple of stories below ground. There are two excavated underground rings inside, the top ring a circle of administrative offices, including all the Laker offices, among them those of Jerry West, Pat Riley, and the owner, Jerry Buss. Off the bottom ring, which encircles the arena floor, are the Lakers' dressing room, the visitors' dressing room, the officials' room, and the press room. It is the catacombs down there. The box office and the entrance lobbies for the public are on a third ring up above ground level. As Italianate as the Forum's exterior is, the behind-the-scenes, below-ground interior is spartan, clean, and sparing in elegant detail, with a lot of exposed concrete and steel. There's rarely anything gilt-edged or glamorous about a professional athlete's workplace, and actually I like it that way. I like the functional simplicity.

Out on the arena floor, a giant four-sided electronic scoreboard hangs from the center of the ceiling high above, and there are no interior support columns to obstruct the view of the action from any seat anywhere in the arena. The basketball capacity is 17,505 and it's about a thousand less for hockey. Like most of the other sports arenas in the league, the Forum alternates basketball nights with hockey nights and other scheduled events. The Kings hockey team shares the arena with the Lakers, and the seasons overlap, the Kings starting and finishing up about a month earlier. The ice on the arena floor is made in September and remains frozen for at least seven months, until the end of the hockey season, which is sometime in the spring. The basketball floor is put on top, with three layers of plywood and foam insulation in between the ice and the hardwood. In four-by-eight-foot pieces, the hardwood floor is assembled like a puzzle, starting at the north end of the court and finishing at the south end. It is disassembled in the reverse direction. There are thirty-two in the changeover crew, and every changeover takes no longer than six hours. After a Laker game, the teardown from hardwood to ice can begin within the hour. The pieces of the basketball floor are the same pieces from back when the Forum first opened twenty years ago, which means that I have played on one floor for all of the time I've been here, and it's the same floor that carried Jerry, Elgin, and Wilt. Every five years the hardwood has been sanded down and refinished completely, and every season small repairs are made.

At the far south end of the court, high up on the arena wall, hang five gold-and-purple world-championship banners, one for the first 1972 title and the others for 1980, 1982, 1985, and 1987. A sixth banner for last year's 1988 title will be hung during this year's home opener. Across from the banners, on the opposite north wall, are the retired jerseys of West, Baylor, and Chamberlain, numbers 44, 22, and 13. And among them is the hockey jersey of Rogie Vachon, number 30, one of the great hockey goalies of the seventies.

Just below these jerseys are the seats from where, high up, Jerry Buss watches the games. With eighty-six seats set aside for himself, friends, and colleagues, everybody has taken to calling this spot the "skybox." Educated as a scientist and self-taught in real estate, Jerry became a self-made millionaire by the time he was thirty-five. He grew up in Kemmerer, Wyoming, moved when he was twenty to Los Angeles, where he got his doctorate in chemistry at USC, *Doctor* Buss, and then in his mid-forties, after making his fortune, bought the Lakers and the Forum itself from the previous owner, another self-made millionaire, Jack Kent Cooke. That was nine years ago. We won the 1980 title the first season he took over. And it's been a long stretch of success and stability ever since. In his mid-fifties now, Jerry has played a large part in that, proving himself to be an astute owner. So often owners can screw things up, wrongly believing themselves to be as expert at basketball as they have been at business. But as much as Jerry loves the team and knows the game, he leaves key basketball decisions like picking talent up to the other Jerry, Jerry West. The stability of a team starts with an owner who backs the general manager, who in turn backs the coach. It's all a tight-knit unit. And Jerry Buss is always there. He has a woman executive, Claire Rothman, to run things on the Forum side of his business. She is one of only two women in the country to manage a major sports arena.

In Los Angeles, no ticket can cost more than a ticket to a Laker game, or be as hard to come by. Season tickets are no longer even available, because the Forum has sold all that it can sell. And over the last ten years, just two spots have been relinquished at courtside, where seats are the priciest and rarest, the Koh-i-noor diamond of seats. There are only 128 of them. In the 1979–80 season, when Jerry Buss bought the team, the courtside seats were $15 each. The next year they increased to $45, then $60, and on upward, until reaching their present figure of $250–$275 for play-off games. Next season, the cost will be a staggering $350 and $375. For an evening out, only Madame LaLa's bordello would cost more. The most expensive ticket for the L.A. Philharmonic, the ballet, or theater in town is $50, and the richest ticket for the L.A. Dodgers, even for club and dugout seats, is $10. And nowhere else in any arena in the league is the ticket price remotely comparable for the choice few front-row seats that exist along the sidelines. In the Forum, just a "good" seat costs $60—in the first tier or two.

The denizens at courtside are largely music- and film-industry people, many like Joe Smith, the president of Capitol Records, who has been coming to Laker games since the beginning, before my time, before there was even any radio coverage and only three thousand fans would show up. Movie producer Mike Frankovich and his wife, Binnie Barnes, who was a screen star in the first talking pictures, have been coming for as long as I can remember. Also cinematographer Haskell Wexler. In recent years, Dyan Cannon and Rob Lowe have been faithfuls, and sometimes the regulars give their seats to a friend on nights they can't make it.

Sean Connery came one night. I had always admired him, especially for his acting in *The Man Who Would Be King* and *The Wind and the Lion,* in which he played an Arab Muslim of both heroic and human dimensions, one of the few positive film images we have of Islam. When I met Sean in the locker room after the game, he said to me, with his Scottish burr, the way he speaks naturally offscreen,

"Metaphysically as well as literally, I can see you stand head and shoulders above the rest of the gentlemen, Kareem." We talked briefly, him telling me he'd been an athlete once, a body builder. I hadn't known that about him. Many come through the locker room, but that meeting with Sean stands out.

Those who pay to be at courtside sit alongside those of us who are paid to be there. The working press have most of the baseline behind the basket at the north end of the court. Dr. Robert Kerlan and Dr. Stephen Lombardo, the team physicians, have seats on the western sideline. And across the floor, on the eastern sideline, are the players, the Lakers' bench toward the south end of the court and the visiting team's bench toward the other end, near the press. In between, at midcourt, is the scorer and announcer's table. The Lakers' public-address announcer is Lawrence Tanter, a former DJ with a deep baritone voice who, at six-six, also used to play basketball back in high school and college in the Midwest. I call him L.T. for short. We have long shared an interest in jazz, even before he began announcing Laker games seven years ago. He used to come back to the locker room and bring me free records. He named his five-year-old son Miles, after Miles Davis.

Immediately to L.T.'s right, tucked in between the scorer's table and the visitor's bench, are six courtside seats. Four of these belong to Jack and Lou, Jack Nicholson and Lou Adler. They have two seats each, the same seats they have had for well over ten years. But Jack and Lou have been coming to Laker games for twenty years, as far back as 1970, the year they met and discovered they had a mutual interest in basketball. They had been coming to games already when I came to town. Together, they started out way up in the rafters, between the foul line and the basket, and as they demonstrated their consistency as fans and as Jack became more successful, over the years they worked their way down toward the floor, until they ended up midcourt, where they are now. By that time, Jack had already done *Chinatown* and *One Flew Over the Cuckoo's Nest.*

From where they sit, Jack and Lou get a good feel for the game. They are able to hear the streams of on-court dialogue, the officials' discussions on calls at the scorer's table, and talk from the opponents' bench. Visiting coaches pace directly in front of Jack and Lou, and over the years, in a kind of respectful detente, Jack and Lou have gotten to know them, and many of the refs as well. Jack and Lou are like sentinels out there. They are serious, veteran fans, and they're there for every game. Rarely do they miss one. They pace themselves like the players do, and keep their own counsel during the season when it comes to the mercurial opinions of the press. They didn't leave during the lean times in the seventies, when the team went six years without getting to the finals, two of those without even making it into the play-offs. They laughed their way through the bad times, they said.

I think Jack and Lou appreciate what we do, the way artists appreciate each other's work. Jack says basketball is the classical music of sport, and that sports is the only place he can go and not know how it's going to end. He usually turns up in some outrageous socks or *film noir* shoes, and Lou in some bohemian hat and sneakers. They are the avant-garde presence at courtside and, affluent as they have become, they bring an element of street. Lou was born in Boyle Heights in East L.A., on the other side of the Los Angeles River, near downtown. Jack was born in Neptune, New Jersey, a small town near Asbury Park, where he grew up around blacks and played pickup basketball games in the playgrounds. Each about the same age, about ten years older than me, Jack and Lou both played high school basketball and both played guard. Jack was the sixth man on his team, Michael Cooper's position with the Lakers.

Lou still plays basketball on a regular basis with friends. He says he's acquired a detachment about almost everything in his life except for his kids and basketball. With his music he can be objective, but basketball gets him in the gut. Starting out as a songwriting partner with Herb Alpert, Lou became a record producer with a streak of hits in the sixties and seventies from talent like Johnny Rivers, Carole King, and the Mamas and the Papas. On Sunset Strip in Hollywood, Lou co-owns the Roxy theater, a music nightclub, and On the Rox, the private club upstairs, where for some years now we have gone to celebrate late-night after winning the world championships. But I think the dancing parties started there with one of my birthdays, way back before my fortieth.

Only recently did Lou reactivate Ode Records, his record label, having taken a long break from music to raise his two sons, Nicolai and Cisco. When Nicolai turned five or six, I remember him coming with Lou to nearly every game. He grew up in those seats in the Forum. Cisco Sam is five years younger, "Cisco" for the Cisco Kid and "Sam" for Sam Cooke—romance and soul, Lou says. I have a photograph of me holding Cisco when he was just three or four weeks old, smaller than a ball cradled in my two hands. Lou tells me that Cisco is real proud of the picture, which makes *me* proud. In age, my oldest son, Kareem, falls in between Nicolai and Cisco, and along with Amir, who was the youngest, we used to visit Lou and his kids at Lou's house on the beach up in Malibu. It was there that I first learned about art nouveau, a turn-of-the-century design style, subtle and free-flowing, emphasizing natural forms. The interior of Lou's house is all art nouveau, and he has a wonderful collection of furniture and art glass from that period. I began collecting myself after I started visiting Lou, but those pieces burned in the fire. I have since replaced many of them, and when rebuilding the house I commissioned the architectural details, the brass, woodwork, tile, and stained glass to be done in that style. Very gentle and back-to-nature, it is a soft counterpoint to the highly structured and ascetic nature of my professional life.

Occasionally, I see Jack off-court too. He lives in the hills up above me, and has a hoop in the driveway. For many years, he has also had a silver tray of torn money sitting on one of the tables in his house, a creation started when the poet Richard Brautigan, visiting one time, ripped up some bills and left them there. Over the years, other friends of Jack's have added to the pile.

Jack is like one of the guys in the neighborhood who would do anything. You laugh at a lot of the stuff he does, like four seasons ago in Boston Garden, when, from a small balcony up above, Jack flashed some obscene body language at the Garden crowd. He and Lou usually travel together to all the road games during the finals, and it was the 1984 finals, the year we choked, the year things got real personal for this generation of Lakers. That was the first time Magic, Coop, Byron, James, and I had faced Boston in world-championship competition. At the point when it became clear we were going to lose, Jack, from his conspicuous spot above the Garden floor, grabbed his crotch in an inciteful gesture toward the whole sea of Celtic fans that were there, an audacious and wonderful act that stole a breath from everybody. He had the whole fifteen thousand screaming at him. The next year they were ready and waiting with choke signs and paraphernalia that said things like "Hit the road, Jack" and "Send Jack back sad." That was the year we won. Subsequently, Boston has come around with some respect for both the Lakers and for Jack, but it was nasty there for a while.

To the team, Jack is like the patriarch or great uncle. From his spot on the sidelines at home in the Forum, he watches intently, and when needed shouts words of encouragement to us or words of discouragement to our opponents. None of the fans resent him because they know he has been here the whole time. He was here when we stunk. After we won the back-to-back last year, he designed a jacket that he had custom-made by his tailor in purple for each of us. On the sleeve are two eight balls for '88 and on the back is scripted the single word *History*, embroidered purple on purple.

This year, Jack will be gone for the first part of the season. He's outside London shooting *Batman*, in which he plays the Joker. He'll have tapes of the games sent to him there.

Wednesday, November 9

Shortly after four-thirty, I left the house for the Forum. The sun had already gone down in the canyon, but once I drove out onto Sunset Boulevard and headed west toward the San Diego Freeway, I could see it still setting, large and red, over the flatter horizon toward the ocean. The game was at seven-thirty, but I like to arrive at the arena early, as I also like the practice of focusing on the game ahead. The mental preparation starts the morning of game day, and I have been doing it for so long, it's second nature. Magic and I usually are the first players to arrive, and usually Magic is there even before me.

The season is five days old, and tonight's game was our home opener. We've played three games so far, two in Texas and one up in Oakland last night. The Dallas game was hectic but we pulled it out. We trailed at the end of each quarter and we were down by as much as eight points until the fourth quarter, when we outscored the Mavericks 10-1, ending up winning the game by three. I was glad to win the first one. We got into San Antonio afterward at 1 A.M., and then lost to the Spurs by fifteen points. This was not only San Antonio's home opener, as it had been for Dallas the night before, but it was the first game under Coach Larry Brown, and they were playing the world champs. Great young athletes, the wave of the future for the game, only three players on the team older than twenty-four, they were flying. We pulled to within four points with only five minutes to play, but we couldn't take it away from them. The San Antonio crowd went crazy. I did all right in the game, putting up sixteen points and ten rebounds, but as a whole I guess we had what Riley calls collective breakdown. We left Texas 1-1.

The game last night against Golden State ended up a win, except for a disturbing incident with Ralph Sampson in the second quarter. Byron was shooting a three-pointer from the left corner when suddenly I took an elbow in the side of the face that sent me reeling to the floor.

Anybody who's played basketball for any length of time knows that, moving as fast and as hard as we do, and in such close quarters on the court, you unavoidably are going to crash into somebody's shoulder or run into somebody's hip or get clipped by somebody's elbow. Those things happen. And everybody realizes it's a physical contest. It's when the physical encounters are intentional rather than accidental that things get torrid. Sampson's elbow felt deliberate to me, and thirty seconds later, while Otis Smith was launching a three-pointer for the Warriors at the other end of the court, I retaliated swiftly by sending Sampson to the floor with my own elbow to the face. From boyhood, I have never had the instinct to fight, but I have always had a temper when provoked, and being prepared to defend myself was something I had to learn in the neighborhood when I was growing up. On the court, normally I am able to channel bursts of momentary fury into more inspired play, but this time I struck back emotionally. I was given a foul and then Riley was given a foul, a technical, for rushing out onto the court toward the melee. For his own part in initiating the affair, Sampson had been spared a foul call. Supposedly the refs hadn't seen his cheap shot, but at halftime in the locker room we watched a tape that showed his blatant move on me.

Ralph is a fine athlete, and I have considered him a friend since he was in college, which probably added salt to last night's wound. Five years ago, through his coach at the University of Virginia, he had asked my advice about whether he should go hardship and enter the pros early or whether he should stay in school and graduate. I told him to stay and get his degree. If his team won the NCAA, his value would go up, and if they didn't, his value would at minimum remain the same and he'd also have an education as well as some seasoning and maturity to help him survive the NBA. He ended up finishing school and becoming the number one draft pick that spring. As with Patrick Ewing later, the pressures on Ralph were enormous, everyone expecting him to be the next me, and when Akeem Olajuwon joined him the next year in Houston, those expectations skyrocketed. The press took to calling them the Twin Towers, and together they were supposed to cut a broad swath through the league. When they didn't, when they failed to win championships for the Rockets and Ralph showed inconsistency in his play, Ralph came under severe criticism, and last December he was traded to the Warriors, missing most of the remaining season because of knee surgery in March, his second knee operation. Perhaps last night was reflective of all the pressures. The incident is resolutely over now, except that my jaw is still noticeably swollen.

.   .   .

From Sunset Boulevard, I turned onto the San Diego Freeway, the 405, and headed south. The four lanes on my side of the road were moving so I didn't have to take one of my alternate routes. You never know what the traffic will be like; it's an adventure. I suppose I ride the L.A. freeways the way I used to ride the subways in New York. I have a kind of guerrilla approach to getting around. I take a certain pleasure in knowing the streets of L.A. and in the deft execution of private shortcuts and pathways.

Off the 405, I passed up the Manchester Boulevard turnoff to the Forum and took the next exit, at Century, instead, making a right onto La Cienega and then another right onto Arbor Vitae, a small street through the neighborhood that goes east the final few miles, dead-ending at the entrance to Hollywood Park, from which you can see the arena. It was dusk by the time I got there, shortly after five o'clock. A slight fall chill was in the air. I made my final turn onto Ninetieth Street and into the high truck tunnel that leads directly down into the south side of the Forum at the arena level, where Magic and I have been given permission to park over the last nine or ten years. Before then it used to be hard after games just to get to our cars.

I saw that Magic was already there, and the guards guided me to a spot next to the west tunnel wall. Some of those guards have been there forever. We've grown accustomed to each other. When Byron was a kid he used to sneak into games at that same entrance, and I have no doubt he put the slip on some of those same tunnel guards. The players' entrance is down there, so Byron just walks right on in now.

I went through the double doors and down the hallway around to the players' dressing room. Normally, for a 7:30 game, Riley wants us in the locker room by 6:00 and wants everybody dressed, treated, and ready to go by 6:45. Then he usually comes down from his office upstairs for a pregame meeting. Everything was moved up half an hour tonight, though, because we had a walk-through scheduled for 5:30. Since we didn't get home from Oakland until 2:00 A.M., this morning's shootaround was canceled, and a thirty-minute walk-through before the game was to be the stand-in for that.

I changed and went out into the arena, where Magic and Mark McNamara were sitting along the sidelines watching the Laker Girls rehearse their routines out on the floor. The Laker Girls are a show-time touch added by Jerry Buss, fifteen talented dancers who have a reputation for being best in the league. You could feel the buzz of opening night in the air.

Chick Hearn was already in his spot in the first row of the upper press box, making his preparations for the evening's broadcast and for the pregame ceremony, in which rings would be given out for last spring's championship. Actually, Chick is always at the arena early, probably earlier than anyone. He likes the quiet before the crowd gets there, and he's always ready. He warms up too. In his twenty-eight seasons of doing play-by-play over the air for the Lakers, Chick has missed a game only twice. He loves the team like he loves the game, but he's not above dishing out his criticism. I don't think there's one of us on the team who hasn't met with Chick's proprietary disapproval on a number of occasions. He says that anybody who doesn't think he wants the Lakers to win is a fool, but that he's no "homer." Jerry West says he can tell by Chick's tone on the radio whether we're winning or losing. Chick broadcasts our games on radio and television both, but he started out in radio, which is maybe why he has one of those rare voices in sports, intimate, colorful, flamboyant, that can draw his listeners up into the sight and sound of a game through words alone. Chick is like a big-city Garrison Keillor in a big-time sport.

Once the whole team had come out onto the floor, Bertka closed the arena to all but the team and Chick, high above the sidelines. Bill Bertka has been the top assistant coach since Riley took over as head coach seven years ago. In his early sixties, with most of those years steeped in basketball, Bertka is the consummate older voice of knowledge and experience in the game. He's like the research-and-idea man for Riley, and he also coaches the big men—me, Mychal T., A.C., and now Mark too. He has a great basketball mind, always looking at the big picture, and always knowing fundamentally why a game does or doesn't work, wisdom that he passes on to Riley. He's the perfect man for his job.

We walked through the offensive and defensive plays that we were expecting to see from Denver tonight, and then shortly after six o'clock headed back to the locker room to await game time. In a corner of the locker room is a time clock that duplicates the one on the scoreboard out in the arena. Once the arena's clock starts counting down, ours does the same. Under the time clock in the locker room is a TV monitor that always has a film edit running of the team we're about to play. Bertka usually slips a tape into the monitor anytime after five. Tonight, the edit for Denver went in after our walk-through. It's a good teaching tool, very immediate.

The locker room is a large, nearly square room, carpeted simply, unadorned, a kind of backstage, only orderly and bare of furnishings except for fifteen metal folding chairs for the twelve players and three coaches and a long wooden bench alongside the wall and underneath the board where Riley does his X's and O's. Off one side of the room is a long narrow supply closet that holds the extra uniforms, ice bags, hot packs, tape, bandages, knee pads, oxygen, basketballs, and goggles for James and me. Off the other side are the showers, and beyond the showers the weight and work-out room. Last, off the far side of the main room, toward the back, is the trainer's room. Inside, along one wall, is a long counter of first-aid supplies backed by cabinets that hold stacks of new basketball shoes, each box marked with a player's name. There are also two treatment and massage tables, along with various treatment machinery and a shorter table for taping. Taping healthy ankles before games to strengthen them used to be a regular practice, but it's rare now and the taping table is used almost exclusively for injuries. I have never been routinely taped before a game, not even back in high school, a time when the practice was common. I also never wore high-tops. From the beginning, I just felt that I could move and cut easier unbound and in low-cuts. And I seemed to know instinctively what everyone believes now, that the skeletal system is built to absorb shock, and if you bind and immobilize the ankle the stress just transfers up to the next available joint, which is the knee, the great nemesis of the basketball player. But I was Galileo out there on this, alone in my approach for a long time.

As you pass through the door from the hallway into the locker room, along the wall to the left are the lockers for Mark McNamara, Byron, me, Mychal Thompson, Tony Campbell, and A.C. Green. Across the room, along the right wall, are those for Jeff Lamp, Cooper, Magic, Orlando, James, and David Rivers. I've had the same spot for fourteen seasons now. The lockers are really small, open cubicles, each with a narrow bench, a clothes rod, a few hooks, and an upper shelf that holds a small metal safe with a name plate on it. Flowers from the fans find their way to one of our shelves every now and then, but otherwise there's little excess here. This is where we dress, where we wait, and where we talk to the press before and after games. The dressing room must be open to the press up to forty-five minutes *before* a game and no later than ten minutes *after* a game. Those are the league rules. So as a team, our private moments here are the half hour just before we go out on the floor, the ten minutes just after we come off, and halftime.

Generally, it stays pretty quiet in the locker room before a game, even with a few members of the press straggling in. It's not unusual to find everybody in uniform and sitting on the chair in front of their spot, in two neat rows, an occasional conversation starting up, the mood sometimes loose, sometimes serious, sometimes in between. I almost always read at this time, and then at six-thirty I start to stretch for the game.

Tonight, the coaches came down about ten minutes to seven—Riley, Bertka, and Randy Pfund, the other assistant coach, the youngest, who starred in high school and college basketball himself and who comes from a basketball family, his father once a head coach in college ball in the Midwest. Riley went over the Denver plays one more time and then Magic talked about not wanting to lose this one; we were 2-2 in the four home openers in which there'd been a ring ceremony this decade. Magic's words on this were an important reminder not to let ourselves be distracted. In conclusion, Riley brought us all together at the center of the room, all hands touching like spokes on a wheel, and in unison we shouted, "Let's go get 'em," an unwavering team ritual that we then repeat out in the hallway leading from the locker room to the floor, and then again out on the court, at the bench, one final time just before the start of the game.

At 7:15, we filed out onto the arena floor, and the building exploded. It was as if the crowd had never left their seats since the last, victorious game of the finals here against the Pistons on June 21. The excitement was palpable. From high up in the arena, the sound engineer began piping in Randy Newman's "I Love L.A.," a pop recording first played here during the 1985 series with Boston that since then has somehow become symbolic of West Coast, Los Angeles, and Laker pride combined. The engineer plays the tape judiciously, saving it for moments just like this, when he senses the heightened emotion of the crowd. Over the years I have seen the L.A. fans become more impassioned, and also more knowledgeable about the game. The team has gained an emotional hold on the city, our collective success having forged some kind of unity in this huge and normally fragmented metropolis, and it cuts across cultural and class lines. I could feel the whole city take us up into its heart for good last year when we became the only team in Los Angeles history to win a championship back to back.

From the court, I spotted my parents in the crowd. They moved here from New York two years ago, and since then have come to every home game, sitting about ten rows up from the floor, near midcourt. I always gesture a greeting once I catch their eye. I have two other seats next to theirs where my sons Amir and Kareem sit, but that is usually on nonschool nights like Friday, and today is Wednesday. I nodded to my parents and then also to my friend Malek, one of my best friends in

L.A., who was standing on the sidelines, camera in hand, watching our two teams go through our warm-ups—Denver had preceded us out onto the court by some minutes. Malek, six-three, is a strong athlete-turned-coach and photographer whom I have known for over twenty years; we first met as students at UCLA. He photographs the games for the Forum, so he will be here every night all season long, sitting on the hardwood behind the baseline along with the other photographers crowded up to the edge of the court.

During warm-ups, I walked to center court to shake hands with the refs and with the captain of the Denver team, forward Alex English, six-seven, one of the top scorers in the league and a twelve-year veteran. This, one of the few formal duties of the team captain, is something I do before every game.

The buzzer then sounded for the start of the ring ceremony, and the Denver players immediately left the arena floor to wait out the festivities in their own dressing room, as other teams have chosen to do in years previous. They don't want to be engulfed, derailed, or demoralized, all imminent possibilities, by a spectacle of their opponent's success on their opponent's home court.

From the announcer's table, in his deep stentorian voice, L.T. directed everyone's attention to midcourt, where Chick Hearn was standing in front of a tableful of rings. Alongside him was David Stern, the NBA commissioner, who is in his mid-forties, and who grew up in New York and, as a city kid, watched the fifties Knicks in the old Madison Square Garden like I did. He went to Columbia Law School, became the first general counsel of the NBA ten years ago, and then five years ago became commissioner, during which time the league has really come of age, the NBA the jewel now in professional sports. After welcoming the fans, Chick showered praise on the commissioner, and then he handed Stern the microphone. Mild-mannered, in gold wire-rimmed glasses, and dressed lawyerly in a dark blue suit, Stern addressed the capacity crowd of 17,505: "Five championships in this decade, three out of four and the coveted back-to-back—these are the statistics that define the dominant NBA team of the decade and one of the greatest in NBA history. It is a personal thrill for me to be here to congratulate this team, its coaching staff, its ownership, the entire organization, and the great fans of what I now understand is the City of Champions." He was referring to Inglewood's having added that moniker officially to its name. "Let's give out the rings, Chick," he said then.

Starting with the coaches and ending with me, we received our diamond rings one by one, as the crowd cheered. Before I could return to the bench, Chick asked me to say a few words as the captain. So, under bright fluorescent lights, jaw swollen from the night before, I took the mike, looked up to the stands, and said simply, "We can try to do it again this year. That's going to be our motivation. We love you. We thank you. Let's get it on." The words seemed to pull the fans out of their seats one more time. Quickly, a spotlight was turned onto a black satin drapery hanging high above the stands on the south wall of the arena and, in a final act of celebration, the gold-and-purple banner for last year's championship was unveiled alongside the five others. It was a nice moment with our home crowd.

The clock on the scoreboard had ticked off about twelve minutes when the Denver team returned to the court and both teams resumed warming up. Riley shook hands and exchanged a few words with Denver's coach, Doug Moe, who is in his ninth season with the team, a very long time to be in one place as a coach in the NBA. Born in Brooklyn, where he played high school basketball for Erasmus Hall, Moe, six-five and age fifty now, has earned a reputation for tirades along the sidelines and gratuitous insults off the court. He's toned down the tirades, for which he used to lead the league in technicals, but the legendary insults appear to continue unabated. Under Moe, who was named Coach of the Year last season, Denver has improved, but they have yet to make it to the finals. The present Denver team plays an up-tempo passing game, probably the most improvisational style of basketball, and what they hope to do is wear you down at both ends of the court. A win against Denver is often a fatigue win, especially when we play them on their own court, which is more than a mile above sea level. The altitude in Denver is worth fifteen points, and I can never sleep there.

At 7:45, L.T. gave the player introductions, and the five starters for both teams walked out onto the floor. Denver forward Wayne Cooper and I set up at center court for the opening jump ball, and I got the tip to James. Seconds later, off a pass from Byron, I made the first shot of the game, a short hook from inside the lane. It was 8–o, Lakers, before the game was a minute and a half old. Four of us had scored, me, A.C., James, and Byron, and then another minute later, Magic made it five. We held the lead for the entire game, except for once at the end of the second quarter, when guards Walter Davis and Fat Lever—Fat for Lafayette—scored two in a row to put Denver up by three. But in the last two plays before halftime, Orlando made a couple of free throws and then an eighteen-foot jumper off an assist from Magic, and we were ahead again by one. For Orlando, tonight was particularly important. It was his debut in the Forum as a Laker, and by the end of the evening's game the fans had shown him their acceptance. With five minutes to go at the end of the fourth quarter, as Orlando left the floor for what appeared to be the last time, the crowd began chanting, in long phrases, the first letter of his name, O, which doubles as the number on his jersey, o. He walked to the bench with a wide smile.

We won the game by a comfortable eighteen points.

Afterward, in the locker room, there was a mood of easy satisfaction. The first sturdy step has been taken at home. I tossed my uniform and whites into the team laundry bin, and was just coming out of the showers when the press crushed into the room from the hallway outside. The media is chiefly male, but for the occasional female reporter, the guard posted at the door generally yells out the warning "Woman coming in!" I wonder how they must feel.

Usually, I'm the first one in and out of the showers and dressed. I like to bypass the postgame quote-gathering as much as possible. Tonight, catching me before I made my early exit, Malek came in and gave me some pictures he'd taken of my place in Hawaii, where he just spent a few weeks bodysurfing. I quickly put them in my bag to savor later, and then slipped out of the locker room, and out of the arena, and into the night air.

I took Kelso, a side street, west to the freeway and then headed north. I felt tired. Conditioning-wise, the Denver game had been tough on me.

I got home sometime before eleven and, as always, Lourdes had a late supper waiting for me. Afterward, I watched some late-night television, then listened to Monk for a while. I imagine I'll get to sleep around two. I always have insomnia in the hours after playing a game. Some nights, many nights, sleep doesn't come until closer to four.

The NBA has made nocturnal creatures of us all.

Practice is tomorrow morning at Loyola. We play Seattle here the day after, on Friday. And then a week from Friday we leave L.A. for our first long eastern road trip.

Thursday, November 10

Tonight I took a friend to the Doolittle Theatre on Vine Street to see August Wilson's *Fences,* a play about an ex–baseball player who, now a garbageman, is living with his small family in some nameless city in

the industrial East. A former star of the Negro baseball leagues, he had
been shut out of the major leagues during his prime playing years and
had been too old by the time the sport was finally integrated in the late
forties. It was a great play. James Earl Jones played Troy Maxson, the
ex-athlete. Afterward, I went backstage to say hello and thank him. He
has remarkable energy, and the discipline in his training is obvious. I
saw him play the Jack Johnson character years ago in *The Great White
Hope*. That was stunning.

Sunday, November 13

Practice today almost killed me. Practice all week, in fact, has been
pounding me into disquiet. It seems my wind comes and goes with no
regard for my needs whatsoever. It feels as though my conditioning
leaves me immediately after working out and has no real impact on my
performance. Sometimes up and down the court I'm fine. Other times,
it feels as if I won't make it another minute. I feel ancient suddenly.

My conditioning has always been something that I have taken pride
in, that has been sure, that has kept me competitive far longer than
anyone believed possible. Keeping myself physically ready to play at the
highest levels of competitive basketball has been a discipline and practice of mine for as long as I can remember. And in years past, as a
professional, I've always been able to get into top condition during the
preseason and have never had problems staying in top shape afterward.
But now, the season less than two weeks old, my conditioning has
turned unfamiliarly capricious, fugitive. I find myself wondering if it's
finally happening, what every interested person has said would happen.
I feel myself disappearing in the games.

Gary, the team trainer, talked to me today about my weight, and
Riley did too. The weight I lost in training camp returned soon after
I came back from Hawaii. I am up to 274, and they want me to drop
the extra pounds for good now. Starting tomorrow, they want me to
add workouts with the blues, the reserves, until my weight is back to
where it should be. Playing fewer minutes than the starters in the
games, and sometimes no minutes at all, the blue shirts do extra
conditioning with Gary to substitute for on-court time. Except for last
Saturday in San Antonio, when I played thirty-one of the game's
forty-eight minutes, my own minutes on the court seem to have dimin-

ished. Riley hasn't said anything openly to me, but I wonder if I am being phased out.

Two years ago, there was a conscious decision to alter my role in the offensive strategy of our team. The change had nothing to do with any evidence of waning skills on my part, but rather with the fact that as a team we'd become predictable and therefore vulnerable to the opposition. Losing to Houston in the Western Conference finals the previous spring had shown us that.

For eleven years with the Lakers, the primary offense had revolved around me in the pivot, in the inside. The play would usually start with me, and I would either take a shot or get the ball back out to my teammates. In itself, the predictability of that scenario wasn't necessarily a bad thing. It worked for a long time. I was successful in that role, able to play with the pressure of that, and the team was successful. We won three championships, and came close to winning others. However, by 1986, certain teams were figuring out how to crack our strengths. In the conference finals that year, the Houston Rockets were finally able to eliminate us by effectively harassing Magic in the backcourt and playing me tough in the middle with Ralph Sampson and Akeem Olajuwon suddenly making our outside, perimeter game bear the main offensive responsibility. We weren't ready, and we lost to the Rockets in five games. Sampson made the last-second shot that ejected us from the play-offs in that fifth game here in L.A.

By the time we reconvened in the fall, the decision to bury the old offense had been made, and it met with no resistance from the team or me. With the support of Bertka and Pfund, Riley had refashioned our game strategy into a more balanced offense, balanced inside and outside, and balanced among all five on the court. The emphasis would still be on an inside-out game, the offense preferably initiated in the territory closest to the basket, the perimeter shots coming off passes from the inside. But the green light to dominate offensively would be spread across the floor, taking maximum advantage of everyone's skills, multiplying our offensive weapons and possibilities, and thereby forcing the opposition to play all of us in a way they hadn't had to before. James and I became equal first-option threats from the inside, Byron a formidable threat from the outside, and Magic a threat from the inside and outside both, first-option or otherwise. In this way, my role was redefined.

I saw the change as a positive move for both the team and me. I've never had to be, or wanted to be, the only one on the mountaintop.

I have never had any problem sharing. It lifted a burden off. That year, the 1986–87 season, turned out to be the easiest year I had in the NBA. I was still strongly involved in the offense, but not carrying the primary load, and I had everything to give when I was needed. It was like a military campaign; we knew exactly what we were going to do, but our opponents couldn't get a fix on how to play us. We went through everybody, ending up with the best record in the league and with another championship, our fourth. In over a month and a half of play-offs, we had only three defeats. So the new offensive concept worked, and brought immediate rewards.

The following year, last year, we again had the best record in the league and again were crowned world champs, for the fifth time, although the play-offs were the exact opposite of the previous spring's. This time, we had nine defeats in three series that each went as far as they could go, the full seven games.

In my own play, I began to feel the downside of my reduced role. My preparation wasn't always evenly matched with the quicksilver demands being made on my game. It was as if I were a first tenor who'd agreed to sing in the chorus, then was asked to sing first tenor again, and whose chops, accordingly, weren't right there. In basketball we call that "rust"! So last season became a tough one for me. The conscious decision that had had nothing to do with the quality of my play began looking more and more like planned obsolescence. And now, at the beginning of this year, it has gotten to the point where I doubt myself. Am I less ready because they are not using me as often? Or am I not being used as often because I don't have it to give? These doubts may be with me all season. I'll be watching myself very closely from now on. So will the coaches.

Sunday, November 27

I am sitting in my room in a quiet waterfront hotel in Philadelphia's restored Society Hill district. The hotel is on the Delaware River and just a few blocks north of South Street, a shop-filled area that bears some resemblance to New York's West Village. It's late afternoon, and it's been raining steadily since we flew in from Detroit shortly before two o'clock today. Upon our arrival, the late-November rain, the gray river, and the darkened eastern sky seemed to match our coach's state of mind. Riley was in a noticeably dark mood over our having lost on the Pistons' home court last night in a stammering performance by both teams. At one point in the evening, he was kicking the press table in frustration. Practice had been scheduled for this afternoon at a gym nearby the hotel, but at the last minute Riley canceled it. We don't know if there was a message in that.

My own mood has lightened considerably over the last two weeks. I have dropped the excess weight I was carrying, and a lot of the doubts. I'm running the floor better, my shot is dropping, and practice once again is merely arduous, not perilous. I just let the weight fall off me and did the extra conditioning I'd been told to do with the blues, which consisted mainly of riding the Bob McAdoo bicycle every day after practice. Bob McAdoo was a great player whose shooting ability wreaked devastation on the court for years. Nobody could take shots from where McAdoo did and hit them. Sharman used to say you had to watch him from twenty-eight feet out. He was unstoppable. On Christmas Eve, 1981, after our then-teammate Mitch Kupchak broke his leg, McAdoo, age thirty, joined the Lakers and became a scoring power off the bench, playing with us for four seasons. He got hurt easily, though, and it seemed he was always on the stationary bike with the blue shirts, recovering from some injury. In my mind ever since, that bike has had his name on it. Now I have been on it.

Five days ago was the big game in the Garden, when we played the Knicks for the first time this season and New York gave me its heartfelt farewell. I played thirty minutes in that game and scored in double digits for the first time since the second night of the season in San Antonio. I feel strong again, and have stopped working out with the blues.

After New York, we played in Miami, a game that I sat out, not because of my conditioning, but because the elbow of my right arm was inflamed and swollen from having nearly hyperextended it in the Knicks game. Over the years, I have developed a bone spur in that elbow, the elbow of my predominant shooting arm, and just in the last few seasons, from time to time, tiny calcium particles that have broken off from the spur or developed independently of it will shift out of place and inflame the joint. In the play-off series against Utah last spring, I played with my elbow throbbing, privately icing it and taking aspirin in between games. It's one of the marks of the game I'll take with me.

The team beat Miami, one of the two new expansion clubs, by a lavish but not unlikely forty-seven points. The next day was Thanksgiving, which we spent in Miami, having our Thanksgiving meal together that evening in the hotel. The only one not with us for dinner was Magic, who had gone ahead to Michigan to spend the holiday with his family there. It was humid and tropical in Miami, and our hotel was sandwiched in between Biscayne Bay on one side and the tense, simmering black section of town called Liberty City on the other. We didn't go for any walks the two nights we were there.

Friday morning we left for Detroit. The Pistons' arena there is an hour outside the city. It was clear, golden fall weather, cool but not cold. Straight from the airport, the team bus took us the extra fifty miles north up to Oakland County, the deep suburbs of Detroit and one of the richest counties in the country, a patchwork of industrial parks and rural Michigan woods, and the home of two mammoth sports arenas, the Palace, which is the Pistons' new state-of-the-art home court, and the Silverdome, which is where we played the middle three games of the finals last season. This was the first we'd been back since then. The rolling country was familiar; we lived out there for a week last June.

On Saturday morning, we went to the Palace for shootaround, passing the turnoff for the Silverdome on our way. This was the first we'd seen the new arena. Large television trucks were already parked outside the back entrance and camera crews were setting up inside for the night's game. It was going to be televised nationally in prime time, the first time in sixteen years for a regular-season game. CBS was billing it as Game 8 of last spring's finals, a rematch, a media strategy and frenzy that was all but lost on the Lakers. For us, last year's games are resolutely forgotten. We are looking ahead. For the Pistons, though, having made it to the finals for the first time ever and then having come so close to the crown in the seventh game, last June still haunts. I read their remarks in the papers while we were there, and they seemed to be reliving last season.

The game turned out to be less than a supreme moment for either team. We both stumbled through the evening, making fewer than 50 percent of our shots, an off night in front of the national cameras and in front of a sold-out Palace crowd of twenty thousand. Riley paced frenetically along the sidelines, as did Detroit's coach, Chuck Daly. The final score was 102–99, Detroit. In an effort to tie, with five seconds to go in the game, Magic was able to get off a pair of three-point attempts, but his first arcing shot bounced off the backboard and the second was swatted away by Isiah Thomas. For my own play, I was able to make more than half of my shots, scoring in double figures once again, but I wasn't a force on the boards.

That was last night.

Sixteen hours later the team was touching down on a wet runway here in Philadelphia, logging our six thousandth mile on this four-city trip. Philadelphia is the final stop. When we play the Sixers in the Spectrum tomorrow night, it will be the twelfth game of the season.

Monday, November 28

At the moment we were arriving at the arena for tonight's game, I imagine Julius Erving was getting ready to make the drive into the city from his home in the outskirts of Philadelphia. Julius was going to preside over my farewell here, just as I had presided over his when he played for the last time in the Forum twenty-three months ago. I hadn't seen or spoken to him since then. On the early end of my long good-bye around the league, with the ceremonies so daunting, I was glad to know that a friend would be waiting for me out there at center court under the arena lights.

Julius Erving and I go back to the summer of 1969. He was still in college at the University of Massachusetts in Amherst and I had just graduated from UCLA and signed with Milwaukee, where I would be starting in the fall. We were both home in New York for the summer and had both ended up one day on Riis Beach, one of the bounties of the Robert Moses era, a public park on the Rockaway peninsula with eight basketball courts on the beach. He was a skinny, bony kid then, six-seven with huge paws. We measured hands that summer, and his were a shade bigger, eleven inches from pinky to thumb with his extremely long fingers outstretched. He played up front, one-handing everything and stuffing over everybody. I didn't know it then, but he had played in the summer Rucker Tournament in Harlem when he was still in high school. Rucker's PA announcer called him the Claw and Little Hawk, the Claw for his one-handed rebounds and dunks and Little Hawk for the soaring and swooping likeness of his moves to Connie Hawkins, who'd preceded him on the asphalt courts by some seven years. Julius was also already called the Doctor.

The next time we saw each other we were both professionals, two New York basketball products who started out in the city playgrounds and high school gyms and ended up on the hardwood courts of the huge modern basketball arenas. Doc grew up on Long Island, and from college he went pro with the ABA, which was still a rival league to the NBA at that time. After the two leagues merged in 1976, he came over into the NBA with the Philadelphia 76ers, where he stayed for the rest of his long career, the next eleven years. He was so exciting to watch that opposing coaches used to admonish their players to keep their eyes off him. He could transfix you with the artistry of his game. He played more than the required notes in his performance; he *invented* in the open court. And he moved like lightning. Always an intelligent, serious, and quiet person, Julius was only extroverted in the highly personal style of his play. Yet this was not at the expense of his team. As a forward in 1981, he was the first noncenter since Oscar Robertson seventeen years earlier to be named the league's most valuable player. Larry Bird has since won the award three times, also from the forward position, although aesthetically speaking, Larry is like a rough-hewn Hemingway compared to the poet in the Doctor.

Julius came into pro ball two years after me, and he left two years before, at age thirty-seven. We used to kid each other about who was going to retire first, something Earl Monroe and I used to do until he left in 1980. Julius would say to me that he wasn't going to retire until I did—he wanted me to leave first—and I would say, Well, I guess I have to stick around then. We also used to rib each other about the greatest this and the greatest that. I would say he was the greatest leaper of all time and he would say I was the greatest hook shooter. We would be children like that together.

Led by Julius, Philly became one of only five clubs to make it into the finals in the eighties, joining Boston, Houston, Detroit, and the Lakers. In four years, they advanced to the championship round three times, and three times it was us they faced. Philly was our chief rival in the early part of the decade, which seems long, long ago now. It started in 1980. The Sixers were favored to win and we were 0–4 against them for the season, but the Lakers had a new configuration of players that year, with a twenty-year-old Magic as the new court general. I was thirty-two then, and it had been a dry eight years between rings. After we won that '80 title, we started our hunt for others. That was me, Magic, Coop, Norm Nixon, and Silk, Jamaal Wilkes. The five of us met Philly in the spring again in '82 and '83, back-to-back confrontations. We won in '82, proving that our previous win hadn't been a fluke, but we lost in '83. That was the horrific season when injuries abounded and when, in midwinter, my house burned down. It was a stinging sweep, 4–0. That was when Julius got his only title.

Last year, the Sixers failed to make the play-offs. That was the first time in the eighties they hadn't made it at least to round one. But this year, the team is looking stronger. Forward Charles Barkley is a big scorer for them and probably the best offensive rebounder in the league. And Maurice Cheeks is a veteran point guard who played alongside Doctor J in all three of our championship battles. He's the familiar face now. In the last week, the Sixers pulled ahead of New York by half a game.

We never take anything for granted when we come to Philadelphia. It has a long, proud tradition of inner-city basketball. Born here, Wilt was one of their own, and he played for the 76ers in the sixties, before he moved west to L.A. The Philadelphia fans are sophisticated and seasoned and go back generations. I've never been one of their favorites, though. I've played on the opposite side in the Spectrum for twenty years now, since I was a rookie and the building was new, and mostly the Philly home crowd has glowered down on me, the same way it glowered down on Bill Russell during the intense years of the great Chamberlain-Russell rivalry.

Tonight I noticed that the Spectrum crowd was gathered early. The rain that started yesterday had stopped falling late this afternoon. The streets were still slick and wet, but in the Northeast that doesn't stop traffic, and it didn't slow the fans from being in their seats by the first buzzer. It was a sellout 18,168. The game was going to be an event—a match against the world-champion Lakers, an appearance by Doctor J, and my last time in the Spectrum, unless we see the Sixers in the finals six months from now. As happened just six days ago in New York, the newspapers here have been full of the night's game.

Before the official start, with microphone in hand, Julius walked out onto the floor and the crowd gave him a sixty-second standing ovation, a very long time for a roar of applause. Wearing a dapper suit and gold-rimmed glasses, his hair graying, his look serious as always, almost scholarly, Julius graciously thanked the crowd and began speaking. I listened from the bench with the team.

"It's an honor for me to introduce a man who has been here many times before," he said, "a man who is the greatest scorer in NBA history, who simultaneously in my opinion is the greatest *player* in NBA history. A man who won gold rings. A man who won banners, and also the hearts and admiration of many. A man who deserves a great Philadelphia tribute as only *you* can give him tonight." And then he asked me to step forward as the crowd rose to its feet and showered me with my own prolonged ovation. Except for its not being my hometown, this was a lot like the crescendo of affection shown me in the Garden. I have been a villain for so long in these basketball meccas, having developed a kind of rhinocerous-hide indifference in order to survive, this late-career appreciation on eastern courts is in the nature of the startling. It's like I'm getting to reap the sweetness now.

Julius and I hugged each other at midcourt, and then tenor saxophonist Grover Washington, Jr., who was set up on the floor with keyboardist Bill Jolly, played a tune by Duke Ellington entitled "In a Sentimental Mood." The piece was emotional and wonderful, but it was also long and lyrical, and as I stood there, the minutes ticking by, I began to feel stiff and grew concerned that the ceremony would distract the team from the game at hand. Back in training camp, we talked about preparing ourselves for a season of these good-byes. Every team around the league would want to make its farewell as I played in its city for the final time. I knew I couldn't just walk out the back door, nor did I want to. Yet to minimize what we know can be a distraction for all of us this year, Riley and the organization wisely sent out a letter weeks ago asking the clubs to contain their tributes to ten minutes. That timing worked perfectly in New York, but tonight's ceremony swelled to twenty minutes at least. It seemed like forever.

When at last Julius handed me the mike to speak, I made my thanks to the thousands in the arena, telling them I'd never come in there without expecting a tough game. And I ended by stealing a few words that I remembered of the Duke's. Whenever an audience gave its praise to Ellington, which was often, he used to always say back to them in a deep, emphatic voice, "I love you madly." "And I do love *you* madly," I said back to the crowd tonight. They erupted at that and also at my publicly remembering their late PA announcer, Dave Zinkoff, who'd been such a part of the building he seemed to have been born there. I always liked the idiosyncrasy of his insistence on speaking what he thought was proper English, the fact that he would never use the word "time-outs" to substitute for "times out," for instance, which was his preference. He would never, ever, say words improperly. I always enjoyed that, and I noticed his absence.

It was a sentimental night. Fortunately, we won the game in spite of that. I got the tip to Magic, James scored the first basket on a lay-up, and we jumped out to an 11–2 lead before the game was two minutes old. We played as if we were at the beginning rather than the end of a long road trip, three thousand miles from home. Detroit hadn't shaken us, although Riley still seemed angry at practice this morning, which went three hours, unusually long for shootaround.

We led the whole way until the Sixers came at us right after halftime and tied it up 70–70, just four minutes into the third quarter, a spurt that aroused the home crowd. Philly had a six-game winning streak going for them at home that they profoundly didn't want broken by us tonight. But we were up again by six at the start of the fourth quarter, and were able to overcome another Sixers' run with less than five minutes to play, finally winning it 104–98. Philly led only once in the game, by one. The Ellington piece didn't hurt us.

We are 9-3 for the season and 3-1 for this trip. We go home with two big road wins, having beaten Philadelphia in Philadelphia and New York in New York, both important teams to beat. We'll have another chance at Detroit in February, when they come to L.A. I played another thirty minutes tonight, but I banged my knee midway in the third quarter, soon after Philly had tied us. Philly forward Ron Anderson had just driven down the middle for a lay-up, his shot bouncing off the rim, and, under a tightly packed Sixers basket, A.C. and I both leapt for the rebound in the same instant and collided in the air with force, kneecap to kneecap. I went down like a shot. My right leg was numb from the knee down, and from the knee up it was all pain. I lay there on the blue paint for what seemed like a long time. Gary stayed at my side asking me questions until the feeling in my leg returned and the pain subsided and I could walk off the floor unassisted to the bench, where he treated me with ice and ultrasound. I felt good enough to go back in the game within a matter of minutes, my knee a dull ache, and I started in the fourth quarter. Gary thinks it's probably a bruise and I'll have it checked out by Dr. Kerlan when we get back to L.A. The bus leaves the hotel for the airport tomorrow morning at 6:45, wake-up call at 6:15. I've been gone ten days, and the first long road trip is over.

The hug from Julius tonight was real. It was from the heart. No one can ever really decide who is the greatest ever in a sport, but I was very flattered for Doc to have said those words about me. It is nice to be appreciated in that way by a friend. And it made me remember our greatest-ever dialogues.

Saturday, December 3

I drove down to Pauley Pavilion this afternoon and noticed that the sycamores are starting to drop their leaves. Pauley is the gym where I played four years of college basketball, and it's only a few miles from where I bought my spot of land after moving back to Los Angeles to play for the Lakers. I live so close to my old campus now, in fact, that were the dam at the top of my street ever to give way, the water from the reservoir would plunge right down the canyon and end up in Pauley, which is built into the ground, bowl-like, at the canyon's natural bottom. My house would be washed right into the hollow of the gym. I didn't plan it that way, but our destinies somehow continue to mingle.

Coach Wooden was already there when I arrived. He and I were meeting for an interview we had been asked to do together. Since it's Saturday, the campus was nearly deserted and the gym empty. This gave us the rare opportunity to have some quiet time together, to exchange a few words and share a few silences. We don't get to see each other that often, and when we do a throng of people usually surrounds us. In the gym today, there was just a small interview crew present. I didn't have a game tonight, so nothing had to be rushed.

The coach hardly looks changed since our days together, except his hair has whitened over the years. He wears his age, like his honors, lightly. He was dressed comfortably in a gray cardigan sweater and I had on my navy athletic jacket, UCLA '69. We were player and coach together here at UCLA in the late sixties. I was eighteen when we first met, and that memory is a vivid one.

He was sitting in his shirtsleeves in an office the size of a walk-in closet. UCLA had just won the national championship for the second year in a row, and the athletic department was in temporary quarters while Pauley Pavilion neared completion. Pauley was already standing then, but awaiting a floor.

"We expect our boys to work hard and to do well with their school-work," he said to me. "I know that should not be a problem for you, Lewis."

He called me Lewis, the formal grown-up version of my name, rather than Lew or Lewie, which was what everybody else called me. This caught my positive attention.

Quiet-spoken, slender, with straight gray hair parted almost in the middle, glasses on, he looked and sounded more like the English teacher he once was than the head coach of the country's preeminent basketball program. He was from the Midwest, from Indiana, and you could hear the traces of his home state in his speech. I had never met anyone like him before. He impressed me immediately as an elder, in the best sense of that word, both respected and respectful, wise but in no hurry to impress, alert to what was in front of him. I trusted him at once.

"I don't expect you will have any difficulty here," he said to me that day.

That was in 1965, the spring of my senior year in high school, when I was visiting campuses and came to Los Angeles for the first time, trying to make a choice about college, about where to go from New York.

I left John Wooden's office that day knowing I was going to UCLA.

"How's your knee?"

Inside Pauley this afternoon, those were the coach's first words to me after we greeted each other warmly, like old friends. He must have read in the paper about the injury from the Philadelphia game. I told him the injury was minor and that the prescription was rest, no practice, until the knee healed.

"Otherwise, you're feeling good?" he asked.

"I had to lose some weight, Coach, for the first time," I said. He nodded and smiled. We were sitting, just the two of us, down on the empty court along the sidelines where a pair of folding chairs had been set up for us, side by side. We looked out across the floor and talked about how beautiful the arena still was, and about the ten national-championship banners hanging from the ceiling above us, three of which I helped to put there and all of which Coach Wooden played a part in. The school hasn't won a championship since he retired in '75, and no other college has ever won more than four.

I could still hear a trace of Hoosier in the coach's voice. I asked him if he had seen the movie *Hoosiers.* I had seen the film on an airplane with my son Amir about a year ago, and had loved it. It was Indiana basketball, but the gym scenes could have been New York. I could smell the gyms. I was back there. The movie took place in the same time period in which I learned to play, the fifties. And the story was like the kind of basketball stories I read as a kid. It was based on the true story of tiny Milan High School's 1954 state-championship upset over mighty Muncie Central, the perennial state power. Indiana plays one-class basketball, which means a single state tournament. The smallest high schools have to defeat the biggest high schools if they want to win the title. In 1954, with a student body of barely 160 or so, little Milan beat the best of the biggest in Indiana, an event that stirred the entire state and that people there still remember. The story, as the movie embellished it, is full of redemption and second chances, for the town and for the characters, a theme in the film that touched me. There can be a lot of redemption in sports.

The coach said yes, he had seen *Hoosiers* too, that he loved the shots

of farmland and country roads, and that he personally had known some
of the people involved in the original story, like Milan's coach Marvin
Wood, on whom Gene Hackman's character was based. It was accurate, Coach Wooden said; Marvin Wood had been new to the town
and ahead of his time as a coach, introducing a new style of play and
philosophy, a disciplined offense in a part of the state that up to that
time had been schooled mainly on free-lance basketball. It was also true
that a player on the Milan team, guard Bobby Plump, who still lives
in Indiana today, hit an odds-defying, game-winning fifteen-foot jump
shot with three seconds to go in that final big game, which was played
in front of a crowd of fifteen thousand at Butler Fieldhouse. Butler
Fieldhouse was long the big-city site for Indiana's high school basketball finals and it was used as the real-life location for the climactic scene
in *Hoosiers*.

The coach told me about how his own Martinsville High School
team had faced Muncie Central in the very same building, in the very
first year that it opened, 1928. Martinsville was a small town, but its
team was one of the finest Indiana has ever produced. They had beaten
Muncie Central the year before, becoming the state champs in '27, but
the next year, the year they helped inaugurate Butler Fieldhouse, they
lost to Muncie, by one, in the final harrowing moments of the game.
Coach Wooden talks about this as the most memorable game of his
playing career. He was seventeen then, and one of the stars.

Back in Indiana, John Wooden is still referred to as "Johnny"
Wooden, one of the state's own, one of Hoosier basketball's greatest.
The roots of the game go far back within this man. He grew up in a
state where the sport has achieved almost mythical status. Alongside
the urban Northeast, small-town rural Indiana was the other cradle of
basketball, where hoops have gone up on the remotest of barns for
generations and young boys play even in the dead of winter, with no
gloves on so they can feel the ball. "You couldn't grow up in Indiana
and not have basketball touch you in some way," Coach Wooden says
now. His own father, who was a farmer, made his son's first hoop out
of an old tomato basket with the bottom knocked out that he nailed
onto one of the walls of the family's barn. There, as a boy, the coach
practiced his first shots with a ball made out of rags stuffed into a pair
of his mother's hose. Like I did, he also loved baseball, but when he
was around fourteen his family lost their farm to hard times and they
moved eight miles into town, where the high school didn't have a
baseball team, or a football team either. That was Martinsville. Basketball dominated the life of the town just as it did the state. The popula-

tion of Martinsville was about fifty-two hundred then and the school gym held about fifty-five hundred, but every seat was routinely filled on the night of a game. Coach says he can remember when it was the homeroom teacher's job to see that everyone in class had a season ticket. If a student was too poor to afford one, it was the teacher's responsibility to find a way to get the student one.

At Martinsville, five-foot-ten-inch Johnny Wooden was All-State for three straight years, and at Purdue he was consensus All-American for another three straight years. There he played under the coaching of Ward "Piggy" Lambert, one of the early advocates of fast-break basketball and the man besides Joshua Wooden, the coach's father, whom he credits with having had the most profound and lasting impact on his life. Joshua Wooden and Piggy Lambert shared a notable quality: They were men interested more in character than in reputation. By the time John Wooden left Indiana for California, having been a coach for thirteen years, most of those in Indiana high school basketball, that same quality of priority-given-to-principles had become an inextricable part of who he was. He was also a fierce, unflinching competitor, which in Coach Wooden posed no contradiction to principles. The keen desire to win was a value he praised highly and looked for in his players. He brought all this west with him when he took the head coaching job at UCLA in 1948. Along with him also came a new racehorse style of basketball. Until he arrived, the West Coast was like a wilderness as far as basketball was concerned. The Minneapolis Lakers, who were just on the verge of becoming the first dynasty team in the pros then, wouldn't move to Los Angeles for another dozen years.

Once he got here, Coach Wooden stayed. He was the coach at UCLA for twenty-seven years, winning those ten NCAA championships in the last twelve of those years, a feat that remains the greatest in college-basketball history. He waited a patient fifteen years for the first title. And he waited a less patient seventeen years for Pauley Pavilion to be built. When he signed his original contract with UCLA, they had promised him a new gymnasium within three seasons. That the three had stretched out to seventeen had become a sore point. But the coach was elated with the new building once it finally was standing, and in the fall of 1965, it was my freshman team that opened Pauley in a game against the UCLA varsity team. Students and fans jammed into the new 12,500-seat arena for the first game ever to be played there. The varsity were the defending national champs and were ranked first in the preseason college polls. So, naturally, no one gave the freshmen a chance. But we had five high school All-Americans on that freshman team, and the game was never close; we beat the varsity by fifteen points. That created a unique situation in which the varsity was number one in the country but number two on its own campus. We took enormous pride in that accomplishment all year, and our team is still the best freshman team in UCLA history.

John Wooden didn't coach the freshmen, so it was the next year that he and I began our close association. I remember in early December, after my first varsity game, a game in which we beat our cross-town rival USC by fifteen and I scored fifty-six points, a school record, Coach Wooden sat down next to me at the postgame interview, patted my arm, and said, "Great start. Keep it up."

Sitting next to him during today's interview, when he was asked about what it was like to have had me as a player, I listened for his answer. "He startled me," Coach Wooden said. "And I'm glad he did." I was the coach's first big man, and I was quick. But we startled each other, I think. Our backgrounds were so different, I a child of the city and proudly black, he a country child from middle America, and a deacon in his church—and we were thirty-seven years apart in age. Yet there was an immediate simpático between our temperaments and a kind of pragmatic idealism that we shared, although I couldn't have put that into words back then. I just knew I was drawn to whatever he had and that the plainness of his demeanor was deceptive. As a competitor, he was unnerving. Many coaches in the then Pac 8 didn't like him because he was too good to be believed. He wanted to win, but not more than anything. Coach Wooden wanted to win *very much*, but within the rules, within the guidelines he had set for the expression of his own and his players' competitive talent. Within those, he went all out. He understood the game totally. He eliminated the possibility of defeat. It was genius.

John Wooden saw basketball as a very simple game. For any measure of mastery, however, he believed the game required supreme conditioning, solid fundamentals, and a commitment to team play. The coach insisted on unselfishness, and within that framework, he understood what it took to teach people how to play basketball. He drilled us in the fundamentals until they became instinctive, able to be executed at full speed, as they must be in basketball. He also told us he wanted us to be in better condition than any team we met. To play fast-break basketball, which everybody wants to do today, you have to be able to run and to sustain a ninety-four-foot game for four quarters, a mistake-inducing pressure basketball played from end line to end line for the entire forty-eight minutes.

All of our practices revolved around the running game and the three pieces of Coach Wooden's system: conditioning, fundamentals, and teamwork. After college, I never again experienced practices like his. Every drill had a precise purpose and was precisely timed. You would advance from one drill to the next and to the next, without stopping or doubling back to repeat a drill. Every workout was a tightly structured grid laid over the anticipated rising fatigue of the players. Every day had its own practice plan, but you knew to expect an exactitude and that practice would end on time, a certainty that eased the toughness of the hour and forty-five minutes, which was usually how long we would go. Everybody did everything. The guards took the big-man drills and the big men worked at the guards' drills. It was my first serious training program and, as it turned out, the best training for the pros I could have had.

Coach Wooden wasn't much for team meetings or blackboard drills, and I notice that I am the same way today. I grow impatient. He also didn't rely on pep talks or charging us up before a game. His consistent message was that each of us must do his best; the win, and ultimately any championship, would take care of itself. No team could beat us, but we could beat ourselves. Respect every opponent, but never fear him. It was the many little things that would make the big things happen. He taught us that if you needed emotion to enable you to perform, then sooner or later you would be vulnerable emotionally and ultimately nonfunctioning. He preferred thorough preparation over depending on the ability to rise to an occasion. Let others try to rise to the level we had already attained; we would be there to begin with.

It was as if John Wooden had read Musashi, the great seventeenth-century samurai-mystic, and vice versa. Musashi wrote about the need to be determined through calm, to cultivate a level mind, to be neither insufficiently spirited nor overspirited, an elevated spirit and a low spirit being equally weak. Coach Wooden talked frequently about his dislike for peaks, which come always paired with valleys, and games could be lost in valleys, he would say. Through his words and by example, he taught a dispassionate attitude that may have been lost on others but wasn't lost on me. Do not let the enemy see your spirit, Musashi would say. Adapt, and be prepared for everything. Be ready. Musashi and John Wooden. East meets West.

The coach started reminiscing.

"Remember the trip from Columbus, Ohio, to South Bend on the bus, and from St. Louis to Chicago on the train?" One time in a snowstorm, all flights grounded, the team had to take the train from Missouri to Illinois in order to make it to the next game. It was one of our more memorable midwestern road trips. More than once on that journey, the rails had to be dug out of the snow, and we were astonished that the coach knew the small towns we were passing through, towns with obscure names like Kankakee. Then there was the time we had to charter a large Greyhound bus to take us from Ohio to Indiana. Coach reminded me of a long conversation on religion that had started up on the bus and that made for a special closeness on that long ride. I reminded him how good it felt to beat Notre Dame at the end of the trip. I also commented on his fine pool game, which was in evidence during stops along the way. "Misspent youth," he said.

"Mike Warren and Lucius Allen, as guards, were two of the best," he continued a few moments later. "They don't come any smarter than Mike Warren." I agreed with him on all counts. Mike Warren—the Great Lover we used to call him—was an incredible ball handler and athlete, with great court vision as a playmaker, another Indiana prodigy. Lucius Allen, as the off-guard, had incredible quickness and was impossible to defend. He was from Kansas City. They were the team's starting-guard combine in my second year at UCLA. We went undefeated that year and won our first NCAA championship, the youngest team in college history to have done so. A junior then, Mike Warren was the only varsity veteran of the starting five, the rest of us sophomores—me, forwards Lynn Shackelford and Kenny Heitz, and Lucius Allen, who had been my roommate freshman year and who later ended up a teammate of mine again on both the Bucks and the Lakers. The five of us were young, but our talent was deep and intense.

In the same combination, we played together for another year, my junior year, which turned out to be the best of the three. Seniors Edgar Lacy and Mike Lynn returned to the team. They had been varsity starters my freshman year but couldn't play my sophomore year. Mike Lynn had gotten into some trouble and Edgar Lacy had gotten hurt and had to have a knee operation, keeping him out of action for a year. Edgar and I were close companions and had an apartment together for a while in Santa Monica. He was the varsity starting forward, and had shown me around the campus and Los Angeles when I was fresh off the plane from New York that first time. We had first met as high school All-Americans.

We lost only one game my junior year, our first loss in two years. Against the University of Houston, it was a game that had been highly promoted because for the first time a basketball game was going to be played in a baseball arena, the immense Houston Astrodome, which held more than fifty thousand. Eight days before the game, which was midway through the season, I had scratched the cornea of my left eye in a game at Cal. That was before I began wearing protective goggles. A Cal player was clawing for a rebound and accidentally clawed my eye in the process. I came home and checked into the Jules Stein Eye Clinic on campus and lay there in a darkened room while my eye healed and while, simultaneously, I lost my wind and timing. At the elite levels of competition, it takes only a week of rest to lose the fine-edged sharpness of your conditioning, even at that age—I was twenty-one then.

Physically, I was off and my depth perception was off, but I felt I could play in the Houston game and the coach did too. We both overestimated me. By the time the game was five minutes old I was exhausted. I missed more than half of my shots. The game was close in spite of that, but ultimately we lost it by two. We were the defending champs so the media made a lot out of the loss, which had been played out in front of a record crowd of 52,693. People who weren't even there still claim to have been in the Astrodome that day. It was one of those games that inspired that kind of hysteria.

For the rest of the year Houston was ranked number one, and nobody gave UCLA a chance of beating them again. Coach Wooden was confident, however, that we would see them again in the spring and, as he put it, would not have a lot of trouble with them at that time. In March, in the NCAA semifinals in L.A., we did have our rematch, and we beat Houston by thirty-two. "We would have been disappointed if we hadn't gotten to play them again, wouldn't we?" Coach said to me today. The day after that win, we faced North Carolina in the finals and took our second title in a row.

Senior year, we lost our guards. Lucius left school and Mike Warren graduated, setting out on the long road to becoming an actor, which ultimately landed him the role of Bobby Hill on *Hill Street Blues*. If he had wanted it, he easily could have made it in the pros. Edgar Lacy was also gone that year. He had dropped off the team after the Astrodome game the year before, never really able to come back to his own satisfaction after the knee surgery. So John Vallely and Kenny Heitz moved into the guard spots, Curtis Rowe moved into the forward spot left by Kenny, and then sophomore Sidney Wicks was one of the reserve forwards. We lost one game that final year, the last game of the regular season, the only loss I ever experienced in Pauley Pavilion, and then went on to win a third NCAA championship by beating Purdue.

We became the first team in college history to win three straight titles. In three years, we had lost only two games, our record 88–2.

After college-championship wins, it's a tradition to cut down the nets from the rims. I still have my nets from those years at UCLA. Fortunately, I sent them to my parents for safekeeping back then, so they weren't incinerated in the fire. I graduated from college with my three nets, a degree in history, and two more inches. I was seven feet when I went into college and seven-two when I left.

During the UCLA years, my confidence in Coach Wooden never wavered. The summer between my sophomore and junior years, the college rule makers outlawed the dunk shot, a move that virtually everyone believed was made in an attempt to lessen my dominance in the game. During my last two years of college ball, that ban robbed me of one of my weapons, and did the same to every other college player who had a dunk shot for the next ten years, until the rule was rescinded. At the time, Coach Wooden told me it would only make me a better player, helping me develop an even softer touch around the basket. This I could use to good advantage in the pros, where I could also, once again, use the dunk shot. He was right. It didn't hurt me. I worked twice as hard on banking my shots off the glass, on turnaround jump shots, and on my hook. It made me a better all-around player.

After I went on from college to six years in Milwaukee, the coach won five more championships at UCLA. He retired thirteen years ago at age sixty-five. He is seventy-eight now, and the only person in basketball who is in the Hall of Fame as both a player and a coach. As a coach, he has no equal; he is in a class by himself. He has proved that to me. He has proved that to everyone else. There isn't going to be another coach like John Wooden, at any level of the sport. It's impossible.

I don't know why fate placed me in his hands, but I'm grateful that it did. My relationship with him has been one of the most significant of my life. He believed in what he was doing and in what we were doing together. He had faith in us as players and as people. He was about winning basketball and winning as human beings. The consummate teacher, he taught us that doing the best you are capable of is victory enough, and that you can't walk until you can crawl, that gentle but profound truth about growing up. Many have tried to imitate his system—he has written it all down for others in a number of books— but I think most fail to grasp the philosophy behind his approach. That waltzes right by people.

Over the years, as I have moved further and further away from our time together, I have gotten a better view of the largeness of this man and his impact on me, the way one can see the full outlines of a mountain from a greater distance. It is a rare experience to meet an individual who affirms the positive values you were introduced to in childhood, as I was by the nuns at school and by my father, who was a cop. You wonder if such values work and then you encounter an individual like John Wooden and see the success he's had as a person, not just in terms of wins and losses, but as a man trying to live his life with some balance and honor, and then you know it's possible. He was the real thing. His example in my life continues to be bright and shining.

Pauley is surrounded by full-grown fir trees and maples now. After we wrapped up inside, Coach Wooden and I walked together for a little ways in what was left of the the early-December sun, the leaves from the maples underfoot. I noticed he still has a lightness in his step. I thought about his wife, Nell, who died four years ago. They'd met back at Martinsville High, in the summer of his freshman year. She was the only girl he ever went with, Nellie Riley. She used to come to every game. They had a son and daughter, and the coach is a great-grandfather now.

The coach and I have never really talked man-to-man. But our communication is such that I feel no loss for that. He knows how I feel about him, and I know how he feels about me.

As we walked and made our good-byes this afternoon, he said to me, "We're all very proud of you."

Thursday, December 8

Doc Kerlan said it was like someone had taken a hammer and pounded my knee. I woke up the morning after the Philly game with my knee swollen and painful from having banged it against A.C.'s in that final game of the road trip. It worsened during the cross-country flight home, so the next day, back in Los Angeles, the last day of November, I went over to Doc's clinic, just a few short blocks from the Forum, to have him take a look at it.

Doc Kerlan, Dr. Robert Kerlan, is *the man* when it comes to any athletic injury on the team, and his associate, Dr. Stephen Lombardo, is next in line for that role as Doc turns more and more of the day-to-day care over to him.

Doc is one of the most renowned orthopedists in the country and another of the rare personages whose daily life is entwined with the Lakers. He has been the team physician almost from the beginning, delicate surgery on Elgin Baylor's fractured left knee having been his first serious repair job. Elgin remembers waking up after the operation wondering whether he would ever play again, and Doc Kerlan standing at his side, reassuring him that he would. A man with a wry, ironic sense of humor, whose eyes miss nothing about the people in his care, Doc has the kind of large and sturdy personality that can stand side by side with a professional player, an elite player, who is having to confront his own athletic mortality. Doc is right there on the razor's edge with his patients. He has had enough experience with the psyches of athletes, even recreational athletes, like runners who are told they can never run again, that he understands the ferocity of that kind of news. Doc has also heard such news himself. When he was eighteen, he began to notice pains in his legs and spine, and five years later the pains were diagnosed as a progressive form of arthritis, not common and not curable, that would lead to the gradual loss of his mobility. Fortunately, and maybe presciently, he had already chosen a career in medicine over sports by that time, because earlier, as a boy, Doc had been an athlete, a nine-letter-man in high school, six feet three and 220 pounds, and he had gotten a basketball scholarship to UCLA. He played college basketball for a year and then opted to turn his energies to premed, following in the footsteps of his father, who had been a country doctor in northern Minnesota. On occasion during his growing-up years, Doc would ride along with his father when the weather was bad. You didn't ever go out alone in the northern Minnesota winters, he said, "when the car heater could conk out and you'd be found frozen stiff as a goat."

After he had been in private practice for a few years in Los Angeles, Doc's love of sports came together with his love of medicine, almost accidentally. In exchange for some free seats at the ballpark, he did the doctoring for the then minor league Angels at the old Wrigley Field. Shortly afterward, the Dodgers moved from Brooklyn, Doc became the official team physician, and the rest is history. In the thirty years since, he has become one of the most distinguished physicians in athletic medicine. He took care of Duke Snider's aging knee when the Dodgers were newly arrived, and became in charge of a long line of golden limbs, including those of pitchers Don Drysdale and Sandy Koufax. It was Doc who diagnosed the traumatic arthritis in Koufax's elbow, the condition that finally forced Koufax to quit rather than permanently cripple his pitching arm.

Two years after the Dodgers came from Brooklyn, the Lakers came into town from Minneapolis and also retained Doc Kerlan. He says his file on Jerry West from that early period remains one of the thickest in his office. If Jerry gets anxious now about a wounded Laker's comeback time, Doc says he just has to remind Jerry that he was out for quite a while with the same injury. With that first generation of players, Doc had to repair not only Elgin's knee in '65, but also Wilt's in '69 and then Jerry's in '71.

Doc enjoys telling the story of the first time Wilt encountered me in the pros. It was in an exhibition game between the Lakers and the Bucks at the Forum. Of course, at seven-one, Wilt had been *the* big man in basketball until I came along. That night, after two quarters on the court, as Wilt left the floor for the locker room, eyes downcast, he said to Doc Kerlan, who happened to be walking at his side, "Jesus Christ, Doc, I have never seen anybody this tall!"

A number of teams followed the Lakers and the Dodgers into Doc's clinic, including the football Rams, the hockey Kings, and the major league Angels, and athletes from all over the country began to show up with problems that couldn't be dealt with in the middle of Iowa or South Carolina. The work is now divided up among the dozen or so associates whom Doc has taken on over the years.

Now in his sixties, Doc focuses his personal attention mainly on the Lakers, the Rams, and the jockeys at Hollywood Park, the Forum's neighbor across the street. For many years, Doc has been fond of horses and horse racing—buying, breeding, claiming, and racing thoroughbreds—and for as many years he has worked closely with the jockeys. In the late 1960s, Doc had to operate twice on the Shoe, Willie Shoemaker, who had until then been virtually unmarked in nineteen years of riding. He got a wicked fracture of the thighbone when his horse took a spill at Santa Anita in 1968, and then a year later having just recovered from the first surgery, in a freak accident at Hollywood Park a filly reared up in the paddock and landed on Willie, breaking his pelvis up into so many pieces that Doc called it a Humpty-Dumpty injury. But in the long second operation Doc succeeded in putting him back together again, and Shoe went on to have another two decades around the racetrack.

I arrived in town to play for the Lakers in 1975, and as my own career stretched out, Doc Kerlan often compared Willie and me. As the tallest and the shortest of his athletes—Willie being four feet eleven and ninety-eight pounds—we seem to be Doc's unusual specimens, and he takes a certain pleasure in that because he has a serious appreciation for athletic talent. He talks about our longevity and the fact that we have both been very good for a long time, much longer than anyone else, in our respective sports, me with twenty years and Willie with forty. By happenstance, Willie and I are ending our careers at about the same time.

Doc was a great surgeon, but gradually he had to give it up, and the major surgery is now performed by Doc Lombardo and by Dr. Frank Jobe, who coruns the clinic. Over the years, Doc had to slowly restrict his time in the operating room as his own arthritis progressed, and as he had to undergo surgery himself more than once. A pair of metal crutches with cuffs that slip onto his forearms are now his second legs. The arthritis has bent his spine, so he walks with difficulty and, in his words, is eligible for pain at any time. Those of us around him don't know much about what he has to live with, but we respect it, just as we respect his enormous talent as a diagnostician.

As the team doctor, during the regular season, Doc sits courtside across from the Laker bench at every home game, in a specially designed chair. Having been with the Lakers nearly from the start, in fact, Doc has probably had a regular seat on the arena floor longer than anyone. During the play-off season, Doc also travels with the team, the likelihood of traumatic injury rising sharply along with the intensity of play. He has been right there with us in the best and the worst of championship times, including those years when we were cut down prematurely by injuries. And, of course, he was there with Jerry, Elgin, and Wilt during the *Lakers Agonistes* period with the Celtics, which perhaps explains why, sitting courtside in Boston Garden four seasons ago during the '85 finals, Doc almost got himself a technical foul.

Doc has always had a dry wit and an unhurried ease about him, sharing a similar comedic, rapscallion kind of attitude with his poker-playing buddy and longtime Laker fan Walter Matthau. Doc and Matthau even look a bit alike. But on this particular occasion in Boston, Doc's normally subtle sense of humor and dignified courtside manner erupted quite suddenly and unintentionally into a larger gesture.

It was during the fourth quarter and final game, somewhere during the last twelve minutes of tension before the euphoria of the win. We had all that history of defeat riding on us, the score was close, and a defensive foul was called on Cooper. Sitting on the Laker bench and close to the action, Doc thought the opposing player had charged into Coop and that the call, a critical one at that point, should have been an offensive, not a defensive foul. In the heat of the moment, in protest, he brought both of his crutches down hard against the floor and, as he later described it, both crutches bounced off the parquet, floating out of his hands as if in a dream, and went flying out onto the court, one landing on the near side of the foul circle and the other sailing clear to the free-throw line, just missing Celtic guard Danny Ainge. Maybe it was some combination of the parquet floor and the rubber tips at the end of his crutches, Doc has speculated since, smiling. Earl Strom was officiating the game that night, *the* veteran referee, with twenty-five years in the league, and he and Doc had known each other for most of those years. Steaming, his face red and neck veins distended, Earl walked over to Doc, leaned into him at eye level, and said, "Doctor, I can't believe it! I just can't believe it!"

Doc said, "Earl, I can't believe it either." Of course, Doc meant the call and Earl meant the crutches.

We all enjoyed that.

Doc examined my knee carefully in his office. He told me that the bruise had bled into the capsule of the joint, that bashed-against-bone as the kneecap had been, a blood vessel may have been broken, but that there was no structural damage to the knee itself, just excess fluid and inflammation. He said I would be out for a few days probably, and in the meantime he wanted no athletic stress put on the knee that might rupture the already weakened membranes inside. Then, as they used to do routinely in Doc Kerlan's office with the Duke's knee, to ease the tightness they drained out some of the fluid with a big long needle, a not too painful procedure. I don't like seeing the needle disappear under my kneecap, though.

That night we played Seattle in the Forum. It was the thirteenth game of the season and the first since Philadelphia. I was on the bench in street clothes. The game was a close call, but we won by four. We allowed a sixteen-point lead to slip away and then Seattle tied us 106–106 with thirty-five seconds left to play. We held Seattle at 106 and then in the final eighteen seconds Magic made two pairs of free throws to give us 110.

In the game's third quarter, on a lob pass to Orlando, who scored the basket, Magic had moved quietly into second place for assists, with 7,212, just behind Oscar Robertson, the all-time leader, with 9,887. This is an incredible feat for Magic, to have achieved the number two spot and to have come within sight of Oscar's record. Assuming health and consistency, Magic may pass Oscar in a few years, doing in twelve seasons what Oscar did remarkably in fourteen. At six-five, Oscar was the first big guard. At six-nine, Magic has exploded all the myths about someone of a certain size having to play a certain position. I think that's gone forever now.

Two nights later, we won again in the Forum, this time in a twenty-one-point blowout against Utah, an important game because there is a rivalry now and the Jazz have just come off the best November in their team's history. Last year, they were serious contenders, taking us to seven games in the semifinals, and this year they will be serious contenders again. My knee was still swollen, still not well enough to play in the game, but Doc Lombardo, who checked it this time, said it was improving. In his forties and a fine orthopedic surgeon in his own right, Doc Lombardo has been the younger, quiet partner alongside Doc Kerlan with the Laker team for fifteen years. Last Friday night, before the Utah game, he told the press, who always clamor for news of an injured player's expected return, that I was on a day-to-day, wait-and-see basis. He and Doc Kerlan still don't want me working out, not even on the bike, until they are positive the knee won't bleed again.

On Sunday we played the Washington Bullets, our third game in a row at home and my third straight no-go with the knee. From the bench, I watched the Bullets outplay us for most of the game, outshooting and outrebounding us, and we couldn't stop their starting forward, Bernard King, who was the game's high scorer, with thirty-seven points.

By game's end, we were down three with one second to go on the clock. It was Lakers' ball, so Riley called a full time-out, and then another, to set up the final shot. Coop was to inbound the ball but then called yet another one, a last twenty-second time-out, when he found no one free for the pass. Finally, no time-outs remaining, behind effective screens set by both Jeff Lamp and James, Magic took the inbounds pass from Coop at half court and, with barely time to turn and shoot, from just inside the center circle, from a distance measured later at thirty-seven feet, Magic launched a one-handed heave toward the basket. I saw it go up and arc tantalizingly through the air, seeming to hang suspended there before it finally started to fall, I thinking as it traveled, "Geez, it looks like it might—" and then, right on target, it plunged straight through the net. I jumped to my feet, as startled as everyone else. Even the veteran beat writers' mouths were agape. The buzzer had sounded during the ball's flight, which had seemed in such slow motion that you could see the ball's rotation. It was one among a small handful of improbable shots that I have seen firsthand in my career. As a three-pointer, it tied the game and sent it into overtime, where we outscored the deflated Bullets by seven. For the opposing team, that kind of last-second shot is like a dagger in the heart.

Magic's face hardly changed expression when his shot dropped. I think that's his maturity and the fact he may have been fed up that we'd allowed the Bullets to do as well as they did. At practice Monday morning, half-serious, Riley said we could all go home if anyone could duplicate Magic's long-distance shot from the night before. He set up the same half-court inbounds play and everyone took turns trying to re-create the thirty-seven-footer, even Magic, who launched an air ball. But then rookie David Rivers made it, and everybody bolted to the door—that is, except the blues, whom Riley strongly encouraged to stay behind, Rivers, Orlando, Jeff Lamp, Tony Campbell, and Mark McNamara. Even though I still can't be on the floor, I am required to be at practices, so I was pleased with the early liberation. I left Loyola and headed over to the clinic for my first day of physical therapy with Clive Brewster, Doc Kerlan's chief therapist. A former college track athlete, Clive is from Trinidad, so he's a special friend and has helped supply my father with calypso albums, music he loves, which originated in the islands.

Tuesday and last night, we had back-to-back games with the Clippers and the Phoenix Suns. Crosstown, in the L.A. Sports Arena, we beat the Clippers on their home court by eight, and in the Forum last night we beat Phoenix by fourteen. We had the game with the Suns well in hand throughout, leading by twenty-seven points early in the fourth quarter, so Riley was able to rest the starters and give the reserves some minutes on the court. In the process of rebuilding, the Phoenix team is one of the youngest in the league, though we didn't take them lightly coming into our first meeting of the season. They are off to a fast start, tied with Seattle for second place in our division. We have been in first place since the second week of November.

Yesterday morning, Doc Kerlan looked at my knee again and said I would probably be out for another week. The knee is better but there has been some deconditioning in the surrounding muscle. He wants me to keep working with Clive, whom I've seen everyday now for the last four days, to bring everything back to full strength. This is always the catch-22 with injuries: The doctors don't want to rush you back into action too quickly, but if they wait too long you decondition. It's always a question of balance. The bruise to my knee was a minor injury and would remain minor were I a musician or a stockbroker. As an athlete, though, such an injury goes beyond its minor status when it starts to take you out of a stretch of games as it has me. We have been home for nine days and I have missed five straight games. I feel restless.

Today I was sitting in the sun up on my cliff behind the house. The Santa Ana winds, the fire winds, have blown the desert air through the mountain passes into the city as they often do this time of year in Los Angeles, so the air is soft and warm, the temperature in the eighties. The sun felt wonderful, and as I soaked it in I thought about the days ahead and about Doc saying I still couldn't do anything and most likely would not be ready to come back for another few games. The team leaves in the morning for the monster road trip that's been on the horizon since October, when we first saw the schedule—seven cities in twelve days. We don't return until four days before Christmas. The November trip back East was really just a prelude for this one. By now, winter will have closed in and the cold-weather cities will have turned arctic. We start and end the trip in the snow division, the Central Division, in Indiana and Chicago. In between, we go to Milwaukee, Cleveland, New Jersey, Boston, and Washington.

Maybe I'll stay here in the sun, I thought. Maybe I don't have to go out into the cold. The mortgage is almost paid for and maybe I don't need to do this anymore.

Subversive ruminations on a Thursday afternoon.

Doc wants me to have one more day of therapy on the knee before I go, so I'll follow the team on Saturday, forty-eight hours from now. Tomorrow I'll see Clive and then pack for the last bad one.

Saturday, December 10

Al picked me up at seven in the morning for my flight to Indianapolis. My father's name is Ferdinand Lewis Alcindor—I was named after him—but he has always been called Al, for Alcindor. For the past two years, ever since he and my mother moved to Los Angeles, Al has been the one taking me to and from the airport during the season. The Laker office sends him the team itineraries and they know to call him with any last-minute changes. He asked to do it, and it has worked out. And because I'm always flying in and out of town, it means we see each other often.

A large man in stature and size, my father was a policeman with the

New York Transit Authority for twenty-seven years, from 1955 until he retired in 1982. He was classically trained in music at Juilliard—I have proud memories of going to his graduation when I was five—but the life of a serious musician was no easier then than it is now, and also blacks weren't being hired in symphony orchestras in those days. He had a family to support, so he became a police officer and played his classical and jazz trombone on the side. As a cop in the subways he worked three rotating shifts, including the midnight run. Sometimes now, many times, he picks me up at LAX at one o'clock or two in the morning and I think about how we have both been night workers, with odd hours.

As I waited for the plane to take off, I read the morning paper and saw in the sports pages that Utah coach Frank Layden has resigned and is moving up to the front office. The article said the move was sudden and unexpected, but in the fragile profession of NBA coaching, nothing surprises. Jack Ramsay resigned just three weeks ago after having coached twenty years in the NBA, ten of those with Portland, which he guided to its single championship in 1977, and the last two with Indiana, a team that has been struggling for a decade, repeatedly falling short of the play-offs. One of the biggest all-time winning coaches, highly respected, Ramsay started his third season with Indiana this year but then announced his retirement abruptly after seven winless games.

Unlike Indiana, Utah has just had its best start on record, but Frank Layden said he wanted to leave before he got either sick or fired. An Irish Catholic New Yorker with a gift of the blarney and a native love of basketball, Layden reminds me of my grade school and high school coaches. At fifty-six, he's a little younger, but essentially of their era. He coached high school and college basketball for nearly thirty years before he came into the pros, and in seven seasons built the Utah Jazz into one of the most powerful teams in the West. I thought they came of age last year. Layden appreciates the players, something I noticed when he coached the West team for the All-Star game in '84. And just a few years ago, I remember him coming into the Forum with the Jazz one night, having gotten up his team's hopes of beating the Lakers, and then we thoroughly blitzed them. Always vocal from the sidelines and quick with the one-liners, Layden got two T's that night and was thrown out of the arena. As he was walking by the Laker bench on his way out of the gym, he said to us, "I've had enough of this. You guys played real well."

Sometimes in a game, coaches have to become a little crazy to get their players to apply themselves, even coaches less naturally flamboy-

ant than Layden. Many times, a team will take an overall attitude of
"This one isn't there to be won." The coach has to sense this and
change the mind-set. Often, taking a technical foul intentionally can
do it. I remember one time when the Dallas Mavericks were playing
uninspired ball against us and the referees had drifted off into never-
never land, giving us a lot of calls that infuriated coach Dick Motta.
When one of the Lakers was given a free throw after having taken steps
on a drive to the basket, Motta verbally attacked referee Terry Durham, accusing Durham of biased incompetence and finally punctuating
his attack with the word "cocksucker." Of course, this outburst got
Motta the desired technical and sobered up his team quickly. As the
free throw was being shot, I slid over to an area on the floor near the
Dallas bench and, getting his attention, said to Coach Motta, "I have
to say you're an excellent judge of character." He stifled a burst of
laughter and lost all the passion that had earned him the T. Even one
of his assistants was smirking. That's the only time I have ever sabo-
taged a coaching ploy with a joke.

But there are fewer and fewer laughs to be had on the hardwood.
About his leaving the coaching spot, Frank Layden said that sometimes
in the NBA you feel like a dog. You age seven years in one. It eats you
alive. And now, for a change, he wanted to enjoy the flowers. He said
he wanted his soul back and that it was time to have his time. I know
how he feels.

It's not the Game, it's the games—the pressure to win, the pressure
to travel, and the very existence of the long season, which just gets
extended every year. My own first championship season, my second
year in the league, ended on April 30. Last year, the season ended on
June 21, our summer shortened by nearly two months.

In the course of my career, I have seen the NBA go through some
serious changes. In fact, as it has turned out, my basketball career has
paralleled the period of greatest growth in the sport; I've seen it all
happen firsthand. I've watched basketball transform itself from a
minor game without much glamour, kept alive by a hard core of
dedicated fans, into the most actively growing game in the country.
As a major national sport, basketball is now unquestionably on par
with baseball and football. It's gained an emotional hold not only in
America, where the game originated, but also outside the country in
places like Spain, Italy, Brazil, Australia, Russia, and the hills of
Greece. Internationally, after soccer, basketball is now the most popular sport in the world. The Europeans, in particular, seem to have
acquired the same kind of reverential appreciation for basketball as

they have for jazz, both being uniquely American forms of expression. They respect our players as they might the virtuoso drummer or trumpeter or jazz saxophonist.

All of this has been thrilling, including the silver lining of increased salaries for those of us who make our living playing the game. But the explosion of popularity and money hasn't been without its price. Basketball as big business has made both the players and the coaches vulnerable to the bottom line. When I came into the league in '69, there were fourteen NBA teams, and only four of those were west of the Mississippi River. We played the same number of regular-season games as we do now, eighty-two, but because there were fewer teams, we traveled to fewer cities, and those were concentrated in the East. Today, there are twenty-five teams in the NBA, scattered across the four corners of the country, and next year there will be twenty-seven. The demands of travel have expanded exponentially with the near doubling of the teams and territory. Doc Kerlan says the road schedule in the NBA would kill the average human being. He emphasizes the tremendous stress of this kind of traveling on the body, and the even greater stress on the mind.

No other major sport has its players travel the way we do. Baseball teams arrive in a town and settle in for three or four days. Football teams travel a mere ten weekends a season, and that's including the exhibition season. Even flight attendants, whose job it is to travel, have protective regulations about air hours and, what's more, once they arrive in a city, their work is done. Ours has only just begun.

Within this context, you are under the constant pressure to perform and to win—pressure from the fans, from the management, from your own high standards. As long as the status quo is profitable, as it has been dramatically in the eighties, the league's owners will never allow the season or the travel schedule to be shortened. So part of your job becomes learning how to play the NBA as well as the ball game. You trudge through the season with as much consistency and equilibrium and snatched rest as you can muster, with the goal of arriving at the play-offs with your physical being and your intensity of desire intact.

This is true for the players as well as the coaches, and in many ways the pressures on the coaches may be the most difficult to manage. They live a precarious existence, responsible to their organization for the whole team. They live with the losses longer. There are more sleepless nights. They receive little recognition until they win it all. And whether they win or lose, the season ages them. Already, the seasons are making Pat Riley old. In flashes, you can see it on his face, which often is a study in stress. One day in the locker room he said that as a coach you are never satisfied until you win the championship, and then you're sort of satisfied. There's another championship to go for the next year, and the year after that, and it never stops. From Riley's point of view, as he has described it, there are two possible states of being in the NBA—winning and misery. And in the last seven years that he's been Laker coach, winning years all of them, on only two occasions have I come close to seeing the state of misery slip completely away from him—when we reaped the back-to-back championship last year and when we beat Boston in Boston in '85. It took the force of those history-making victories to lift off the angst that otherwise seems to cling to Riley, another Irishman, only forty-three years old.

A few days ago, I was killing some time in a bookstore on Melrose Avenue before a parents' meeting at Amir's school and I bought Riley a copy of Musashi's *Book of Five Rings*. I've seen some of the works of the great military strategists like Rommel and Patton and Sun-tzu on his bookshelves at home, and I thought he might like to add Musashi's more subtle warrior philosophy to his collection. I brought the book along with me to give to Riles on the road.

With a stop and a three-hour time change, it was late afternoon by the time my plane descended into Indianapolis. From the airport, I went straight into the city to Market Square Arena for the night's game. There was a light snow on the ground and on the war memorial in the center of town, and the temperature was just below freezing, expected to drop to 8 degrees by morning. For me, that will be a drop of about 70 degrees from the Santa Ana weather I left behind.

At the arena, I was reunited with the team, who had already come over on the bus from the hotel just a few blocks away. The mood was quietly confident inside the locker room. We left Los Angeles for our long journey undefeated at home, at the top of the West, and with a 14-3 record, several wins ahead of last year's pace. Our last loss was in Detroit. For the daunting schedule before us, with the exception of my maimed knee, we could hardly have set out under more favorable circumstances.

There was an air of excitement inside the arena. Basketball remains a sacred trust in Indiana and, with all that tradition, the Indiana fans embrace the game and the players, even the players on the opposing teams, with an ardor that's special to this state. So during the player introductions before the game, the sellout Saturday-night crowd gave a warm welcome not only to its own team but also to the Lakers. I saw a lot of red-and-white in the stands, not the colors of the Pacers, Indiana's pro team, but the colors of Bobby Knight's Hoosiers at Indiana University.

The game was almost a blowout. The Pacers came into the evening with their worst start in club history and with an interim coach filling the hole left by Jack Ramsay's recent departure. Their seven-foot center, Steve Stipanovich, was also missing, having just had surgery on his left knee, and seven-foot-four-inch rookie Rik Smits was starting in his place. The Pacers looked a genuinely weakened team, although we knew better than to be complacent going in. We have the experience to understand that even weak teams can emerge as fierce to an opponent caught unawares, however strong. And besides, regardless of the shape of the team we were facing, we wanted to win this first one on the tour, and we ultimately did. We were up by seventeen at the half when Indiana got back in the game. We struggled every minute of the last quarter, but finally pulled it out by seven.

This was my last time in Indiana as a player, so before the game began the Hoosier crowd and I exchanged our formal farewells. I talked briefly about the two personal connections I have to their state: a guy from Martinsville High who is considered one of Indiana high school basketball's greatest, John Wooden; and a guy from Crispus Attucks High who is considered *the* greatest, Oscar Robertson. Oscar was born in the South, in Tennessee, but he ended up in Indianapolis, where he led Crispus Attucks to two straight state championships and the first unbeaten record in Indiana basketball history. Named after the black who was among the first Americans to die in the American Revolution, Crispus Attucks High was an all-black school when Oscar was there in the mid-1950s. In '56, it was an all-white school that they defeated in the state finals. Traditionally, Indiana's winning team is feted with a parade through the center of their hometown, but that year, "to avoid racial incidents," Crispus Attucks was advised to take its celebration to a remote corner of town. I imagine Oscar has not forgotten that slight.

At my mention of him and John Wooden, the crowd exploded in appreciation. They then clamored to see a last skyhook, even though I was in civilian clothes, in jacket and tie and street shoes. So to a thunder of applause, Magic threw me the ball, I nailed a ten-footer, and the scoreboard above the floor registered two points, one assist. The scoreboard stayed that way until game time.

First stop, 1-0.

Sunday, December 11

You know it's cold in Milwaukee when there's steam on the lake. I could see it rising off of Lake Michigan as we flew into town this morning. The Midwest is heading into a deep freeze, the newspapers say. Why do I always seem to be here in the worst Wisconsin weather?

I can remember times when I lived here that it was 50 degrees below and you didn't dare go out of doors. There was a window facing north in my apartment and I came home one night, went to draw the curtains, and found the window a solid sheet of ice. This was early in my stay in Milwaukee, and I said to myself, "Oh, my goodness." Sometimes we'd have snow as late as my birthday in April, and it was four years before I stayed in Milwaukee between basketball seasons. Once I did, I discovered the country roads north of the city, and found that it was almost as nice in summer as it was bone-chilling in winter. But I never grew accustomed to the cold. Even for people born and raised here, it's too cold.

Milwaukee is where my pro career started. It was my first experience with having to go to a place where I wasn't particularly eager to be. It forced me to learn to make adjustments. Growing up in New York and playing college basketball in Los Angeles hadn't done anything to prepare me for Wisconsin. Young as I was, I had lived a kind of gilded, urban, and relatively sophisticated existence up to that point, and Milwaukee was then a quiet, conservative factory town. I felt transplanted into a completely foreign environment. I felt like I was living in a place that was on the edge, the periphery, of everything, and that made me extremely uncomfortable. In the beginning, I wasn't mature enough to handle it. I used to drive ninety miles south to Chicago just to sit in a friend's living room for an hour and a half.

I remember arriving in the fall of '69 at the Bucks' training camp in Janesville, a small farm town southwest of Milwaukee. We stayed at the Holiday Inn, and I remember there was corn growing right up to the edge of the hotel parking lot. That was my first camp. Our home court in Milwaukee, the Milwaukee Arena, was the third oldest building in the league, after Chicago Stadium and Boston Garden. It seemed a dark, gray kind of place after the brightness of Pauley Pavilion, which held even a few more thousand seats, but it was a solid, well-tended facility and you had to have that kind of basementlike structure to protect against the elements. My first few years there, I lived in an apartment about three blocks from the arena. And in my last few years, I lived in an old nine-story Art Deco building on the lakefront. It was well built and had privacy and character. I loved that apartment.

I was twenty-two when I got to Milwaukee. The Bucks were a new team heading into their second year in the league, and they had just completed their first year in next-to-last place. By finishing at the bottom, they had earned the right to a coin toss with Phoenix, the other new franchise then, to determine who would have the first pick in the spring's NBA draft. In almost biblical fashion, this is how the league corrects for imbalances of talent: The last gets the first, and the first gets the last. The Bucks won the coin toss, I was the top player coming out of college that year, and so my first major career move was decided on a coin flip. At the time, the ABA was still in existence, and there was the possibility of my playing with the Nets, who were out on Long Island then. That would have meant returning home to New York. But the outcome of the negotiations pointed in the direction of the NBA and Milwaukee, so I headed inland, into the center of the country.

For me, the cultural transition was more difficult than the basketball transition from college to the pros, although the differences between those two worlds are marked. In college, you're playing against guys who have just come out of adolescence. In the pros, you're playing against mature, muscular, highly trained men, and there are no average players. From the twenty thousand or so in the college ranks, the best are distilled for a very small number of professional slots. There were only 168 players in the NBA when I started and there are only 300 players now. In the pros, in addition to the heightened level of talent, there's just the more physical nature of the game, the intensity, and, of course, the impact of the schedule and the road. I played more games in my first year with the Bucks than I played in the entirety of my college varsity career.

We started winning in my first year. Traditionally, the prognostications for a new team are zero, but there was a lot of excitement about us in that season because in six months we became one of the best teams in the NBA. We beat everyone in the Eastern Division except New York—the great 1970 Knicks team.

There was healthy rivalry between our two clubs that year and that's when, as a rookie, I became a villain in the Garden. The Bucks and the Knicks finished the season with the two best records in the league, and much was made of our games together. In the play-offs, we advanced past Philadelphia and set a play-off-game record of 156 points, which still stands. We then lost in the next round to New York, who went on to the finals against the Lakers to win their first, long-awaited championship.

This wasn't a punishing defeat for us, though, because we had gone farther than anyone expected. We went from being the doormat of the league to being a *very good* team. And then the following year, my second with the Bucks, we got Oscar, and that was it. We went over the top. We won the world championship in '71, sweeping Baltimore in the finals in four games.

Working with Oscar Robertson was working with the best, and with the epitome of court generalship. He had great vision, great timing, and he understood how to make things happen in the big picture and in the little picture simultaneously. That takes a certain talent; the preparation has to be exact, and Oscar knew exactly what he was doing at all times. He kept the game simple, which was the first secret to his genius, as it was for Bill Russell and for John Wooden. A perfectionist on the court, Oscar would whip the team into shape. He would yell at you in a second if you weren't doing what you were supposed to be doing. I was elated when I was told he was coming. Just as my first season was ending, I got a call at home from the team's owner, Wes Pavalon. Wes had been a basketball star in high school, uncommon among NBA owners, and he had kept an unbridled enthusiasm for the game.

"We got help! We got help!" he said.

"What help?" I asked, not knowing what he was talking about.

"We got Oscar!" he said.

Oscar was thirty-two by then. One of the greatest players to ever play the game, he had been in the NBA for ten years and had never won a championship. In fact, Oscar hadn't experienced that particular elation since high school, at Crispus Attucks. A championship had eluded him in college and then afterward in the pros. He played with the Cincinnati Royals for a full decade before coming to Milwaukee, and Cincinnati hadn't made it to the finals in all that time. So, hungry for a title, Oscar got himself traded to us, to a team he perceived rightly as having a chance to go all the way.

On that championship team, it was Oscar and Jon McGlocklin, an All-Star guard, in the starting backcourt. The frontcourt remained the same as the year before, with Bobby Dandridge, Greg Smith, and me. Our sixth man became Lucius Allen, my former teammate at UCLA, who joined the Bucks at the same time as Oscar. Lucius, Bobby, and

My first love was always baseball. This is me fielding on 111th Street and Seventh Avenue in Harlem. Note the double-decker bus!

Grandmother Venus Alcindor and me.

Me and my dad at the beach, a place I have always loved.

My very first basketball season, fourth grade.

Me and my high school coach, Jack Donahue.

"Rhythm-a-ning." Thelonious Monk and me (age nineteen) in the kitchen of the Village Vanguard.
(© *Andrew D. Bernstein/NBA*)

Oh, those were the days.
(*Malek Abdul-Mansour*)

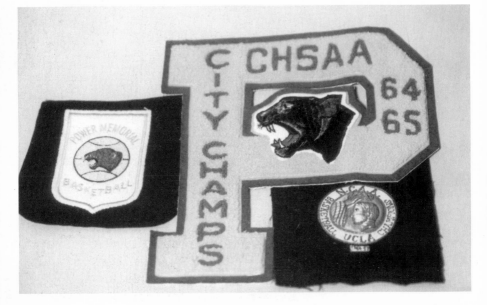

Left to right: Wilt Chamberlain, Oscar Robertson, me, Jerry West, and Elgin Baylor. This is the only time we were all on the court together. *(AP/Wide World Photos)*

Apprentice to the Wizard, John Wooden.
(UCLA Athletic Department)

The season begins at training camp in Honolulu. That's Tony Campbell on the left. *(Malek Abdul-Mansour)*

Behind the scenes in the hallway at the Forum, preparing to go out on the floor. *(Malek Abdul-Mansour)*

My pregame ritual.
(Malek Abdul-Mansour)

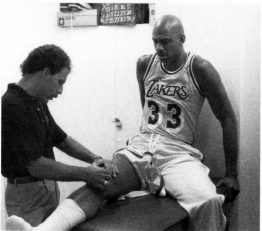

With trainer Gary Vitti,
making sure the wheels
work. *(Malek Abdul-Mansour)*

The very beginning of the
Laker fast break.
(Wen Roberts, Photography Ink)

This shows how you can get the
hook off even against great
defense. *(Malek Abdul-Mansour)*

Opposite page: Me and Josh Rosenfeld, Laker publicist, dealing with one of many pregame requests. *(Malek Abdul-Mansour)*

Magic and me at Chicago Stadium in 1988, our last All-Star game together. *(Malek Abdul-Mansour)*

And miles to go before we sleep. *(Malek Abdul-Mansour)*

Michael Cooper: situation specialist. *(Malek Abdul-Mansour)*

The James Worthy
floating show.
(Malek Abdul-Mansour)

Pat Riley, certainly
underappreciated.
(Wen Roberts, Photography Ink)

FACES IN THE CROWD

Richard Pryor. *(Malek Abdul-Mansour)*

Bill Murray. *(Malek Abdul-Mansour)*

Jack Nicholson and Lou Adler, courtside at the Forum.
(Malek Abdul-Mansour)

Nate Thurmond and me at my last game against Golden State in the Oakland Coliseum. *(Bill Beattie)*

FAREWELL TO OLD FRIENDS

Me and Julius Erving.
(© Greg Lanier/The Philadelphia Inquirer)

Moms and Pops at my last regular-season game at the Forum. (*Chris Carlson*/The Orange County Register)

Amir singing the national anthem at my last regular-season game. (*John McCoy*/L.A. Daily News)

Somehow they kept me from
seeing my gift, a Rolls-Royce.
(John McCoy/L.A. Daily News)

My last steps on the court.
(© Andrew D. Bernstein/NBA)

Still dreaming about baseball.
(© *Andrew D. Bernstein/NBA*)

Me and the gang in Hawaii.
Left to right: Kareem, me and
Amir, Habiba, and Sultana.
(*Malek Abdul-Mansour*)

Thanks for the good times. You were the tops.
*(Nancy Lane/*Boston Herald)

Greg were relentless runners, I was in the middle, and Oscar, who controlled the ball, directed us.

Having passed that magic age of thirty, which usually marks the tip of the down slope for a guard's career, Oscar had lost maybe a step, but his mastery on the floor was full compensation. Oscar was a deadly shot—there were half a dozen seasons when he'd averaged thirty points or more—but his special gift was his passing, the skill that is the real foundation of the offense. In the swirl of players jostling for position on the court, Oscar would get you the ball in the precise place you needed it, through all obstacles, and in the precise moment. I could receive the pass and turn and hook in one unbroken motion. When you play with someone of his caliber, it does a whole different thing to your game.

Oscar was six-five and 220 pounds, and no playmaking guard near his level had ever been that size before. Bob Cousy, the first great playmaker, had been six-one. Guy Rodgers was six feet and Jerry West six-three. All three were under 200 pounds. And so, breaking precedent, Oscar became the prototype of the big guard. Few people realize that playing opposite him was like playing a fullback. He'd knock you on your heels, or he'd fake and then knock you on your heels, and he'd do that over and over, running into you, or faking and running into you. Oscar was Jim Brown on the basketball court.

After our ascendant moment in '71, Oscar and I were together for three more years. We came within a game of winning it all again in '74, this time facing Boston in the final with the league's best record. The nucleus of the team had remained intact except that Greg Smith had been traded to Houston for forward Curtis Perry, a management move with which I was unhappy. Greg had been my best friend on the Bucks. He and I had been able to talk about virtually anything, our home lives, women, being black and lonely in Milwaukee, and it left a big hole in my life when he left. The core of the '74 team without Greg was me, Oscar, Bobby Dandridge, Jon McGlocklin, Lucius Allen, Curtis Perry, and also forward Mickey Davis, who spelled Bobby from the bench.

We had a team deep with talent, but I think the Celtic ghosts were stirring that season. A few games before the play-offs began, Lucius slipped on a warm-up jacket left too close to the court and his knee wound up in a cast. He was out for the season and he watched our combative, closely contested final series with Boston from the bench.

Neither team was able to establish dominance and, oddly, we were both losing on our home courts. For us, it came down to a memorable sixth game in Boston Garden. Many said that this was the Celtics' most dramatic contest since they'd gone four overtimes in '53. We were down 3–2 and had to either tie the series on Boston's home court or lose it all. We were facing elimination. We *had* to win.

The game went into two overtimes that included two tied scores and twelve lead changes. With seven seconds to go in the final overtime, Celtic John Havlicek, one of the great forwards, hit a shot that made it 101–100, Boston. The Boston crowd was screaming; the title looked to be theirs. We called a time-out and set up a play for Jon McGlocklin, who then couldn't get open for the inbounds pass at half court. Seeing this, I darted from the inside to out past the free-throw line, took the pass, broke down through to the baseline, and shot a hook from fifteen feet. The clock read 0:03 as the ball dropped through the net, and now we were *ahead* by a point. We won the game 102–101, tying the series 3–3.

I couldn't sleep at all that night. It was a tremendous victory for us, and that final-seconds winning shot would turn out to be one of the most unforgettable of my career. Over the years, I have taken pleasure in the fact that Boston hasn't forgotten it either. But ultimately they prevailed that year. The series returned to Milwaukee, where, in the seventh game, they defeated us by fifteen points on our home court.

I remain convinced that with Lucius healthy we would have had another title. That was my first raw encounter with the wrenching role injuries can play in the outcome of championship battles.

Oscar retired after that season, and without him I played one more year with the Bucks. I remember getting to training camp in the fall and the first thing Bobby Dandridge said was "I can't wait for this season to be over." I said to myself, "Oh, no, it's going to be a long one." And it was. Lucius was traded ten games into the season and I missed the first sixteen, having broken my hand in an exhibition game. In a tightly packed scramble for a rebound, my left eye had been accidentally pawed by an opponent groping for the ball, giving me my sixth corneal abrasion. In a flash of pain and anger, I threw a hard punch at the metal stanchion supporting the backboard and broke two bones in my right hand, compounding my injury, an action that I regretted instantly and for the duration of the six weeks it took my hand to heal. The eye was better in a matter of days, but when I returned to play, the cast finally off my hand, I was wearing protective goggles. They caused some stares and talk but I have worn them ever since, and that particular injury was the last one to my eyes. Like the knees, they are acutely vulnerable in basketball, especially for centers and forwards, who play closest to the basket, where the play is the most physical. Adjusting to the goggles took awhile, as did finding a make that allowed me the peripheral vision I needed, but eventually I found some that worked, and every now and then I will feel the click of someone's nails on the lenses and know it's been worth wearing them all these years.

Oscar was conspicuous by his absence in that last season, which turned out to be a losing one for us—my first since I was a twelve-year-old at St. Jude's. I had another year left on my contract with the Bucks, but by that spring I had decided that I'd paid my dues and that it was time to move on. It was 1975; I had been in Milwaukee for six years.

I asked to be traded in March and by June a deal was made with the Lakers in Los Angeles.

Once again, I had tried to go back to New York, this time with the Knicks, but once again it hadn't worked out. The Knicks didn't have the players Milwaukee wanted and a few conversations between the two clubs left everyone with the impression that a trade couldn't be made. With New York out, both the Lakers and the Washington Bullets emerged as possibilities, and I was faced with either choosing between the two or playing out my contract with the Bucks. I chose L.A. I was traded for four quality ballplayers, Junior Bridgeman, Dave Meyers, Brian Winters, and Elmore Smith, all of whom were early on in their pro careers. Bridgeman and Meyers were about to be rookies, Winters had just finished his rookie year, and Elmore Smith had just finished his third year in the league. Their youth looked promising for Milwaukee. At the time, the Bucks' general manager, Wayne Embry, was quoted as saying, "Kareem is twenty-eight and these four young players will be around when Kareem is long gone." Looking back, Wayne laughs at those remarks now because, as things turned out, it's the others who are long gone, not me, a fact at times strange to contemplate.

It was Wayne Embry who handled my trade to the Lakers. Wayne has the distinction of being the first black general manager in the NBA, or in any major team sport. He broke the color barrier by going into the top front-office position with the Bucks in 1972. There are now three black GMs in the NBA, all former players, Bill Russell with Sacramento, Elgin Baylor with the Clippers, and Wayne, who eventually moved on to Cleveland. There are still none in either baseball or football.

Wayne and Milwaukee helped to make my professional transition as painless as possible. The city let me leave with the same open arms with which it had welcomed me. It was as if the fans knew I didn't really belong there forever, and they let me go with all the appreciation they had always shown for what I did on the court. This made it both easier and harder to step away.

Milwaukee fans extended far beyond the city, to all of Wisconsin, upper Michigan, and even parts of Minnesota. These fans used to listen to the games on the radio and root for the Bucks like we were a local high school. They were the salt of the earth. When I left Milwaukee, I left with their goodwill, a championship ring, and some friendships that have lasted. I also left with a new name for my shot. Early in my years there, the Bucks' radio announcer Eddie Doucette had taken to describing my hook shot as the *skyhook*. It was a name that stuck, a little gift to my game from Milwaukee.

The afternoon and evening were full of these memories. When I left here thirteen years ago, I certainly never dreamed I would be saying good-bye again to this city. As a rookie, I remember having a conversation with Jon McGlocklin in which we were trying to look into our professional futures. I said then that I would probably play eight years, ten years tops, and he suggested twelve. *Twelve?!*

Jon was at tonight's game, as were Bobby Dandridge, Greg Smith, Mickey Davis, and two other former teammates, Sam Williams and Dick Garrett. Wayne Embry was also there, and Larry Costello, who was our coach in those early years.

The game was held in the Bucks' new arena, right across the street from the old one, which is about half the size. The place was so newly finished you could smell the paint. Filled to capacity, the house went dark just before the game and I was asked to walk out to center court for my farewell. As I made my way, a long thunderous ovation rolled down toward me from the stands, the applause amplified by the darkness, the only light in the arena the spotlight I was standing in. I had been through the team's infancy with this crowd, and they were letting me know that the years I'd been gone had done nothing to dim their memories. It moved me powerfully. I said a few words, the Bucks gave me gifts, and they rededicated the two banners that now hang in the new building, both of which I had a hand in winning for them, the '71 world championship and the '74 Western Conference title.

After the game, Bobby and Greg came up to my hotel room, and we talked late into the night.

It was tough not being able to play in the actual game. We were looking for our eighth consecutive win and our second on this trip. Three minutes into the second quarter, on a drive to the basket, Byron stepped on the foot of Milwaukee's Ricky Pierce and badly twisted his own right ankle. Unable to continue playing, he joined me on the bench, from which we watched the Lakers struggle and then fall behind the Bucks by ten points in the third quarter. The game looked to be sliding away from us until we regained the lead in the fourth quarter, which was tense. It came down to the final three seconds. We were up by one, the score 94–93, and it was Milwaukee's ball. Riley's instructions were to deny the inbounds pass to Terry Cummings, Sidney Moncrief, and Jack Sikma, the three Bucks on the floor most likely to deliver a clutch shot. We ably blocked those options, so the ball was passed instead to reserve guard Jay Humphries, who somehow found an opening between Coop and Magic and hit a sixteen-foot jump shot at the buzzer. The Bucks got two and won by one, the final score 95–94.

These are the ones that hurt, when the win slips through your fingers.

Second stop, 1-1.

Monday, December 12

This morning, I was up at dawn. The windchill outside was minus 6 degrees.

Our flight to Cleveland was at eleven, but before leaving Milwaukee I was scheduled to have my knee tested at a sports clinic located on the outskirts of town. The news was good. The tests showed the week of rehab had done its job, restoring nearly all the muscle strength I'd lost, enough for me to get back on the floor. At last. From the clinic, I went straight to the airport and boarded the plane. I handed the test results to our trainer, Gary Vitti, and he said that now we'd just have to see if the knee swelled in practice. Gary had been up twice during the night, at two and four A.M., to rewrap Byron's ankle, which was still throbbing. It's thought to be only a minor strain, but it's unlikely Byron will be able to play in tomorrow's game.

For Gary, being up in the middle of the night with a wounded player is nothing new. On the road several years ago, I was seized in the dead of night with one of the piercing migraines that used to plague me, and it was Gary I called, howling in pain. He's the one you call at those times. He's the point man for all our physical mishaps and spills, working hand-in-glove with Docs Kerlan and Lombardo on player inju-

ries. Day-to-day, he concerns himself with keeping us healthy while the
schedule does its very best to wear us down. Gary is also responsible
for the team equipment and for handling every detail of travel on the
road. Like all trainers in the NBA, in spite of his advanced degree in
sports medicine, he has these non–athletic-training tasks tagged onto
his job.

In his thirties, a first-generation Italian American from New England, Gary probably puts in the longest hours of anyone associated
with the team. For flights in and out of Los Angeles, Gary will be the
first and last at LAX. For flights on the road, his wake-up call will
precede ours by an hour at least, and he'll go on ahead to the airport
to turn our batch of tickets into boarding passes and to make sure we
all get the right seats. Upon arriving in a city, while the players and
coaches board the chartered team bus that's always waiting curbside,
Gary counts our fifty-plus pieces of luggage as they pour off the baggage
carousel—both personal luggage and equipment trunks. Patiently, he
matches claim checks and has the pieces loaded into the bottom of the
bus, which then takes us all to our hotel, where Gary then sees that
every bag makes it to the right room. Through all this, Gary manifests
a kind of low-key uncomplaining unflappability that gets the job done,
city after city. He's our liaison with the endless hotel clerks, bellboys,
skycaps, airline agents, and bus drivers who line the NBA circuit. He
helps to soften the NBA travel nightmare into just a bad dream.

This morning, Gary got me my usual first-row aisle seat on the left
side of the airplane. This has been my aerial spot for years, the seat with
the most leg room, seat 1B. Generally, the team fills the entire first-class
cabin, and our seating arrangement rarely varies. The less we have to
think about on the road the better. The routine simplifies; we can just
walk onto the plane and sit down. I don't even have to look over my
shoulder to know that behind me in the second row are Magic and
Cooper, who have been seatmates now for going on ten years.

Behind Magic and Coop sit Byron and Mychal T., and then Mark
McNamara and Jeff Lamp. Across the aisle are Orlando and A.C., and
in front of them sit James and Tony Campbell. James always sits in the
first aisle seat on the right side of the airplane so he can stretch out his
bad left knee, the one that has the two screws in it. We call this the
Blue Heaven seat because James went to the University of North
Carolina, whose colors are baby blue, and because for five years before
James the seat belonged to our former teammate Mitch Kupchak; he
also went to North Carolina and also had a bad left knee, often aching,
that he would stretch out in the aisle the same as James. Until his knee

finally forced him to retire, Mitch was one of the best backup centers I ever had, the kind of player who would break his nose, fracture a finger, or otherwise run through a wall, if necessary, to win. Before his major knee injuries, he was a starting power forward. He's in the front office now with Jerry West.

Rookie David Rivers has been assigned this season to the shortened bulkhead seat next to mine and sometimes to a seat farther back with the rest of our group. We are seldom fewer than sixteen altogether. Riley and Bertka always sit together in a spot behind the players, Bill usually at the window and Pat in the aisle seat. And Gary sits with Chick Hearn, one of the most restless travelers among us, because he's been at it so much longer. During waits in terminals, he paces the floor, and on planes he passes the time with endless crossword puzzles, while Gary reads. Since Hawaii, Gary has been lugging around a thick hardback copy of *War and Remembrance*. I think he manages a page or two a day on the road.

We landed here in Cleveland around one o'clock, and an afternoon practice was scheduled for two at the Cavs' home arena, which is way out in the middle of nowhere in a little town called Richfield, midway between Cleveland and Akron. After we got off the plane, it was almost an hour's bus ride into the country. It had snowed, so from my seat in the back of the bus I watched the white Ohio landscape pass by outside the windows.

We have our regular seats on the team bus too. I have the very last row that stretches across the back, and Magic and Cooper share the row just in front of me, Magic on one side of the aisle and Coop on the other. The back of the bus is the players' domain, far removed from the coaches, who sit all the way up front. Riley always takes the first pair of seats closest to the door and Gary sits opposite, behind the bus driver, so he can give instructions. The assistant coaches are behind them, and then Chick, sometimes the beat writers, any team staff, the team doctors when they're with us, and rarely anyone else. All riders must be okayed by Riley, who guards the team bus like an inner sanctum.

The team was tired and still feeling the sting of last night's loss to Milwaukee, so the long ride out to the gym was quiet. In three days, we have been in three time zones and three different cities.

Practice turned out to be one of those that will be remembered for the rest of the season, three hours long and brutal. Riley's agitation over losing the way we did last night was evident, and we had tomorrow night's game with Cleveland facing us. There's been a lot of talk about Cleveland being the toughest challenge for us on this trip because the Cavs have surprised everyone by jumping into the early season's upper echelon. As of today, three teams are tied with the fewest losses in the league: the Lakers, Detroit, and Cleveland.

So Riles was tightly coiled and ran us extra hard and extra long. It was after dark by the time we got back to our hotel. Gary announced from the front of the bus that it was leaving again at eight in the morning for a nine o'clock shootaround back at the arena. With the game in the evening, that means two trips out and back tomorrow, almost four hours on the bus. We tried to put that out of our minds.

It was iron-cold outside; we filed off the team bus with the navy hoods of our warm-ups pulled up over our heads. We could see our breath. Filing into the hotel lobby, weary with fatigue, we could have passed for an order of Druid monks, twelve hooded contemplatives, very tall.

We dispersed to our separate hotel rooms, too tired to do anything but sleep.

I slept about four hours, waking up around eleven, and had a midnight supper in my room. I'm pleased to see no sign of swelling in my knee. The practice was exhausting for me, as long as it was, and being my first time back in two weeks. But the knee has withstood the test on the floor.

I am back to work.

I have missed a stretch of seven games, the longest I have been out of play in eleven seasons, the longest I have been out of play *ever* for an injury to my knees or to my legs.

Wednesday, December 14

Cleveland turned out to be the worthy opponent we'd anticipated, but in the end we beat them by a comfortable nine points in front of a crowd of twenty thousand, the Cavs' largest home crowd of the season. In the final quarter of the game, we built a fourteen-point lead that the Cavs quickly slashed to five, but then A.C. Green hit an improbable three-pointer that lifted us to an eight-point cushion with only a minute left to play. In his four seasons with us, A.C. has been only one for fourteen from the three-point line, and this was only the second such shot of his career. It sealed the night's win. As it dropped through the basket, from twenty-five feet out, Riley went racing down the bench with his fist pumped into the air. It was a rare moment of exultant abandon for Riles, but this road game had been especially heavy on his mind. It ended 111–102.

Third stop, 2-1.

That was last night.

And by tonight we were in the Meadowlands Arena in north Jersey playing the Nets in front of another opposing home crowd of twenty thousand.

The Nets came into the game toward the bottom of their division, so for us this should have meant a straightforward win. Instead, it was as if all passion had been spent in the game the night before. We were leaden, and allowed the Nets to remain close throughout. The full four quarters were a struggle. In the end it came down to a mortal final seven seconds in regulation. I had just made a pair of free throws, which gave us a three-point edge. The score was 106–103, and it looked like we had it won. The Nets' only hope was a three-point shot that we knew we must deny them. After a last time-out, Nets rookie Chris Morris inbounded the ball to point guard John Bagley, who then appeared to drive for a lay-up. Mychal Thompson left his position on Morris to double-team Bagley, but then Bagley flipped the ball back to the now-open Morris, who launched a shot from behind the three-point line with three seconds to go. The shot went in, the crowd went wild, and the score was tied 106–106. The game went into overtime, where we lost it by five, the final score 118–113.

It was an emotional loss.

And it was so much like the last-second defeat in Milwaukee only three nights ago, that the Cleveland win went into immediate eclipse; Cleveland was suddenly forgotten and Milwaukee remembered.

"That's two gifts in a row," I heard Riley say to the press afterward.

Gifts are the games you give away, the games that haunt. You hate to lose that way.

Now we are carrying two such losses on our backs.

Postgame, I showered and then slipped out early to the empty team bus that waited by the rear entrance of the arena. I settled into the seat in the far back and switched on the small light overhead so I could read until everyone else had gotten on and we took off for the hotel. That's a usual practice of mine after games on the road.

I played twenty-eight minutes in tonight's game and seventeen minutes in Cleveland. I got winded—I could feel the effects of two weeks of inactivity in my legs and lungs—but all my conditioning should be back in another two or three games.

Orlando boarded the bus a few minutes after me. I knew the evening had been particularly rough on him because this was his first time back in New Jersey since leaving the Nets to go into drug rehab last winter and since becoming a Laker this fall. His former home crowd had given him a most unwelcome reception, booing him loudly when he first came onto the court in the first quarter and continuing to berate him up through the fourth quarter, when he missed four free throws in a row. Orlando said he started listening to the crowd's jeers after missing the first one. He'd expected to be booed upon his return, but hadn't expected to be affected by it as much as he was. Nor was he ready for the slurs about his drug problem. Preparing to shoot the foul shots, he was hammered with taunts from the stands like "Don't snort that line, Orlando!" And this won't be the last time this season that such messages rain down on Orlando in a league arena. Like people anywhere, sports crowds can be cruel, intolerant, and ignorant about addiction.

I noted Orlando's calm in the face of all this. I must admire him for handling these situations with a lot more serenity and reason than I believe I could muster up.

I put down my book and the two of us talked for a while in the quiet of the back of the bus, which had the team back to the hotel shortly after eleven.

Fourth stop, 2-2.

Thursday, December 15

Boston next.

We flew up to New England late this morning and remet the snow we'd left behind in the Midwest. New Jersey had been covered only in a gray-brown winter smog, but Boston was covered all in white, including red-bricked Boston Garden, which passed by out the window as we drove through the city's North End on our way in from Logan Airport. The sun was shining, but the cold front had followed us here, so the temperature outside was icy, bracing, that kind of wet-cold you get in the East.

We are going to be here for two days, staying in the city's Back Bay, a district adjacent to Boston's South End.

An afternoon practice had been scheduled for shortly after our arrival, but as the bus pulled up to the front of the hotel, the Marriott Copley, Gary announced that practice was canceled. All of us were surprised by this because after last night's debacle in the Meadowlands we thoroughly anticipated a brutal workout along the lines of the one that followed Milwaukee. For Riley, practices can never be too often or too long, especially after a bruising loss. He wants them to be worse than the games, and they are. Many are the times on the practice floor that we go to a point where we're too tired even to pay attention. Riles will say, "Okay, we'll go over this one last play and that'll be it." But no way. Several other subjects will emerge and practice will run at least another hour or forty-five minutes. At least in a game you know when it's going to end; it runs on a clock. In practice, we never know when it's going to end—or sometimes even begin. One time, when a court appearance was going to keep a player from making our regular 10 A.M. Loyola practice, the hour was changed to 7 A.M. I am reminded of the saying "Neither snow, nor rain, nor heat, nor gloom of night . . ." It certainly has applied to Laker practices.

But every now and then, Riley reads the signs of diminishing returns and eases up. By the time we got here to Boston, he must have realized how fatigued we really are. We need to practice, but we also need to catch our breath. We've just been through back-to-back seesaws, first in Indiana and Milwaukee, then in Cleveland and New Jersey. Both ended in demoralizing moments for the team. So Riles appears to have yielded to a day of restorative rest.

We stepped off the team bus, and the hotel quickly swallowed us up.

My room, high up, has a big, north-facing window from which I can look out to the partly frozen Charles River and, across the river, to snow-covered Cambridge. I drank in the view for a while before I drew the heavy drapes, turning the day to night, so I could sleep. My body clock is all disoriented from the spinning changes of geography in the five days since I left Los Angeles. You get a sense of vertigo when you're on the road this long. You don't look back even to yesterday or you get dizzy. Yesterday already has moss on it. It's like it happened a hundred years ago.

I dropped off to sleep, thinking about my history with this city and remembering the time in this very same hotel when the fire alarms kept going off in the middle of the night. This was at the start of the 1984 championship series with Boston, the one that got away. The same thing had happened the year before in Philadelphia during the 1983 finals with the Sixers; we had to evacuate our hotel after someone set a wastebasket full of paper on fire in one of the stairwells. In Boston, the hotel alarms began waking us up on the Saturday night before Game 1 and continued waking us up nightly until Thursday, when we played Game 2. There wasn't a doubt in my mind or in the team's mind that the alarms had been intentionally triggered to disrupt our sleep. Celtic fans weren't above that kind of guerrilla tactic, especially that year, and we knew it. That was the first year the Lakers and Celtics had met in the finals in fifteen years, and in all that time the force of the rivalry had not abated, on either side.

Boston has always been a heated and hard-boiled kind of place in which to compete, but things got out of hand that spring. The tripped alarms were only the beginning. The series went a full seven games, and by the day of Game 7 we needed a police escort just to get out of our hotel and onto the bus waiting to take us to shootaround practice. By that time we'd switched hotels, but there's really no way for the Lakers to hide in Boston, for our whereabouts to remain unknown in this city.

As we came down from our rooms the morning of the last game, a mob of Celtic fans was barricading the hotel entrance and the Boston police department had to give us two huge police dogs and six cops on motorcycles for protection. It took our bus ten minutes just to turn out of the hotel drive and into the street. That night in Boston Garden, the security force wasn't fully prepared for the brawl-like behavior in the stands, either during or after the game. The crowd hurled trash and wet towels, pelted us with a storm of verbal abuse, and at the final buzzer couldn't be restrained from pummeling us as we left the court. Somebody ripped the glasses off my face and tried for my jersey. I had to defend myself.

The thing was that Boston had won the night's game and therefore the season's championship, but there was no grace-in-victory for the Celtic fans. They were savage victors that year.

As our bus tried to pull out of the Garden's truck tunnel sometime before twelve that final night, hundreds surrounded us—pounding on the windows, throwing rocks, and rocking the bus side to side as it literally inched its way forward. Sitting inside, we thought the windows might shatter.

In hindsight, this jarring, explosive scene was an apt backdrop for the loss of that championship. It was Boston's worst and most ignoble moment as a host city, and it was our worst and most painful moment as a team. We had gone all the way to a seventh game—played on June 12, the longest the NBA finals had ever gone until that time—only to lose by one point. The blow of that defeat was deepened by the fact that we all believed we would have beaten Boston if not for two critical mistakes—twice in the series, at crucial times, we had thrown the ball away. Sometimes, oftentimes, it all comes down to that: a matter of a few errors. We had beaten ourselves, and we knew it.

We also had the past weighing heavily on us. We had inherited a long history of having the Celtics kick sand in our faces. The '84 defeat became the seventh time in seven meetings that the L.A. Lakers had lost to Boston in the spring. We were now 0-7 in our finals together. Boston had been the eye of the needle through which the sixties Laker team had failed repeatedly to pass. And now the eighties Laker team had fallen. Besides me, on the team at that time were Magic, Coop, James, and Byron, who was a rookie then, Mitch Kupchak, Bob McAdoo, Mike McGee, Larry Spriggs, and Jamaal Wilkes, whom we called Silk because his moves were that smooth. Silk was poetry in motion.

We ended that season hungry for another shot at Boston, and we got it exactly one year later, in the '85 finals. All of us—the Laker roster was virtually unchanged, and we faced the same Celtic starting lineup as we had the previous spring: Robert Parish, Kevin McHale, Dennis Johnson, Danny Ainge, and Larry Bird. It was a rematch, and we were motivated in the extreme.

This time the Boston security forces were ready. Uniformed policemen and security guards were visible everywhere, beginning with Game 1, which turned out to be a game to remember, the final darkness before dawn.

It was an afternoon game on Memorial Day, and we were decimated, losing by a staggering thirty-four points. The press took to calling it, rightly, the Memorial Day Massacre. It was the worst defeat ever suffered by a Los Angeles Lakers team in a championship-series game. My play was terrible, the most terrible, and it went down throughout all levels of the team. Nobody was really able to play his game the way he should have. The next-day's *Boston Globe* headline read FIRST BLOOD: CELTICS CUT UP LAKERS. The final score was 148–114, the Celtics setting a new finals standard for most points in a championship game, a record that still stands.

We had three days to recover before Game 2, on Thursday, and it was during that time, between those opening games, that I think Pat Riley had his greatest moment as a coach. After our Game 1 loss, he could have gotten hysterical or, alternately, morose about our predicament. Instead, he calmly but determinedly got us organized. His vision was very clear. He was his coolest and ablest as far as his hands being on the wheel, and for that, in my book, he'll be remembered. Collectively, we pulled together and made the decision that we were not going to give this championship away; the Celtics would have to win it. And if they did, we could accept that. But there would be no handouts this time.

As Riles tells the story, Game 2 became the most important, backs-against-the-wall game in the history of our team. He had carefully prepared a pregame speech that he says he was then inspired to throw away on our way to the Garden that night. It involved my father, who'd come up from New York. I'd asked Riles if he could ride over to the game with us on the team bus, and he'd given his permission. Somehow, seeing my father and me together on that occasion triggered thoughts of his own father. He remembered back to his father's last words to him, spoken not long before a fatal heart attack: "Just remember what I always taught you. Somewhere, someplace, sometime, you're going to have to plant your feet, make a stand, and kick some ass. And when that time comes, you do it."

It was that message, unplanned, that became the theme of Riley's talk before Game 2. For me, the words weren't as significant as the attitude—resolute, unflinching. Pat's approach was directly on the money, and we not only came back from the brink to win the second game, but we went on to win it all, in a sixth and final game in Boston Garden.

We played that last game on an exquisite June Sunday afternoon, and the final score was 111–100. As time ran out and it grew obvious we'd won the title, the feverish Garden crowd fell silent. After a quarter century of futility, we'd finally shut them up. In victory the year before, the Celtic fans had been like animals. In defeat this year, they were like saints, better losers than winners, clapping civilly for the efforts of their vanquished team, and yielding to us our hour of glory.

I fouled out of that last game with fourteen seconds to play. At that point, though, I knew it was ours, and all I remember is running up and down in front of the bench, screaming, my fist raised to the Garden rafters, my finger pointing number-one skyward, my teammates surrounding me as the final buzzer sounded. After seven consecutive world-championship losses to the Celtics—eight if you count the Minneapolis Lakers' loss in 1959—we finally found a way to beat that team, and that's when *our* team became great. We'd removed permanently the green-and-white East Coast albatross from around our necks—for ourselves and for all the Laker players in that losing tradition.

Afraid he'd jinx the outcome by his physical presence in Boston, the site of past despond, Jerry West had stayed behind in Los Angeles and watched the game from home, almost too nervous to watch. During the first half, his television cable cut out, so he switched to an old black-and-white set still able to pick up the transmission. Sometime during the second half, the cable returned, but Jerry kept the small black-and-white screen running alongside the color one, not willing to risk turning the team's luck by turning off the tube on which we'd been winning. Superstition runs deep and serious in Jerry. As a player, before every home game, he'd tear a stick of chewing gum in half, then place each piece on either side of his locker in the Laker dressing room. He believed that helped.

So safeguarding our destiny with the televisions was entirely in character for Jerry, watching our victory from his house in L.A. that June day. He said that afterward he walked alone out into the quiet of the hillside streets, assimilating privately, after all those years, the delirium of the win.

The delirium was intensified for all of us by the fact that we'd beaten Boston *in* Boston. Boston had never lost a title in the Garden. And, of course, they'd never lost one to the Lakers. We beat a lot of history that day.

The only comparable event in sports had been the 1955 World Series, when, after decades of frustration, the Brooklyn Dodgers beat the New York Yankees for the first time. I remember that Series well because, at eight years old, I was already a committed Dodger fan. After beating the Celtics, I knew how the Dodgers must have felt that day. And I was like Johnny Podres, the Dodger pitcher who won the seventh game in '55, because I had the honor of being named MVP of the '85 finals. I was thirty-eight then, and the oldest player to have ever appeared in the play-offs, the oldest player to have ever earned a championship-series MVP award. To be the key ingredient in that final breakthrough, to have led the team in the first win over Boston, was deeply gratifying to me. It has to be the highlight of my career as a professional basketball player. I could have walked away forever then, with no unfinished business.

In the wake of that final game, I remember talking to the press for an hour or more afterward, unusual for me. My father came back to the team dressing room to share the moment, and also Jack and Lou, who usually keep their distance from the postgame locker-room scene, even when they've come three thousand miles.

The following day, *The Boston Globe* ran a large front-page photograph of Kevin McHale, who'd fallen to his knees at the final game's end, his body bent over in a kind of prayerlike position, his massive hands and forehead touching the Garden floor. It seemed the perfect representation of the Celtics in defeat. Back in Los Angeles, the *Herald Examiner's* banner headline read LAKERS! in giant type. During the celebration in downtown L.A. a few days later, I noted the marquee of a Spanish movie theater along the parade route: *"¡Saludos a Lakers! ¡Campeones mundial!"* I remember thousands coming out that day: people from Koreatown, Chinatown, East L.A., South Central L.A., the Valley, the Westside—everybody.

We beat Boston again only two seasons later, but the sense of achievement was of a different kind. In '87, we really just tied the bow; in '85 we satisfied a blood feud. Like Musashi, who killed his archenemy, Sasaki Kojiro, we'd also slain our archrival. One story had it that Musashi wept a little at his foe's passing. Kojiro had been the last person left who could really challenge him and help him improve. It was a little like that between us and the Celtics, only for us there has been no weeping.

Friday, December 16

Shootaround this morning was at nine o'clock at Hellenic College in Brookline, a wealthy Boston suburban enclave where the Celtics routinely practice. As a visiting team, we've been there many times before. Our practice went until about eleven, when we had to be off the court, but Riley hadn't finished, so we met again six hours later for a five o'clock walk-through at the hotel before leaving for the night's game in Boston Garden. Riley rented one of the hotel ballrooms and had a half court taped out on the ballroom floor, with key and baseline. Our team always travels with ten rolls of thick white adhesive tape expressly for this purpose.

When we finally arrived at the Garden around six-thirty, I wasn't surprised to find the temperature in the arena near freezing. The sixty-year-old building appears to have no heating in winter, just as it definitely has no air-conditioning in summer. None of us have forgotten the fifth game of the '84 finals, when the temperature on the court here in early June was a smoldering 97 degrees, *before* game time. The heat and humidity were so oppressive that we were forced to take oxygen during the game—Laker and Celtic players alike. It didn't help much. One of the refs became so dehydrated after the first half that he had to sit out the second.

Tonight we had the opposite situation. Outdoors, the December temperature was a raw 15 degrees, and the Garden was like an icebox. Our hands and fingers stayed cold and stiff until the heat of the game and the packed house warmed things up, well into the first quarter. Fortunately, no one had left any of the windows of our dressing room open. That wouldn't have been unusual at this time of year, nor to walk in and find some of the showers not working. One will be broken and a weak stream of tepid water will be coming out of another. The locker rooms in Boston Garden are the worst in the league, as every player in the NBA knows well. They're small, old, and tired, like the building itself. The plumbing is antiquated throughout, and rats now inhabit the back corners of this proud survivor from another era.

Boston Garden was built in 1928, above the city's North Station, which is still in operation today. The Garden was designed by the same man who built the old Madison Square Garden; it is just a little smaller, but otherwise has the same type of ceiling and the same double balcony of steeply inclined seats, which give great sight lines and a sense of intimacy with the action on the court. You enter the arena and get that same feeling of tradition and intimidation that New York's old Garden once inspired. Sixteen green-and-white world-championship banners, going back to 1957, hang from Boston's rafters, as do two sheafs of retired Celtic numbers, including Bill Russell's number 6, Bob Cousy's 14, John Havlicek's 17, and Bill Sharman's 21. These hang high above the Garden floor, which is composed of many small pieces of oak hardwood, fitted together in alternating patterns parquet style, the only one of its kind in the NBA. The wood is cut across the grain, which is supposed to enhance its hardness and durability—the current parquet floor is forty years old—but because the Garden begins on the second level, standing above ground, many of the support beams underneath have either broken or sagged with age, and consequently the court surface is uneven and full of dead spots. The ball hits the floor in these places and doesn't spring back to your hand as it should off the hardwood. This can be unsettling, especially for the guards who bring the ball up the court. The Garden floor, like the locker rooms, is also the worst in the league.

Tonight, as a player, I experienced them both for the last time— unless we meet in the play-offs—as I did the Garden crowd, which is a force unto itself here. Celtic fans have been exposed to great basket-

ball for so long, for so many years, they act as if they've been born to
it. And playing in Boston, as a result, is like singing opera in Milan. The
audiences in Milan are knowledgeable and discriminating. They have
standards. They're going to know if you screw up or step on any of the
lines.

I didn't know what kind of farewell to expect from this crowd,
especially given the competitive nature of our long association, and the
explosive championship battles of which I'd been a part. But they gave
me a long, standing, good-bye ovation tonight. I received an ovation
that strong on only one other occasion here in the Garden—when I
broke Wilt's record for field goals in February 1984. (It was two months
later, in April, that I passed Wilt's big one, the all-time scoring record.)
After a decade and a half of combative relations, the spontaneous
appreciation from Boston in that moment was a shock, a round of
applause that came out of nowhere, it seemed to me then. I was so
moved that I wrote a thank-you letter to the Celtic fans that appeared
soon after in *The Boston Globe*.

Tonight, from the floor, I just talked to them about how I had
followed the Celtics as a kid, and how Bill Russell and the Celtics teams
of the fifties and sixties had helped me my whole career. I also spoke
about how rivals get to know each other better than others who just
pass in the night, and how respect and admiration come grudgingly in
this kind of rivalry, but that it does eventually come, as it had between
our two clubs.

Red Auerbach came out to center court, where I was standing. As
hard-boiled as they come in Boston basketball, Auerbach has been
connected with the Celtics for forty years, almost from the beginning,
the coach behind the first nine Celtic crowns before moving into
management, where he is today. He was Cousy's coach, and Bill Russell's coach. I have known him since I was fourteen years old and his
team practiced in Power's gym when they were in New York to play
the Knicks.

"You've gone up and down this floor so many times," he said to me
over the din of the crowd. "It's got to happen. We've got to give you
a piece of this floor." And with that he handed me an inscribed chunk
of the parquet.

"We don't want you to forget anything about this building," he said.

After the ceremony, which preceded the evening's game, we resumed
our warm-ups, and I noticed that Larry Bird, watching his team from
the bench, was in street clothes. He had on a light-colored pair of huge

plastic shoes that looked like ski boots, the soles curving front to back like rockers. I've never seen anything like them before. They can't be too easy to get around in. Last month, after playing only the first six games of the season, Bird had major surgery on both heels to remove bone spurs that had begun pressing painfully against the Achilles' tendons in each of his feet.

Larry Bird is one of the most totally prepared basketball players I have ever seen. His mind is 100 percent in the game 100 percent of the time. He always knows where he should be on the court—and he's always there. Last season, in '88, when I caught some of the Celtic play-offs on television, I noticed that he *wasn't* always there—he wasn't always in the right place at the right time. And that's when I first knew there must be something physically wrong with him. And four weeks ago, when the operation was announced, that suspicion was confirmed. Official word is that he's out until spring; he can't return until mid-March at the earliest.

In Bird's place, the Celtics started Brad Lohaus, a young second-year man, alongside its nucleus of veterans, Kevin McHale, Danny Ainge, Dennis Johnson, and Robert Parish. Robert Parish is a great team player, an agile seven-footer, and a superb center who's been under-rated for too many years and who, in spite of that, has worked hard and successfully to develop his game. I have always respected him as an opponent. He, McHale, and Bird have been an outstanding front line for the decade they've been together, all three top-shelf.

Boston has been reeling for a month from the loss of Bird, but none of that was in evidence in the Garden tonight. Boston played its finest game of the season to date, and we played our worst. We didn't do anything well at the defensive end, and, except for Magic, we didn't make our shots. This was Byron's first game back after having missed the last two in Cleveland and New Jersey, and he was three-for-nine from the floor while I was five-for-thirteen and A.C. three-for-nine. In the first half, James missed all seven of his shots. The stat sheet said we were 38 percent overall.

We tied the game eight times in the first period alone, but then the Celtics pulled ahead to a ten-point lead in the second, at which point the Friday-night Garden crowd erupted with play-off intensity. Riley and I both had technicals before the half finished with us down by fourteen. We came within four near the end of the third quarter, but that was the closest we were to come for the remainder. The press called it a slaughter, and it really felt like that. The final score was 110–96.

We don't talk publicly about it, but this is the toll the road takes. With two losses in a row—three in five days—a gloom has now settled in.

I could hear a number of Boston fans yelling, "Good-bye, Kareem" as I filed off the court with the team tonight.

Fifth stop, 2-3.

Wednesday, December 22

The rest of the trip was like one long dental appointment. Two days after Boston we lost again in Washington, this time to the Bullets, a club in last place in its division, a team that had won only five of its last twenty games. We had a comfortable lead of twenty in the first half, continued to lead by fourteen in the third quarter, but then things fell apart in the fourth, and we lost to them by five.

From Washington we flew to Chicago, where we also fell. The Chicago Bulls outscored us 10–1 in the first three minutes of the game, and when we came within a close five points with five minutes left to play, they made a 13–0 run that sent us into a tailspin from which we were unable to recover. We had started and finished poorly. The game ended at 116–103. The Bulls hit a club-record eight shots from three-point range, a scoring avalanche that helped bury us.

The only thing good about Chicago was that it was the last stop. Also, for me personally, it was nice to be given a warm send-off by the city, with Jesse Jackson and the mayor participating at center court. Chicago Stadium is as intimate and old as Boston Garden, and my mind went back to the early seventies, when the Bucks and the Bulls had some great games there. We would come the ninety miles down to Chicago from Milwaukee, as would a sizable number of our fans to cheer us on. We'd look up to the stands during games and there'd be fantastic fights going on, people getting punched out and diving over rows of seats—some serious brawls. The Bulls fans didn't like the joy the Bucks fans would take in our winning down there, which was a frequent occurrence in those years.

Yesterday morning, subdued and exhausted, we came home from our odyssey, having lost five of our seven games on the road, including all of the last four. The team was bent low from the experience, and the

four-hour plane ride back seemed quiet and long. Some of the players—
Magic, Byron, Orlando—began prowling the aisles as we got about
thirty minutes outside of Los Angeles. The pilot hadn't yet announced
our descent, but when you travel as much as we do, you get a visceral,
animal-like sense that you're nearing home.

We landed at about 11 A.M. California time, and I was first off the
plane, as always, the rest of the team behind me. I walked straight
through the terminal to the car outside, able to escape the purgatory
of having to wait for bags. Long ago, I learned the wisdom and skill
of traveling light in this profession. I never carry more than one bag,
no matter how long we'll be away, and I never check my bag. It's part
of my survival, of becoming expert at arrivals and departures. I can slip
in and out of the airport in a matter of minutes.

Al was waiting for me curbside, I tossed my bag into the backseat
of the car, and we were gone.

The last bad one was over.

Wednesday, December 28

It's late, and I'm in my room waiting for sleep to come after having
played Philly at home tonight in the Forum. We won the game, but
let a big lead evaporate again, until we were only three points ahead
with six seconds remaining on the clock. We've been having a serious
Jekyll and Hyde thing happening in our level of play. It's been blown
entirely out of proportion by the doomsayers in the press, but there's
no question we're weathering a storm. We have yet to lose at home,
but since we returned from the East a week ago, we've lost two more
away games, and when you're losing on the road the way we've been,
things are exaggerated tenfold. Players can get into a collective cringing
about the road, and I think we're experiencing some of that now. The
team is down.

The days have shortened, and it's as if winter came to Los Angeles
overnight while we were away. I'm remembering that it was around this
time three years ago that Silk went down. He'd been hurt in February,
traded into obscurity with the Clippers in the fall, and he was gone
before Christmas, retiring at age thirty-two. He'd been a Laker teammate for eight years—a shooter, real quick, and with a great first step.
An opponent would be trying to catch up and Silk would just come and

take five in a row. Silk could be devastating. But he went down with the Clippers and the December blues.

After returning home seven days ago, we had three wonderful nights in our own beds and then flew to Utah on Christmas Eve for a game in the Salt Palace on Christmas Day. An afternoon sellout, this was our first regular-season game in the Palace since the Jazz took us the full seven games in the semifinals last spring, almost bumping us out of the play-offs in round two. The Jazz were one of our toughest competitors in the West last year, and so far they look just as tough this year. Karl Malone is a tremendous athlete and the second-leading scorer in the league after Michael Jordan; John Stockton is like a jackrabbit running the court and one of the best point men in the NBA after Magic; and Mark Eaton is like the altitude in Salt Lake City—he hurts your game just by being there. At seven feet four and nearly three hundred pounds, he makes it tough, very tough, to shoot inside.

I remember that when Eaton was in college, on the UCLA varsity, he didn't get a whole lot of playing time—only forty-some minutes total for the entire season in his last year. He was so awkward on the court, so bungling then, the whole Bruin student body used to ridicule him. He was seriously uncoordinated, his body fat probably over 30 percent, and heckling him became part of going to the games.

But Eaton became a great example of somebody who's excelled through sheer determination. After UCLA, he was drafted by the Jazz, and in the six years since, through relentless effort, he's gotten his body-fat percentage down to under 20 and his coordination to the point where he can run easily up and down the court. And that's just the result of hard work. Progress like that has nothing to do with bolts from the blue. Eaton has remade himself.

As massive as he is, he still lacks agility and quickness—I get to feel svelte when I go up against him—but he has become highly effective on the inside. Not pretty, but effective. He just gets in there under the basket and does his job. He plants himself in the lane, immovable and wide as a city block, like one of those Easter Island monoliths. He can drape those three hundred pounds on you like a lead coat, and he has enormous reach. Eaton has led the league in blocked shots for four of the last six seasons. For the big men, it can be trying. I saw a film clip a few years ago of a game in which Houston's Akeem Olajuwon, in frustration, threw a startling punch to Eaton's groin. Otherwise occupied, the refs didn't see the jab, but the camera picked it up. They had to send that one in to the league office.

. . .

The game stunk for us.

Utah established a lead in the first quarter, never relinquished it, and we lost by fourteen. We didn't lack in effort, just in execution. We have to play intense, mistake-inducing defense in order to score off our fast break, but our defensive moves were off and we got zero points from our transition game. Half consciously, you say something to yourself like, "Okay, I'll get him at the *next* step," and then your opponent just runs by you and lays in the ball.

We're struggling to get everybody playing well at the the same time. Even Magic, whose play has been the most consistent, shot four for thirteen from the floor in Utah.

It was our fifth straight road loss.

After the game, we caught a 5 P.M. plane to Phoenix, where we were to play in the Veterans Coliseum the following night. Geographically, the drop from Salt Lake City to Phoenix is almost straight down, and that seemed a metaphor for both me and the team. I've been struggling ever since I came back from the layoff with my knee, and Phoenix was to be our sixth straight road loss.

For the Lakers, this marked the longest losing streak on the road in ten years. I was around for the last one, and for far worse, but neither Magic, Coop, James, nor Byron had ever had the experience of losing six in a row away in the regular season before. Late in the fourth quarter of the Phoenix game, the frustration began to show. An out-of-bounds call went against us, Magic refused to give up the ball immediately to the Suns, saying something inaudible to referee Billy Oakes, and then bounced the ball behind his back, nearly hitting Oakes in the leg. That was enough to get him two technicals and tossed out of a game for only the second time in his career.

Practice at Loyola the next morning was like combat. After playing the Phoenix game, we'd gotten back to L.A. around midnight.

Among other things, the coaches think we've been playing too much of a perimeter game, too little of the pivot, so bodies and elbows and shoulders were flying in practice as we worked for two long hours on our inside game. A lot of guys got hit in the ribs, in the head, everywhere, and a couple of players went down. I almost quit myself during the running. Riley talked to me about diminishing returns, about not getting what they need from me. They want more.

That was yesterday.

Today is exactly a month since I injured my knee in Philadelphia, and, coincidentally, tonight we played the Sixers again, but this time at home. I ran well in the game and tried for a lot of offensive rebounds, but I'm still not back. The final score in the game was 128–123.

Around two, I'm ready to turn off the lights.

Thursday, December 29

Scott Ostler wants to bury me.

Before practice this morning, I opened up the sports section of the *Los Angeles Times* to the headline EARLY RETIREMENT WOULD BE KAREEM'S CLASSY WAY OUT, and Scott's article went on to advocate my leaving the game earlier than planned. Midseason, at the All-Star break in February, would be the perfect time, he thinks. He wrote: "Retirement with dignity is something Kareem deserves. But how dignified will it be for him to finish the season riding the pine, starting games but essentially playing a backup role, playing fewer and fewer minutes, sitting out the crucial last minutes of each game, facing the inevitable critiques of his diminished skills?"

The column wasn't meanspirited—I think Scott wrote it out of appreciation and respect for what I've contributed to the game. But it was the first public sign of panic over how I'm doing on the court in my last season.

This isn't my first experience with a story like this. Speculation that my career was ending began over ten years ago, when I passed my thirtieth birthday. There's been a preoccupation with my age on and off since then. I've had a decade's worth of premature burials, of having the press throw dirt on my face—usually when the team is struggling.

By hanging on to my form longer than my contemporaries—all of the guys who broke in with me are gone today—I've paid the price of being called "old." *El Viejo*. I've been the oldest player in the league for five years, ever since Elvin Hayes retired at age thirty-eight in 1984. But my whole life I've had to bear the weight of being different, and being over forty in the NBA, playing longer than anyone has played the game before, is just another wrinkle on that.

Some days I feel ageless, and others—as in recent days—as though I were here before Buddha. But I can remember expressing that as far back as my early years in Milwaukee. If I'd listened to the opinions of the press about when to quit, I would have missed the experience of some or all of five world championships. I wouldn't have received the honor of the finals MVP award in Boston when I was thirty-eight. I wouldn't have had the personal fulfillment of "pushing the envelope" in this game.

I look around me now and there's just such a big gap between me and the next guy. There's seems no earthly reason that I should still be here. It seems like voodoo or something. Yet, here I am. It's not about how old you are—you either start or you don't start. Playing, and playing well, is the great equalizer.

Before this final season began, I knew my every step would be closely monitored by the press. I hadn't anticipated the knee injury or the question marks about my conditioning, but I had anticipated the increased glare. It's like being in the eye of a hurricane, and as soon as you move in any direction you're buffeted by crosscurrents. I've been playing under that kind of microscope and pressure since I was twelve years old. Other people's expectations, and learning to keep my own principles in the face of those, have been constants in my life.

My only professional concern now is to improve and to help the team win. The great statistics are no longer important. I have my own personal standards to maintain that are higher and more exacting than any outsider could know. I'm not concerned with how the world sees me, only with how I see myself, and I believe the adage "That which does not kill one will make one strong."

I don't want to go out meekly because the press, however well or ill intentioned, is calling for my early retirement. The challenge of turning things around is what drives me now. I have to believe that the journey is not yet over.

I almost had to quit during the running again in practice today, another tough one.

Sunday, January 1

New Year's Day.

Riley gave us the weekend off, and Amir has been here with me since Friday night. I slept most of the afternoon yesterday, listened to Amir run up and down the stairs, and then he and I went out to the movies.

So often, from the time Amir was born, I've caught glimpses of myself as a boy in him. I was outgoing and curious and open as a kid, the same way he is. For me, that easy openness went under wraps over time as both my height and notoriety grew. We'll have to wait and see what's in store for my son in that regard. I know he's confident that his mother and I both love him and, as his father, that's important to me. People mistakenly think children need toys and other material things in order to thrive, but what they really need is your attention and your love. If they're confident they have that, they do all right.

Today, Amir and I went over to spend a little time with my mother and father, who live just a few miles away. It was an unusually clear, watercolor kind of L.A. day, and from town you could see the snow on top of the San Gabriels to the east. I was standing at my parents' window looking out toward the mountains when my mother told me she'd read the *L.A. Times* piece and asked me how I was feeling.

My mother has always been as outspoken and expressive as my father has been soft-spoken and quiet. Because he frequently worked around the clock when I was growing up, I ended up under my mother's thumb a lot, and her influence was a strong one. She was always supportive and gave me clearly defined goals to reach for. She had a vision of excellence and wanted me to be intelligent and courageous and charming, a renaissance kind of man. My mother is proud, and her attitude was always "Anything you can do to advance, go do it." Six feet tall, she was never comfortable with her size while she was growing up and was determined that that not be the case with me. When I first started to dramatically outgrow my friends and questioned her about it, she told me to appreciate myself the way I was and to take pride in my height. She was emphatic about my standing up straight and walking tall. And her overall message was "Don't let anybody intimidate you."

We kicked around the recent press talk about my status and the team's status and she offered her thoughts on the subject: "You can't beat these people. You can't fight them head-on, so don't. The way to fight them is to win. Go out there and play ball, and they won't have anything to write about. You just have to concentrate, and things will get better for you and for the team."

Good advice.

The two days off have been a much-needed rest, for me and for everybody. Since the start of training camp, we've spent sixty of the first ninety days of the season on the road. If the road stops slapping us around as far as wins and losses go, the worst of it should be behind us. We're away only five times in January, and four in all of February.

Ironically, given how we've been beaten up of late, our end-of-December record, 19-10, came out right on the mark—exactly the goal that was set three months ago by the coaches in camp.

Practice is tomorrow morning at nine, and we leave for the airport directly afterward.

We play the Sonics in Seattle on Tuesday night.

Thursday, January 5

It was a charcoal sky with rain today, which seems appropriate. At this late moment in my career, I feel as if the sea is up just at the moment I should be cruising safely into harbor. I have an image of having sailed upon the seas for nineteen seasons, having been out there for so long and gone through the best and worst of everything, and now, just as I'm trying to come into port, in my last and twentieth season, a typhoon hits. A tempest.

We lost in Seattle, for our seventh straight road loss, and Riley kept me on the bench for the entire fourth quarter. I played only fourteen minutes altogether, and Cooper played only three, so it was me and Coop at the end of the pine there.

That game and my dismal performance has inspired another newspaper article clamoring for my early dismissal, this time written by Doug Krikorian, not my favorite sportswriter, in today's *L.A. Herald Examiner.* I haven't read the piece, but I recall he wrote a similar obituary a year ago, in early 1988, a few months after which he printed a retraction.

Debate and controversy over my play are now in full swing. With five metropolitan dailies tracking the team, two having already had their say, it is, of course, a journalistic imperative that the others respond.

Throughout my career, my relationship with the press has been strained and many times almost hostile, though things started out innocently enough. The first articles to appear about me in the paper were written in 1961, when I was in the eighth grade. And I remember my dad buying about fifteen copies of the *New York Journal American* the next year when I was featured as a frosh phenom at Power Memorial. It was fun to see my name and picture in the pages of the press, along with flattering comments about my potential. But the spotlight was something that wouldn't leave me from that point on, and my early innocence turned out to be pretty short-lived.

The first education I got about the press came from my high school coach, Jack Donahue, who'd seen firsthand some ugly incidents involving high school athletes and gamblers, with the media as middlemen. Gamblers used members of the press for information about and access to the kids, and Donahue took immediate steps to eliminate any problems. To the team he issued stern warnings that really hit home about guys who might want to exploit us. And he also notified the press that we wouldn't be available for interviews, a step that had a particularly profound impact on me. I was All-America throughout high school, and the press was after me as much as every college in the country was. But Donahue hid me completely. The pressure for interviews grew enormous after we became nationally ranked from my sophomore year on, but the coach held his ground during all that time.

It was virtually the same for me when I got to college: a huge demand for interviews and an athletic department at UCLA that was determined to shield me as much as possible. I didn't talk to the press at all in my freshman year and had only limited contact in the three years after that as we won a string of national championships.

So I came out of high school and college with a significant wariness toward the media, and, as I later learned, with an inadequate preparation for the level of public scrutiny that awaited me in my professional life. This is not to assign blame to my first coaches. Particularly in high school, a milieu that included reporters screaming loudly and openly about point spreads, I think the coach's policy did more good than harm. Still, in retrospect, I believe I would have benefited had I experienced more back-and-forth with the press, especially in college. I was enlightened about the nature of the monster we deal with; I saw its insatiability and also its ability to twist words and the truth. But I'd also met a number of journalists who were honest and ethical people. I think I would have learned a lot about dealing with both the good and the bad had I had the opportunity to interact more early on.

Instead, I took my suspicion and shy nature with me into the NBA, and it wasn't long before I was branded "reticent," "enigmatic," "aloof," "taciturn," "a tough interview," and other less flattering descriptions. No writers got close to me then, or really got to know me. I had my guard up, I was unapproachable, and mostly said as little as I could—monosyllabic answers, no embellishments. This had been my training, and also I believed that the press was a distraction. I thought that if I did my job well, that would be sufficient.

It was, and it wasn't.

In my early years with the Lakers, for instance, I was hailed by the press for winning back-to-back MVPs in both 1976 and 1977, and yet was dismissed for not being able to bring the world championship to Los Angeles in those same years. And that kind of appreciation laced with criticism has repeated itself many times over in my career. I bridled at it, and at the media's habits of inflaming unrealistic expectations in the fans and creating controversy for its own sake, regardless of the human consequences.

I remember when the Houston Astros' great right-handed pitcher J. R. Richard was having serious health problems. After first calling him a malingerer, the media started the speculation that his problems were drug-related. At the time, even Richard didn't know what was really wrong. Eventually, doctors discovered a blood clot in his pitching shoulder, a condition that nearly cost him his life and did cost him his athletic career. By that time, though, the rumors of drugs had greatly damaged his reputation. He had to suffer through that alongside the uncertainties of his physical health. All a player can do in that kind of situation is try to ride it out. When you see a professional athlete like Richard decide not to speak to the press while some controversy is boiling up around him, it's usually because he can't cope with the scrutiny and distortions and do his job effectively at the same time.

Invariably, the media's excuse is "We meant no harm." The journalist walks away, and the athlete is left with the wreckage. It's the player who suffers. The press's mistakes and excesses go uncorrected, whether they were intentional or not. There's very little a player can do to protect himself.

I was involved in one such situation with a former beat reporter of the *Herald Examiner,* Rich Levin. He was one of the first to write of my so-called drastically diminishing powers in an article entitled KAREEM MAY BE PAST HIS PRIME. It was the late seventies; I was thirty-one.

Some time later, he wrote a piece that I felt crossed the boundaries of principled journalism. I had been approached through my business agent to speak to a group of local boys at a youth house. This was during the regular season, and when my agent explained the impossibility of my schedule, the request became more emphatic, and in the course of the discussion my normal public appearance fee was mentioned. Irate at the outcome, the youth representative called Levin at the *Herald* with the story that I demanded dollars to speak to their kids, a story Levin printed without contacting me to verify its accuracy or to learn my version. My efforts to publish my side of the story later in the *Herald* were refused. Peter Vecsey of the *New York Post* finally put my story in his column, which the *Herald* ran along with an editorial renouncing my characterization of the events as lies.

It was not until a few years ago that some of the ill will underlying this incident came to light. In a book about the Lakers called *Winning Times,* Levin is quoted about his coverage of me: "When it came time in a game story to evaluate his play, I took advantage of the opportunity to rip him, when normally I wouldn't have. It was easy to take shots at him. I know it was unfair, that it was immaturity on my part, on both our parts." That last phrase was Levin trying to spread the blame around.

The original attempts I had made to correct the situation had been turned away by Levin and his sports editor at the time. The editor mouthed a lot of sanctimonious b.s. about journalistic integrity, professional attitudes, and objectivity. No retractions, of course, were ever forthcoming from the *Herald* after Levin's disclosure, and the damage to my reputation had been done.

In the final analysis, the impact of the media on the sport is mixed. I've observed both good and bad effects during my career, in both print and television. When I started in pro ball, ABC had the TV contract with the NBA, and the network's coverage was many times sporadic and dominated by the belief that it couldn't make money televising the finals unless either New York or Los Angeles were on the court. Even after CBS took over, the game didn't get all that much respect in the beginning; I'm sure every fan can remember having the beginnings or endings of games lopped off by a golf or sailing event. And key games were still not shown if the home market of cities like Cleveland or Atlanta wasn't the size the network wanted.

Fortunately, the cable industry had the foresight to sell games as a package, and the sport was soon on cable outlets all over the country. The popularity of the NBA rapidly expanded, and the men at the top of the league, David Stern and company, did a great job in helping the process along. By both cable and network, the game is now broadcast not only throughout the nation, but overseas as well.

Only one nagging complaint remains. Three weeks ago, when we were on the road in Cleveland, I read for the first time the behind-the-scenes story of the MVP selection in the 1980 championship series. In his column in honor of my farewell, Bill Livingston of the Cleveland *Plain Dealer* came forward with the revelation that he'd been pressured that year to change his vote and that he wanted to get the incident off his journalist's conscience. He had been a beat reporter for *The Philadelphia Inquirer* at the time; the 1980 series was with the Sixers.

It was back-and-forth wins for the first four games, so when we came back to L.A. for Game 5, I was very pumped up, as was everybody. Philly wanted the championship as much as we did. They'd been coming close for years.

Late in the third quarter of that fifth game, I got a nasty ankle sprain. The game was still very much undecided, so when Doc Kerlan gave his opinion that I couldn't injure the ankle further if we taped it, I shut out all the pain and just focused on the job at hand, going back into the game in the fourth quarter. Desire and adrenaline carried me through on virtually one leg, and we ended up winning and going ahead in the series 3–2.

Game 6 was back in Philadelphia two days later. My ankle was too swollen even to travel, so I stayed in L.A. to rest it in the hope it would be better by Game 7, should we go that far.

After calling the team on the phone and telling them to go for it, I watched the sixth game from home, which was almost terminal for me. I had to turn off the sound. I was chewing on the pillow and crawling under and over the covers. And at one point, after a three-point play by Silk in the fourth quarter, I hobbled out into the backyard and had to yell a little bit.

That was the only time I have ever sat out a finals game.

We won it by sixteen points and took our first world championship of the eighties. Magic, who was a rookie then, had been incredible in that final game, and a couple of other Lakers, like Silk, had pro-career highs. Livingston wrote that before the fourth-quarter balloting for the MVP, he and others had seen the official news release that had my name typed into a blank space on one copy and Julius Erving's on another. Because of my stats in the first five games—I averaged thirty-three points—and because of my role in winning Game 5, there had been a consensus that should the Lakers take the title rather than the Sixers, I should receive the play-off MVP award. But it was not to be.

Toward the end of the sixth game, Livingston said that the seven writers and broadcasters who voted the award were pressured by a publicist, either from the network or the league, to switch their vote to Magic. My not being there in Philadelphia to receive the trophy on camera was a major inconvenience as far as the television people were concerned. "CBS didn't want to present the MVP award to an empty chair," Livingston wrote, "so enough of us saps changed our votes, in the heat of the moment, to deny Kareem the award, by a 4–3 count."

The outcome was never a problem between Magic and me, but I wondered about how that vote had taken place, and I'm grateful to Bill Livingston for setting the record straight more than eight years later.

· · ·

Over time, the imperfections of the press notwithstanding, our relations have gotten noticeably better. I've outlasted my most severe
critics. And I've come to a better understanding of how my own
wariness, the caution I developed so young, drew the wariness of others
toward me. I've made a conscious effort to stop generalizing about the
motives of the press, and I've found that if I give them a chance, they
give me one too, and that seems to work out better for both of us.

Late this afternoon, I left the house for an early-evening taping of the
Arsenio Hall show on the Paramount lot in Hollywood. Arsenio has just
this week begun playing on Johnny Carson's court with a late-night talk
show of his own.

 This was only Arsenio's third show, and he had me on with my friend
Quincy Jones. A trumpeter, pianist, composer, and big-band arranger,
Quincy is a musical genius who goes all the way back to Billie Holiday
and Count Basie and Louis Armstrong. A Seattle native, he was only
sixteen when he first left for New York. He toured with Dizzy Gillespie
and played with Lionel Hampton, and he knew my dad as a big-band
trombonist. I would have been around three years old then. Quincy and
I became friends later, in L.A., when we discovered we were neighbors
on the same street, and then, when he and his wife broke up, we really
became close. He'd come up to the house at odd hours, just wanting
to talk. I was glad to see him and share a few words tonight.

 On the air, Arsenio asked about the Lakers' recent road woes, what
all the fans are wondering about, and I told him that what both the
team and I are going through is a very emotional thing. He said, "If
you never score another point, if you never shoot another skyhook,
you've already given us so much joy."

 I savored those words on the way home. With this typhoon howling
all around me, they were good to hear. I sometimes forget that the fans
don't abandon us in hard times.

Friday, January 6

After shootaround this morning, I went upstairs to talk to Jerry West.
One level up from the Forum floor, Jerry's office is on the small side,
but its walls are full of memorabilia, including a prominently hung

framed copy of the *Herald Examiner*'s front page from June 9, 1985, proclaiming our triumph in Boston. I called Jerry yesterday to tell him I wanted to come by and talk with him about recent events.

Jerry and I have a long history of weathering the criticisms of the press together, and he's always been the first to take me aside when the turbulence hit to let me know that he was with me, and screw everybody who was calling for my quick and immediate dismissal to the woodpile.

Because Jerry had one of those playing careers in which he was outstanding every year, in which he felt the burden to be great every time he walked out on the court, there's an identification between us. We've both experienced long losing seasons, and we've both been to the finals many times—nine times for Jerry and nine times so far for me. Having been there, Jerry understands the mental demands, the pressure to be stupendous every night, the unseen effort, the skills that underlie the ease with which we seem to play the game. And in a game dominated by blacks, Jerry had the added weight of people wanting to make a racial thing out of his success, wanting him to carry the standard for the white guys, the way they're doing now with Larry Bird. And Jerry didn't feel comfortable at all with that.

So, over the years, Jerry and I have stood by each other. I *was* the team for the three years he coached the Lakers in the late seventies, and he was always acutely aware of that and respected me for it. He's gone to bat for me when every sportswriter wanted to see me gone, supporting me through all those earlier calls for my retirement. Even when no words are exchanged between us, I always feel his presence in the background, in my corner. And I stuck up for Jerry during his lean times as a coach and later when he first took over the helm in the front office. People were always trying to say, "Jerry West should have done this; he should have done that; he's just lucky." Well, he's proved himself to be a genius now, but it wasn't always that way.

Jerry started out our meeting by telling me he didn't like the flogging I was taking in the press. "It bothers me," he said. "But one thing you can't do—you can't hide. You have to play. The only way you can shut these people up is to play your game."

He then went on to say that I seemed a hundred miles away on the court and that I wasn't playing worth a damn. Jerry is a soft-spoken man, but he always speaks his mind—it is a candor I appreciate. He told me that he didn't want to see me go through this and if I did want to retire early, he would understand, that he was behind me in whatever I decided to do, and that there wouldn't be any issue with money. He'd spoken with the owner, Jerry Buss, and there would be no problem paying me the remainder of my contract. His main concern was that I not get hurt.

Jerry's raising this option disconcerted me a bit because I hadn't been thinking at all about retirement when I asked for the meeting. I'd just wanted to tell him that I didn't want to put him in a tough position defending me or make it hard for him to justify having me out there if they could use my space on the roster. I wanted him to know that I would cooperate if they felt they had to do something. And even though I'd suffered financial losses through poor professional management a few years ago, my salary has never been the deciding factor in whether I kept playing or not.

I told Jerry that I would think about what he'd said, and that my plans were to keep doing all I could to improve. I said that I would like to finish the year out, but that I didn't want to finish it limping into the future either. We agreed that it will be clearer in a few weeks just how much I can contribute.

Thursday, January 12

I think we're waking up.

The team was delivered another knockout punch on the road two nights ago, and, for me, the realization has come through that, mentally, I didn't come into the season fully prepared to compete, and it's the mind that makes everything else work.

Tuesday night, we were up in Sacramento and lost to the Kings, a team in last place in our own division, a team that has lost three quarters of its games so far this season. It was our eighth straight road loss; we've now set a new record for the longest losing streak on the road in the club's history.

I think that evening was our bottom.

I was reminded of what happened to Roberto Durán when he fought Tommy Hearns. Hearns hit him so hard that Durán was knocked from his feet unconscious; he was awakened by his face hitting the floor.

After the game, Magic came into the locker room livid. "That's it! That's it! That's it!" he exploded. He knew that Sacramento had no business beating us, like a lot of other teams recently. He'd had enough of it. He went on a tirade in the dressing room, slamming furniture around and hitting the blackboard so hard it cracked, almost falling on him. It was out of character for him, but, at his peak of frustration, he was making a point. He knew we could play better and it was time to draw the line. Something had to change. Something had to be said. I thought his outburst was good.

In the showers afterward, Magic and I talked. I'd had an abysmal game, shooting under ten points and playing under twenty minutes. "I'm doing nothing for the team," I said to him. He said that it wasn't just me who was having problems. "Cap, you've just got to keep working on your game," he said. "Just work on your game."

Back at the hotel, in the hours after the game, I began to sort through the events of the last few months and the input of the past several weeks. When we played the Sixers at the end of December, I had a conversation with a former player, Steve Mix, that hit home. Steve and I had been rookies in the same year—he started in Detroit— and we played together briefly when he signed with the Lakers for the entire 1983 play-offs, after James, who was then a rookie, broke his left leg just before the first round. At that time, Steve was the only other guy left from my first pro year who was still playing. And that was his last season.

Now a color man for the Sixers' road games, Steve asked me to do an interview with him before the Philly game. Before we went on camera, he asked me what it had been like trying to prepare for my final year, and then he told me what it had been like for him. He said that he'd come into training camp not quite ready. After gearing up mentally and physically every summer for thirteen years, he'd experienced a letdown in desire. The spark that makes everything else happen just hadn't been there in his off-season. His sprints were more like fast jogs, he said. But he didn't realize any of that until he got to training camp and found himself out of preseason shape.

I didn't say much, but I heard what Steve was saying.

I look back on last summer now and realize that something similar happened to me. My training didn't have the sense of purpose it had had in other years. I was thinking of other things and not the competition I had to get ready for. I was thinking about the twenty-five cities' worth of good-byes, the twenty-five cities' worth of press questions about my going. I spent a lot of time wondering whether I could go through with this long public farewell. Mentally, I was one step from sitting down, and that destroys your incentive to go out there and compete hard. It takes something away. I didn't do anything on par in the off-season. But I didn't know that then.

I came into the season prepared to contribute, but not to dominate.

This showed in my physical and mental presence on the court. I was in shape, but I wasn't crisp, and the underlying conditioning wasn't there. Ultimately, that was debilitating. When the knee injury forced me to take a layoff, the conditioning I'd just rebuilt went all the way down to the bottom again. And, I think now, I gave in to burnout. And not just burnout from last year's championship campaign, but all the burnout I've been carrying for nineteen years. I gave in to it without being consciously aware of it.

Now that I understand what's been going on, I can do something about it. I have a good idea of how far I have to go, and knowing where to go is half the battle. It's up to me. I feel like I've been sleepwalking, and now have found myself outside in my pajamas, awake and feeling silly.

As far as the team goes, I don't think it's a coincidence that we've been struggling in lockstep. Maybe my teammates have been feeling like I'm already gone, like one of the wheels is missing. I also think the team is experiencing the residuals from achieving our goal of back-to-back world titles. You come away from winning a championship title with a successful team concept—you're playing better than any other team at the beginning of the next season—but the fatigue and mental burnout carries over too. And, after reaching any hard-to-obtain professional goal, like finishing a novel or achieving a breakthrough in science, it's human nature that there be a letdown. We all had a letdown from last year, some more intense than others. We've had a drop-off, and I think it happened on the long road trip, starting with that demoralizing one-point loss in Milwaukee.

I returned from Sacramento with the belief that if I can raise my game, then I can help to lift the team. If anything is going to change, it has to start with me. I've always led by example, through my play, so if my thing comes together, there will be something for my teammates to rally around. We have a thing about the team being greater than the sum of its parts.

Today at practice, we had a long team meeting in which I told the team what I'd been thinking and in which I asked the coach for more minutes on the court. Ordinarily, I don't think team meetings accomplish much—you can't lick these things with rhetoric—but this morning's was an exception and I felt it was important that I speak. At the start of the meeting I told the team that I thought I was the main reason for the fact we were struggling. I said that I hadn't been holding up my part, hadn't come into the season as mentally or physically prepared as I should have; I thought I was ready, but it was a minimum kind of ready. I then told them that I was ready to make the commitment from here on in.

I tried to make my statement as emphatic as I could, to let the team know that I was with them and wasn't going anywhere, and that I planned to work hard and to pick up the slack.

The other players spoke after me, verbalizing all the frustrations we've been dealing with over the past weeks and discussing the problems in their own play—almost everybody's numbers are down. It was a good collective look at ourselves.

Riley and I are going to talk tomorrow about my playing time.

On our way home from the airport yesterday morning, after Sacramento, Al had a few words to say to me about Ted Williams, one of the finest natural hitters the game of baseball has ever known, who hit an epic home run at his last turn at bat. "You know what you have to do," my father said. "Do your best and you'll go out on a positive note. You could go out like Ted Williams."

The Splendid Splinter.

Al was planting a seed of inspiration.

Saturday, January 14

Riley's office at the Forum is a few doors down the hall from Jerry West's. He has the same *Herald* headline framed and hanging on his wall, and, also like Jerry, the only championship ring he wears is the one from 1985.

A former player, nine years in the NBA and five of them with the Lakers, Riley has learned coaching in the heat of battle, so to speak. He came on as Laker coach in the midst of chaotic circumstances in the early 1980s.

In 1979, the year Jerry West moved up to the front office, the Laker team was sold to Jerry Buss, who then brought Jack McKinney on as the new head coach. McKinney had been an assistant at Milwaukee when I was there and at Portland later with Jack Ramsay. His concepts of team play were both progressive and effective, and they were responsible for us getting off to a good start that year.

That was Magic's first year too, and McKinney was impressed with his floor leadership, his ability to see the whole court and to set things

up for his teammates. McKinney devised a highly improvisational offense that minimized the number of set plays and enabled us to flip
between our running game and half-court game as conditions war-
ranted, which is exactly how I love to play.

In early November, however, one month into that 1979–80 season,
Jack McKinney had a nearly fatal bicycle accident that knocked him
out of the Laker coaching role permanently. Paul Westhead was selected to take over the job. Fresh from coaching at La Salle, he had
been Jack's assistant for a matter of weeks when the accident happened.

With Paul, we decided to make no new moves, to stay with McKinney's game plan, and as a result the year was fantastic. Every player got
behind the approach, so that even when Paul was hospitalized with a
kidney stone, the team played smoothly, and we took home the world
championship—the Lakers' first in eight seasons.

The following year Paul Westhead decided to experiment some, and
we were eliminated from the play-offs in round one. At the beginning of
the next season, Magic was so alienated by Paul's insistence on sticking
with an ineffective approach that he came out publicly against the
coach, a move that created much controversy. As popular as Magic
already was, the fans didn't take to the idea that a player might break
rank and try to get a coach, any coach, fired. For weeks afterward, Magic
was booed everywhere he went, and it was exceedingly hard on him.

Magic was only twenty-two then, in his third pro year, and he didn't
know yet that you never go to the press with private discontents,
because the press will invariably run with them in exactly the opposite
direction and in the reverse spirit that you intended—that's almost
guaranteed. Magic could have gone to Jerry West or come to me for
help, but he didn't know about those options either, so he had to learn
a hard lesson, one I was sorry he had to suffer through.

After all was said and done, the Laker management decided to
replace Paul Westhead, and it was into that heated quagmire that Pat
Riley, only recently Chick Hearn's color man, was advanced from
assistant to head coach. That was in November 1981, almost two years
to the day since Jack McKinney's bicycle accident. That season, once
again, the team pulled together. We transcended the controversy,
Magic putting the criticism behind him, we went back to the basic
McKinney game plan, and we ended up taking home another world
championship. There have been three more since, all with Riley as
coach, and he has never been given full credit for what he has been
able to accomplish. The presence of Magic and James and me has

contributed to the team's success and to Pat's success, but Pat has been a dedicated and hard worker at his job. As to his being obsessive and neurotic about practices, I suspect that his stay in Kentucky during college with the legendary disciplinarian Adolph Rupp ingrained some of that eccentricity into his style.

In Riley's office yesterday, when I talked to him about my playing time, he told me that he should take as much blame for my performance as anyone else. He said that he had gotten caught up subconsciously in the whole matter of my age and upcoming retirement, and, consequently, had fallen into just trying to maintain me, trying to save me for the end of the year. Without realizing it, he said, he'd just kind of let me float. He got into the habit of not demanding more, of not using me enough to keep me conditioned as a player. When you've been a scorer and a starter all your life, you can't suddenly play five minutes and then sit down for fifteen and expect to stay warm and keep your rhythm. I told Riley that I was confident I could contribute more, that I could turn things around, but that I needed to have more minutes in order to do it.

"You're right," he said. "You'll get more time." And last night he kept his word.

It was a big game at home against Cleveland, and I was in for twenty-eight minutes, the most playing time I've had in the last dozen games. It was an important game for us because since we last saw Cleveland a month ago, back in the Ohio snow, the site of our last road win, the Cavs have shocked everyone to death by having the best record in the league.

Riley played all twelve of us in the game, and we beat the Cavs by a convincing nineteen points, outrebounding them and holding them to a little more than 38 percent from the floor. The crowd was really into it. We're now 14-0 at home, still the best home record in the league, and Riley reminded us before the game that we're still number one in our division and in the Western Conference. "Don't believe you're as bad as the media are saying," he said.

In the wake of our win, Jerry West made a rare appearance at practice this morning at Loyola and addressed the team. "You may have been reading things in the papers," he said, "that we are thinking of making trades or thinking of asking Cap to retire. But I want you to know from me that nobody's head is on the trading block, and Kareem is not retiring, period. *This* is our team. If we're going to sink or swim, we're going to do it with you guys right here. You are the team we're going to finish out the season with."

He talked about the level of our performance of late and said, basically, that we were all accountable. It's not just Kareem, he said, and then singled out others by name whose games haven't been up to par. "You're a team with great players," he said, "and you should be doing it." No major threats—we were just to go out there and play. It was the voice from the top.

Sunday, January 15

We broke our road-loss streak without even leaving town today by beating the Clippers in an afternoon game in the Sports Arena. Personally, I don't think it was that big of a deal. We just have to get back to playing well every time we go out on the floor. Once we do that, it doesn't matter whether we're at home or away. Our problems have been that we go out and play very well for the first quarter and a half, cruise into halftime, come out of halftime still cruising, and then get caught in the second half. Today was the first time we've had a winning fourth quarter in over a month. Normally, the fourth quarter is one of our strengths.

I played thirty-some minutes, and while I'm not thrilled yet, I'm no longer feeling winded. My shots feel like they are going to go in, and, whereas before I'd be jogging into a play that had already started, now I'm there when it starts.

The game might have been closer today if the Clippers had had the services of their rookie Danny Manning, whom they'd been counting on to save the franchise. But just yesterday he underwent reconstructive surgery on his right knee. Doc Lombardo did the operation, and Manning's definitely out for the rest of the year and maybe some of next. The Clippers seem to be good at bad luck.

Shortly before the owner, Donald Sterling, moved the Clippers up from San Diego in 1984, he sought my advice about where they should go. I suggested Orange County, where they could develop their own base of fans and appreciation. Plus, a regional rivalry, like the one between baseball's San Francisco Giants and Oakland Athletics, could have been to the benefit of both the Lakers and the Clippers.

When Sterling asked me what I thought about the L.A. Sports Arena, I hoped he was kidding. I told him it wasn't the greatest facility, nor was it the greatest neighborhood. But he apparently fell in love with the idea of selling the team as the cut-rate Lakers, offering the same entertainment for a cheaper ticket price. But being the worst team in the league in the same city with the best team is not good for either the players or the fans. It seems like you're settling for second best. And as it turned out, no NBA team has ever gone as long without making the play-offs as have the Clippers; they seem to be a genuinely star-crossed organization.

With twenty-eight points, Byron was the high scorer in today's game. Last year, in the '87–88 season, Byron finally realized he had the green light to shoot, and because he's a great marksman and accurate under pressure, the points naturally followed. He led the team in scoring for the first time—the only other Laker in thirty years to do so besides me, Magic, Jerry West, Elgin Baylor, and Gail Goodrich. You give Byron open jumpers and he's going to nail most of them.

Within the team, Byron is known as "Baby B," a nickname inspired by his almost juvenile appearance. Twenty-seven years old, he's often mistaken for a high school or college student. Of all of us, his journey to the Lakers has been the most direct because he lived in Inglewood from about the age of seven, at 104th Street and Sixth Avenue, only fourteen blocks from the Forum. He used to dream of one day playing basketball for the Lakers. He and his school friends used to sneak into the Forum with a simple but effective technique: One of them would distract the guard in the security booth at the entryway to the truck tunnel leading to the players' entrance, as the others ducked beneath the booth window and sprinted for the door. They alternated who did the talking because the kid who distracted the security guard was the one who couldn't get in that night.

I can remember noticing Byron back in the late 1970s, when he was a high school star, an All-American at Morningside High. From there he went on to Arizona State University, where he was also a standout; he left in 1983 as the school's all-time scoring leader. The Lakers got him through a trade with the Clippers the day before the preseason schedule started—and that was really one of Jerry West's shrewder moves, although it also put a lot of pressure on Byron because he was replacing Norm Nixon, a very popular player of All-Star caliber who'd been with us for the previous six years. In Byron's first season, 1983–84, we suffered that disappointing loss in Boston in the finals, and everyone second-guessed Jerry's judgment. The following year we came back and took the '85 championship from the Celtics, and all criticism of Byron dried up.

Byron is now in his own sixth season with us and has had the locker next to mine in the Laker dressing room for all this time. There's a fourteen-year age difference between us, but I feel close to Byron—we talk, and we also laugh a lot. Byron is the team's resident comedian and mimic. He has memorized entire songs and whole monologues, in dialect, of people like James Brown, Eddie Murphy, Richard Pryor, and Redd Foxx, and the dialogue from just about any movie you can name. On our way to Miami around Thanksgiving, he and Tony Campbell wore us out with their reenactment of *Scarface*.

Byron is a lot of fun because while he has scored on us with some great one-liners, he can take the same stuff he puts out there. It's very hard to get down with him around. For a while, I was practicing how to pick pockets with him as my victim. We would go on road trips and I would steal his pocket square or new hat. Or I might hide his dress shoes or try to take his jewelry—though I would warn anyone not to go for Byron's jewelry. You might lose a finger, or worse.

On the western edge of the South-Central ghetto, Inglewood is a tough place for a young boy to have grown up in. The thing that makes me feel best about Byron, aside from our personal friendship, is the stable role model he is for young kids in the neighborhood and the way the people of Inglewood have responded and supported him all these years. Byron could just as easily have gotten involved in gangs as in sports, but, fortunately, through strong relationships with his mother, stepfather, and real father, who was once a basketball player himself back in Utah, where Byron was born, Byron was able to escape that destructive alternative. Anytime I make a public appearance in Inglewood, the kids always claim some connection with him. It's "He's my cousin" or "He used to live down the street from my aunt" or "He used to play with my brother's friends at the park." The people of Inglewood are proud of him and proud *for* him in a very special way. And that's appropriate, because Byron is a special guy.

Monday, January 16

It's Martin Luther King Day. There was a moment of silence before our afternoon game with Houston at the Forum, and then George Howard played the national anthem on the soprano sax. Later, I saw on the news that riots had flared up in the Liberty City area of Miami after a policeman killed a black motorcyclist. It's true that there has been a lot of progress, that the legal basis for racial discrimination has pretty much been eliminated, but the battle for people's hearts and minds continues. For every positive step there are a hundred negatives that keep things at the status quo. When you're trying to horn in on the American pie, people just don't give up their share easily.

I met Dr. King once. In the summer of 1964, when I was in high school, I interviewed him as part of a journalism workshop at HAR-YOU-ACT, a Harlem antipoverty agency. At the time I didn't subscribe to his philosophy of nonviolence, believing results would have to come some other way, maybe even through violence. In retrospect, though, I've come to realize that his way is probably the only way. Dr. King, in every way, was a great American.

When I was a kid growing up in New York City, though, the black man in public life I looked up to most was Adam Clayton Powell, Jr. In 1936 he succeeded his father as pastor of Harlem's Abyssinian Baptist Church, the oldest and largest black congregation in the North, and in 1945 he became the first black congressman from New York.

Adam was the congressman from our district, and, except for one term, he served continuously until 1970. He was a brilliant man, and the older I get the more I admire him, because he led the way in knowing how to deal with the power structure at a time when blacks had very little political power. He wasn't any nickel-and-dime kind of guy; he'd amassed so much seniority by the 1960s that he wielded real clout. People had to listen to what he had to say, especially if they wanted to get a bill passed or wanted money to fund something. He made sure that the interests of women and minorities were taken into account, and in those days that took courage.

When my family got into housing difficulties, it was Adam who helped us out, not directly, but through his influence on city officials. My mother wanted to move uptown to the Dyckman projects, but the New York Housing Authority had decided that Dyckman was going to be lily-white; they wanted to send all the blacks down to the Alfred E. Smith projects on the Lower East Side. But Adam didn't let that go down—he made it possible for us and other black families to move up to Dyckman. He may be mostly forgotten today, but not by me.

The first time I really became aware of myself as a black person was when one of the kids at St. Jude's brought a Polaroid camera to school and took a picture of all of us standing in the back of our third-grade classroom. When I looked at it, I realized how different I was from everybody else; I was darker. Up until then, I hadn't felt that difference, but once I did, it stuck with me.

As I progressed through grade school, civil rights became a serious issue, and I became more and more conscious of racial conflicts. I remember when the black church in Birmingham was bombed, and four little girls were killed. That got me for months. And in the fall of 1955, when I was eight years old, Emmett Till was murdered because he spoke back to a white woman down in the Mississippi Delta.

Emmett Till was from Chicago and had been visiting relatives in Money, Mississippi. When he went to buy something in one of the stores in town, the woman behind the counter became exasperated with him, and he then sassed her back. Later he was found beaten, shot, and dumped in the Tallahatchie River, the fan of a cotton gin tied to his neck with barbed wire. He was only fourteen years old.

My parents had always subscribed to *Jet* magazine and I remember vividly a photograph they ran of Emmett Till in an open casket. My parents talked about it a great deal; they were outraged, and the whole episode had a real impact on me.

The local authorities in Mississippi probably *knew* who'd done it, but at first the death was called a suicide. Then they changed that to death at the hands of persons unknown, and finally those responsible were brought to trial. It was the first time any white people had been brought to court on the basis of testimony by a black person. Of course, the trial was held in a segregated courtroom with an all-white jury and the accused were acquitted, but the incident was one of the sparks that ignited the civil rights movement.

The other day, I saw *Mississippi Burning,* the film about the murder of three civil rights workers. It brought Emmett Till's story back to me all over again. Even though it was inaccurate about the extent of black involvement in the movement, I thought it was a significant picture because it attempted to take the gloves off and be realistic about racism. In the past it's seemed to me that movies have always looked for some way to explain people's racism, and, through explaining it, to excuse it. *Mississippi Burning* was the first time I'd seen racism portrayed as fundamentally odious. You came away with an understanding of how totally ridiculous, irrational, and hateful it is.

When I was fifteen, my parents sent me down by bus, to North Carolina, where my mother was from, to attend the high school graduation of the daughter of a family friend. It was 1962, and I saw Jim Crow "Whites Only" signs all the way through Virginia and North Carolina. It was hard to understand that black people couldn't drink at the same water fountains, use the same rest rooms, or eat at the same restaurants as whites. And the more of it I saw, the less I trusted white people, except for the ones I'd personally known. But Jim Crow was under attack.

It's hard for young people today to grasp the enormity of the racial and social tension that plagued the country back in the sixties. In July 1964, riots swept an eight-block area of Harlem, between Eighth and Lenox avenues and 123rd and 127th streets. I was seventeen years old. I remember stepping off the subway right into the middle of it. It was chaos, wild and insane, and I just stood there trembling. Cops were swinging nightsticks at everybody, bullets were flying, windows were being smashed, people were stealing and looting. It was a scene I'll never forget. All I could think was that I wanted to stay alive, so I took off running and didn't stop until I was at 137th and Broadway.

I sat there huffing and puffing, absorbing what I'd seen, and I knew it was rage, black rage. The poor people of Harlem felt that it was better to get hit with a nightstick than to keep on taking the white man's insults forever. Right then and there I knew who I was and who I had to be. I was going to be black rage personified, black power in the flesh. I was consumed and obsessed by my interest in black power, black pride, black courage. I thought that that, for me, would suffice. It was immature thinking, but that was me at age seventeen.

I came to understand that the history books I'd read throughout grade school and high school had contained absolutely nothing about what black people did for this country. The only thing I'd learned was that black people were slaves until Abraham Lincoln freed them. I was almost an adult before I found out that a black man, Crispus Attucks, had been the first American to die in the Boston Massacre in 1770. And it wasn't until I was playing in the NBA that I found out that the Battle of Bunker Hill wasn't decided until Peter Salem, a recently freed slave, shot the British army's Major-General John Pitcairn.

We've always been involved in meaningful things in America, but without credit. Black people get recognition only for urban crime and welfare fraud, with a little rhythm and blues and sports thrown in. Which is why blind rage at whites is a part of the black condition; most black people reach it. Some pass through it to a higher plateau of understanding, but some never get out of the rage, and their lives are blighted by it. I understand them and I don't turn from them, because I went through it myself. But I eventually found that angry racism made me ill. Emotionally, spiritually, I could not afford to be a racist. As I got older, I gradually got past believing that black was either the best or the worst. It just was.

The black man who had the most profound impact on me was

Malcolm X. I had read *Muhammad Speaks,* the Black Muslim newspaper, but even in the early sixties their brand of racism was unacceptable to me. It held the identical hostility as white racism, and for all my anger and resentment, I understood that rage can do very little to change anything. It's just a continual negative spiral that feeds on itself, and who needs that? I knew these Black Muslim dudes from uptown, and when they tried to recruit me, I didn't like that aspect of their message so I stayed away from them.

Malcolm X was different. He'd made a trip to Mecca and realized that Islam embraced people of all color. He was assassinated in 1965, and though I didn't know much about him then, his death hit hard because I knew he was talking about black pride, about self-help and lifting ourselves up. And I liked his attitude of nonsubservience.

Malcolm X's autobiography came out in 1966, when I was a freshman at UCLA, and I read it right before my nineteenth birthday. It made a bigger impression on me than any book I had ever read, turning me around totally. I started to look at things differently, instead of accepting the mainstream viewpoint.

Part of it had to do with the fact that I *was* different—I was too tall and too dark to really *be* mainstream. Plus, Malcolm clearly showed what was right and what was wrong about what was happening here in America, and he opened the door for real cooperation between the races, not just the superficial, paternalistic thing. He was talking about real people doing real things, black pride and Islam. I just grabbed on to it. And I have never looked back.

It's hard to believe that the twenty-fourth anniversary of Malcolm X's assassination is going to be next month. It's even more amazing to me that both Malcolm X and Martin Luther King were younger than I am now when they were killed—they were both thirty-nine. What a loss they were to us, to everybody.

Someone once said that being black in America is like playing your home games on the opponent's court, and I can obviously identify with that. But a lot of black people seem to favor handouts. The Republican agenda seems basically indifferent to people's hardships, but I agree with its position that handouts are not the solution to social problems. There are no easy solutions. As blacks, we are going to have to do, or continue to do, from within our own community; we're going to have to start to work at changing what's happening.

There was an interesting segment on *Nightline* recently about a Nicaraguan refugee. The dude came up here and cleaned toilets, swept streets, worked at McDonald's. Many black people won't do that. They want to go from the gutter to Easy Street. It doesn't work like that.

And, unfortunately, failure has been internalized by the black community to such a degree that people expect to fail. As soon as they're challenged, they go back to the old bromide of "Well, we got really screwed during slavery."

One of the advantages that I've had is that when my grandparents came over here they were just like that Nicaraguan guy. My grandfather studied to become a dentist—he worked in construction to pay for the equipment he'd need, and was still working construction when he died. But he always took advantage of whatever was available. And it's been our family tradition to see education as a key to getting ahead.

That tradition is why I'm not happy with the tremendous emphasis put on sports in the ghetto as the only means of escaping the cycle of poverty and ignorance. The NBA isn't a realistic hope for most people. I'm not comfortable being preachy, but more people have to start spending as much time in the library as they do on the basketball court. If they took to the idea that they could escape poverty through education, I think it would make a more basic and long-lasting change in the way things happen. When we set up unrealistic goals and then don't achieve them, that's another example of internalized defeat.

What we need are positive, realistic ideas and the willingness to work. Hard work and practical goals.

Since today's Houston game was in the afternoon, during the drive to the Forum I could enjoy a perfect L.A. winter day, clean and clear; I could see all the way to the mountains. The Rockets came into town leading the Midwest Division with a 22-12 record. But we were at our finest—and unbeatable. We shot a very impressive .653 from the floor, our best and probably the best in the league so far this year, and that made the 124–113 victory seem simpler than it was.

I think our game is recovering. All five Laker starters scored in double figures and I made good use of my twenty-eight minutes, going six for eight from the floor. In all, a good game.

There's always a special challenge in playing well against the Oba, the Rockets' Nigerian center, Akeem Olajuwon. I always call him the Oba, a Yoruban term referring to the local person of highest esteem in any village, like the mayor. It seems to fit Akeem and his stature in the game. Because my roots go back to the Yoruba, I know a little bit about it, and it really mystifies him that I, an American, would be this knowledgeable. Once when Akeem came into the Laker dressing room, I sang him a few bars of a song from Lagos that my father used to play on records. Akeem didn't know quite what to make of that.

Though he's listed at seven feet, the Oba is more like six-ten, but no matter what height he is, he's one of the strongest rebounders in the NBA. He's not a massive guy, but he's strong, with great leaping ability and quickness, and he's explosive, really fast up and down the court—an incredible athlete overall, his endurance and footwork coming from all the soccer he played as a kid.

Physically, Olajuwon is probably the best center in the league right now. If he has a weakness, it's that he doesn't find a way to help his teammates; it's just a matter of maturity, I think. The key to playing him is to keep him off the offensive boards. I blocked somebody's shot today and he went up and got it while it was still in the air and dunked it. If you let him put in his teammates' misses, he can really dominate the game, so you want to get him to shoot the ball from the outside. If you do that, you can have a good game against him.

Friday, January 20

We nearly blew a twenty-seven-point halftime lead against Dallas tonight, allowing them to within seven points early in the fourth quarter before pulling away to a 115–99 victory—that makes five wins in a row. I had eleven points and six blocked shots, a season high, and this was the first game this year that I've really had fun. People aren't feeling sorry for me anymore.

A friend of mine sent me a copy of a *Sports Illustrated* cover story on me, with its big headline KAREEM'S LAST STAND. I like the idea that the article now appears ill timed. It's not appropriate anymore—it's already history. And my mother said Scott Ostler has reneged. He wrote a column with the headline IT MAY NOT BE TIME TO GIVE HIM THE HOOK. That's why journalists think I'm no fun; I've been too unpredictable my whole career. It's satisfying to prove your critics wrong sometimes. My friend Malek says I'm like Jason in *Friday the 13th* because I absolutely refuse to stay buried.

Mike Tyson was at the game and came into the locker room afterward. He's from Brownsville, where my father's family is from, and my uncle had him pegged when he was just coming on: "a guy from the neighborhood who should be pretty good." Was that ever an understatement.

Tuesday, January 24

Our home streak finally ended tonight. We had a perfect 17-0 record at the Forum, which was the team's best start at home since the Lakers moved to Los Angeles. But the New York Knicks beat us 122–117. Two months ago, we had handed them the only home-court loss they've had this season, so they were totally inclined to pay us back.

Still, it was a curious kind of loss, because in many ways we should have won. We shot better than the Knicks, outrebounded them, totaled more assists, and never were behind until two Patrick Ewing free throws put them out in front, 114–113, with 3:56 left in the game.

But if we did a lot of good things, they did the right thing at the crucial time, outscoring us 31–18 in the final quarter. That's the mental aspect of the game, and this particular time we didn't rise to the occasion.

As far as the home streak ending, that's part of the game. Every streak ends. You never feel good about losing, but if you turn defeats into learning experiences, they won't bother you very long. You've got to prepare to play again.

Right now Cleveland has the best record in the league, we've moved into second, and Detroit is in third place.

Friday, January 27

Tonight, at halftime of the game with Charlotte at home, I was made an honorary Harlem Globetrotter by one of their legendary players, Curly Neal. I've known Curly since I was in college and he went to Johnson C. Smith in North Carolina. And the Globetrotters as an organization go even further back with me. They were the first basketball team that I ever admired. In the very beginning, I didn't know anything about the Celtics, the Knicks, or any of them. I knew only about the Harlem Globetrotters.

When I was in the third grade, my mother took me to see *Go Man Go,* a movie about the Globetrotters and how they got started. It's got one scene that nobody who's seen the picture ever forgets. Dane Clark played Abe Saperstein, the team's founder and a guy in desperate need of a good dribbler. Marques Haynes wants the job, and to get it he has to get the ball past Saperstein in a tenement hallway. The hallway is narrow as a toothpick, and Saperstein is so much on the wide side that it looks like even a fly couldn't get by him, but, almost magically, Haynes dribbles right around the man and gets the assignment. From that point on, I wanted to play basketball. I went in to Coach Hopkins and told him I wanted to be on the team.

While some people aren't comfortable with the Globetrotters because they think the team is like a minstrel show, I've never thought their style was degrading. But I've also never forgotten the fact that the organization began as a barnstorming black team that played serious basketball for more than two decades. The original concept was to go out there and play a little minuet against the system, to bring a new dimension of individual creativity to the game with guys like Haynes, who would drop to one knee and sometimes two, easily weaving in and out among defenders, sometimes even bouncing the ball between their legs.

In 1948, two years before blacks were allowed in the pro game, the Globetrotters beat the then-world-champion Minneapolis Lakers and the game's first big center, six-foot-ten-inch George Mikan in an exhibition game before 17,853 fans. They were as good as the best, and black people always admired them for that. And in the early 1950s, after the NBA had completely taken over the professional side of basketball, the Globetrotters changed from being a competitive team to entertainers. They would go out and beat the pants off of people and make it into a show. What's wrong with that?

I got nineteen points against Charlotte, my season high so far. My passing and defensive play have gotten better as well. I think I'm doing a better job of fitting in with the team. The more I can do, in a varied kind of way, the better. I'm at the middle, reaching up, and if we can continue to improve as the season ends, which is usually what we do, I think we have a chance to win the Western Conference.

Sunday, January 29

Byron is out sick. He missed Friday night's victory over Charlotte at home as well as tonight's game in Dallas, not even joining us on this three-game road trip, and there is no telling when he'll be back. The problem appears to be with his kidneys. He hadn't been himself the last few games he played, and this must be why.

With his absence, the Mavericks looked to be a tough opponent. Plus we hadn't won a road game outside of California since Cleveland back in mid-December. But not only did we beat Dallas fairly easily, 118–93, we handed them their worst home-court loss in the history of the franchise. And a lot of the credit has to go to Michael Cooper, who started in place of Byron and scored a season-high eighteen points. The importance of the sixth man in the NBA cannot be overestimated, and in Michael Cooper we have one of the best in the league.

Within the team, we all have our roles. I'm kind of like patriarch. Earvin is like number one son. Byron is the jester, the jokester, A.C. a jokester and moral force combined. And James and Cooper are the strong silent workers.

Cooper has been able to show the world what determination and team play can contribute to a winning effort. Usually, players are assessed by their ability to score or create plays. Cooper does not excel in either of these categories but he has been a crucial player with the Lakers despite that. He has made a career of being the person to take a specific job, a very tough specific job, and deliver what is needed for us to win. Michael always ends up guarding the opposition's toughest offensive player. He's been able to take key scorers like Larry Bird, George Gervin, Rolando Blackman, and Freddie Brown out of the game at critical moments. After a while, all they think about is Coop. He's *on* them, his chest attached to their shoulder, and they can't get rid of him. In fact, Bird has said that when he practices by himself in the summers, he imagines it's Coop who's guarding him. "My games," he's said, "are always against Cooper." So it's hardly surprising that he won the Defensive Player of the Year award after the 1986–87 season. His eyes have teeth.

Cooper will do anything to distract, annoy, unnerve, or intimidate his assignment. He reminds me of a wolverine: He's got that kind of tenacity and aggression, and he will go for it. Feisty and combative, he's also got a crazy streak; you don't even have to drop the hat—he's already going for it. For being reed-thin and only weighing 180 pounds, he's a very muscular six feet seven, and that wolverine mentality doubles his strength.

Cooper has other physical attributes that serve him well. His cardiovascular training has enabled him to run the whole time he's in the game, and being a lightweight, the running game will not wear him out.

Cooper has also done the little things to improve his game. He worked on his ball handling and, when he saw a need, he developed a three-point shot to complement our inside game. Cooper, Magic, and Byron work on their three-pointers together before practice every day. They go out and play for money, matching shots at $5 apiece, at least. If one of them is down a few shots, it's very quickly $20 or $30, plus they rag and heap all kinds of abuse on each other when one of them misses.

I liken Cooper to a commando or special-forces type of operative, doing the dirty jobs behind enemy lines with very little recognition. But the other guys on the team are aware of his tenacity and his willingness to do the tough, unglamorous jobs that help a team win. He's the stopper, the guy we turn to to shut people down. We all have seen him blocking shots, making steals, or forcing bad shots at critical times to help us seal a victory. It's often been true that in twenty minutes Michael has turned a game around by this kind of play. And the fans love him, often chanting, "Cooop, Cooop, Cooop," when he walks onto the floor.

I remember one especially big play. It was in Game 5 of the second round of the play-offs against Utah last year, when Michael had the game in his hands. If we'd lost, we would have had to win the next game in Salt Lake or be eliminated,. There were less than ten seconds left when Magic drove the lane, but he got double-teamed. Cooper was the only guy open and Magic hit him with the ball and he took the shot, a jumper from near the top of the key. The ball went in with seven seconds to go for a 111–109 victory. It was not just Cooper's only basket of the day; it was the first game-winning shot of his career.

Off the court, Michael is a quiet guy. He's been married forever, since he was a senior at New Mexico, and he and Wanda have two kids. He's got all the old games on tape at home, and he watches them and pays attention to what he needs to do to be more effective. He and Magic are close. They sit together on the plane and hang out together when we're on the road, and they've had lockers next to each other for ten years. Magic has the social confidence and Coop is real shy, so they complement each other very well.

Before the game came the Dallas farewell ceremony, the first one since Chicago in December. I feel a special warmth toward the crowd at Reunion Arena because six years ago, two nights after my house burned to the ground, the fans gave me a prolonged standing ovation. "Thank you for reaching out and giving me the ovation when I was at one of the low points of my life," I told the fans tonight. The Maverick organization gave me a sculpture of an elephant carved in verdite by an African artist from Nairobi, Kenya. The inscription read, "Dignity, strength, durability." It was a beautiful and thoughtful gift.

Wednesday, February 1

Surprises, I've found, come in all shapes and sizes. Yesterday, right before the tip-off against Houston, Morganna, a.k.a. the Kissing Bandit, an exotic dancer who makes a habit of kissing sports celebrities, ran out on courtside and kissed me on the cheek. It was a silly kind of surprise, a brief sensual flash, and then it was over. When I saw her coming, I was trying to figure out what she was doing on the court. Hey, I thought she was a *baseball* fan.

After beating the Rockets 125–114, we moved on to Phoenix, last stop on the road trip, where several members of the press were waiting for me in the locker room before the game tonight. They told me that the Western Conference coaches had voted Mark Eaton and Kevin Duckworth to back up starter Akeem Olajuwon as center for the February 12 All-Star game. That wasn't much of a surprise. Naturally, they wanted my reaction. I told them it was appropriate that I had not made the team. The game is supposed to honor the best players of this season, and I haven't made a big enough contribution to the Lakers. My play has improved somewhat the last two weeks, but two weeks doesn't cut it with me. If I had made it, something would have been wrong. I'd just be taking the spot of a more deserving player. I told them I'd agreed to be the personal guest of David Stern, the NBA commissioner, at the All-Star banquet the night before, and that would be enough of an honor for me. As most of these guys know, I've never been one of the All-Star game's biggest fans, feeling that everybody gets breaks that weekend but the All-Stars.

The game with Phoenix was a blowout. We scored a strong thirty-eight points in the first quarter, but were held to only eleven in the second, our lowest quarter since 1982, and ended up on the short end of a 114–97 score. The Suns may be a young team, but they're right on our tails, only two games out in the conference standings.

Friday, February 3

Back at the Forum, the Trail Blazers are in from Portland, which gives me a chance to chat with Clyde Drexler. He's not just your average jock type, but a bright and very aware young man, a nice dude. And he's got as much athletic ability as Michael Jordan. He can run as fast and leap as high, and has a fine shooting touch; he's just a great player. This year was his second selection in a row for the All-Star team, but recognition has been slow in coming. Part of it is that he's stuck up in Portland. Unless they're going to be winning the world championship, he's not going to get the attention he would if he played back East.

Monday, February 6

It was 34 degrees today, the coldest day in Los Angeles in 102 years. Every winter, I'm grateful that I don't have to struggle through ice and snow or through the grayness of a winter day in either New York or Milwaukee, except when we're passing through. Today there was ice on my windshield when I went to practice, though. And it was *thick* ice, too. I'm glad we only get frost here every century or so.

There was no game tonight, so I had my three oldest children over for dinner—my son Kareem, who is twelve, and my daughters, Habiba and Sultana, who are sixteen and nine. Habiba, my oldest, will be going to college next year, probably UCLA, a fact difficult for me to grasp. It doesn't seem that long ago for me. Quiet like I am and a great reader, Habiba scored in the top 2 percent nationally on her SATs. All of my kids, including Amir, do well in academics, and I'm very proud of that. Each of them is also involved in some type of athletics—Kareem has developed into a serious basketball player—but I haven't wanted to make the mistake of pushing any of them to follow my footsteps into sports. I try only to encourage and influence them in the direction of their education. Other than that, I want them to be free to make their own choices.

All my children live and go to school in Los Angeles, but, during the winter, because of my schedule, it's very difficult for me to see them and always has been. So this was a rare family evening together.

Wednesday, February 8

Tonight's game with the Warriors was a wild one. Don Nelson, the Golden State coach, benched both Ralph Sampson and Manute Bol and started a "small" team against us, with no one taller than six feet eight. And these midgets gave us our second Forum loss of the season, 121–118.

Byron Scott, having missed six games, came back to the lineup tonight. His problem turned out to be a kidney stone. But then we lost Magic. He was driving the lane late in the third quarter, and though he hit the basket, when he came down, he grabbed his left leg. Apparently, he partially tore his hamstring while planting his left foot on the lay-up. It's not clear how long he will be out, but he will definitely miss Sunday's All-Star game. Losing Magic, even briefly, hurts the team more than anything else can.

Describing Earvin Johnson is more complicated than one might guess, because the man himself is more complicated than he at first seems. The whole world knows about his sense of showmanship and his flair for the spectacular, but the inner man, the fierce competitor with the iron will to win, is often concealed by the smile and the easy demeanor.

My first contact with Earvin—and I called him Earvin for a long time until I realized no one knew who I was talking about—came when he was about eleven years old, still in grade school. It was at Cobo Hall, in downtown Detroit, and I was still with the Milwaukee Bucks. We'd just beaten the Pistons, and Earvin, who'd traveled an hour and a half from Lansing to see the game, came into the locker room and got my autograph. Magic tells this story, so it must be true.

We met formally eight or nine years later, at Laker training camp in the fall of 1979. Playing off somebody like Magic, who creates confusion by running the ball upcourt really fast was what we did every day at UCLA, so doing it with him was almost second nature.

Our first game together was the opener of the 1979 season at the Sports Arena against the Clippers. With the score tied in the closing seconds, I got the ball about fifteen feet out and made the winning basket at the buzzer. Magic just went crazy, leaping up on me and hugging me; he was so fired up and enthused it was like he'd won the NCAA all over again.

In the locker room afterward I said, "Earvin, do you realize that we have eighty-one more games to play?"

His face said something like, "Gee, I'm sorry. I just got excited." But that was Magic's kind of commitment, I learned.

I've always believed that you can learn a great deal about a player's personality from the way he executes the fundamentals of the game. Oscar Robertson's game, for instance, was based on his ability to get a step on you and use that advantage to either get to the basket, draw help from the rest of the defense and pass, or unexpectedly pull up for a shot, many times drawing a foul in the process.

Oscar was very unemotional in his execution and delivery, his style quite similar to a symphony conductor: all business, no frills, the model of efficiency. Much is made of the triple-double statistic these days. It means a player went into double figures in points, assists, and rebounds in one game. Well, Oscar had *seasons* where he averaged triple-double stats for the entire year. Such dominance and ability from someone in the guard position was not fully appreciated in those days.

At the time I thought that what Oscar gave to my game only comes once in a lifetime. But then it came twice, with Earvin. His style, based on his ability to get to the basket under any circumstances, is completely different from Oscar's. Magic will drive the ball to the hoop and force the defense to collapse. His 225 pounds makes it impossible to guard him with a small body, and, at six-nine, he can shoot it over any average-size guard they put on him. This has forced more matchup difficulties for our opponents than I could enumerate.

But the quintessential Earvin experience doesn't start until, having passed his man and heading in for an easy lay-up, he has to deal with a last-second attempt to block his shot. That's when the Magic Show really begins. Sometimes it's a pass to an undefended Laker left open because of reactions to Magic's penetration. Sometimes it's a fake to the open man and a lay-up for Magic. Magic can combine real threats with fakes to real and imaginary teammates in almost infinite combinations. He determines in an instant how a play might develop, and can automatically make the most of slight, fleeting advantages. Doing what he does under the pressure of competition has been one of the greatest continuous athletic feats ever, one that I'm proud to have been a part of.

Magic runs the game like a disco DJ. He wants the fans and his teammates to enjoy every success on court. And he wants his opponents to know that they've been bested and that it'll happen again if they don't tighten up. The challenge in his look is obvious; it says, "Fooled ya! You should know better!" If he is going to respect you on the court, you're going to have to earn it.

Earvin Senior, Magic's father, is six feet four and he was his son's hero, a working man, father of ten, who held two jobs. Magic has told me that when his dad played him one-on-one as a kid, he purposely played him unfairly, pushing, grabbing and holding him all over the court. He wanted Magic to know early that he wouldn't always get his way. He wanted him to understand that even though something's not right, there will be many times when nothing will be done about it. And you can't quit; you simply have to play harder. My dad did the same thing for me, made me come to grips with the fact that it doesn't have to be fair and it probably won't. Black people really have to get prepared for that.

Magic is so competitive he can become overbearing. Early in his career with the Lakers we would almost come to fisticuffs because of the intensity he brought to meaningless practice games. Magic doesn't like losing at *anything,* and he will argue all day to avoid it. The rest of the Lakers could not help but be positively affected by that, and our level of play rose accordingly. Our opponents, too, were forced to raise their level of competence and desire when they played us. Getting the best of Magic and the Lakers became an irresistible challenge, and around the league people came to expect an intensely competitive game when the Lakers came to town. I think that's one of the reasons the NBA got to be as popular as it has been in the 1980s. We've all been able to enjoy what Magic has brought to the game.

For all his easy charm, it takes time to really get to know Magic. It took us three years before we were fully able to communicate as men. It's a task to know and understand someone when there is a twelve-year difference in your ages, but there was never any jealousy or resentment between us. From the beginning, people expected our egos to clash, the presumption being that I would be threatened by Magic. But I've never had to be the only one on the mountaintop; everybody gives me all these prima-donna-type attributes I don't have. And Magic's playing personality is as far away from being egotistical as you can get. All he wants to do is get the ball to somebody else and let him score. If you're a basketball player, you've got to love somebody like that.

As Magic has matured, we've grown closer, and now I feel that we are family. I even taught him how to shoot what people call the "junior skyhook." I showed him how to set it up with his hands and explained the special triangulation of the shot: ball, eyes, rim. He's shared in most of my records; for instance, he gave me the assist back in 1984 that enabled me to shoot a hook over Mark Eaton and break Wilt Chamberlain's all-time scoring record. This season, Magic's been the first person to greet me on the bench after I finish my farewell-ceremony speeches. That's no accident.

Magic also has roots in North Carolina, so he shares in the bond I have with James Worthy and Bob McAdoo. His mother, Christine, is from there. She's big-hearted like her son, and when Magic first came to the Lakers she sought me out and asked me to keep an eye out for him. Christine cooks for us every time we go to play in Michigan, and for me, it's like going home. I'm sure I'll dream of Christine Johnson's sweet-potato pies and Magic's first-class smile long after I've retired.

Sunday, February 12

I flew to Atlanta last Thursday to sign autographs for L.A. Gear at a sporting goods manufacturers' show. As soon as I walked into my hotel room, the phone started ringing. It was Lorin Pullman, my assistant. She'd been calling me every fifteen minutes, because the league office had been calling *her* every ten minutes. What none of them knew was that my plane to Atlanta had been delayed two hours en route.

Apparently NBA commissioner David Stern wanted to appoint me to take Magic's place on the Western Conference's All-Star squad. After I hadn't been elected to the team, I was unofficially approached and asked to consider a strictly honorary, thirteenth spot on the squad, but I made it clear then I wasn't interested in that. Now I felt I had to say yes. Being a good soldier is ingrained in me, so I agreed. I must have had some premonition that this was going to happen, because I'd brought my sneakers with me. Fate wanted me at that game.

I arrived in Houston about 6 P.M. Friday. Lorin met me at the airport and told me she'd arranged for me to go up to my room at the Hyatt via a back elevator so I could avoid the carnival atmosphere in the lobby. Lorin is terrific at things like that. She handles many of my business and personal affairs, as well as arranging my schedule. I'm fortunate to have someone who's as able and intelligent as she is who also grew up in the world of sports: Her dad played college football and later coached in the army.

It seems that nothing about me and this game can escape controversy. I heard that Doug Moe, the Nuggets' coach, had written a column for *The Denver Post* personally blasting me. I was surprised to have him on my case, because I don't know him at all and I've never had any run-ins with him.

We played the game today in the Astrodome, which is like playing on a prairie—it's that big. There are no fans within one hundred yards of the court on either side, and despite all the media and the 44,735 fans, an All-Star-game attendance record, the place was almost quiet. Noise in the Astrodome simply dissipates and dies in the air.

Even for an All-Star game, this one was not especially exciting. The West, after building up a lead as big as thirty-one points, held on to win 143–134. I played thirteen minutes, and hit on two free throws in the third quarter, but with the game almost over, I still hadn't scored a basket. With 1:31 left, Riley, who was coach of the West, asked me if I wanted to go back on the floor. Clyde Drexler said he was intent on getting me the assist, and with time running out, twenty-four seconds left on the game clock, I took a pass from him and hit an eight-foot skyhook from the left side of the lane. I smiled when it went in.

It was a nice way to end it, but it had been a long weekend.

It's appropriate that that final shot was a skyhook, as was my thirty-eight thousandth career point, which came against New Jersey just a week ago. I've done so well with it that some people think I invented the thing, which obviously isn't true—it's just that I was in the last generation to learn that shot. Most kids nowadays don't learn to play with their back to the basket, and if you don't have your back to the basket, you can't shoot a hook shot. Young guys today want to be like Doctor J and Michael Jordan. They think it's great to put on those athletic moves, and the girls think it's great, too, the brilliant acrobatics more sexy than backing up and making a hook.

The skyhook has definite advantages, however. I don't have to rely on brute force or blinding speed to utilize it. It doesn't require a good pass, but if you're moving and you get one, it's easy to shoot it before anybody can react. You grasp the ball, take a step, coil, launch yourself into the air, extend your arm, lengthen your body, and then release the ball. You can't defend against it; nobody can get a hand on it—I can shoot it over Manute Bol. Successful shooting is all in the touch. The release has to be consistent, the same each time. It's an artistic shot, but I am blessed—or cursed—that a lot of the stuff I do looks easy.

I had the form and release of the hook by the time I was a freshman in high school, but my coach there didn't emphasize it. At UCLA, Coach Wooden made me shoot the hook hundreds of times daily. Those sessions improved not only the mechanics of the shot, but also my overall concentration. Shooting it is a very Zen activity: You center on your inner calm and your target, isolating everything else until you and your objective become one.

Sometimes people don't understand what I'm talking about when I discuss the hook in those terms because they really haven't tried to discipline themselves like that. People have been sent to study Zen archery just so they can learn to concentrate. There's a whole system of getting physically ready, having your equipment ready, knowing the target, becoming part of the target, and sending the arrow from yourself to the target, which is really just sending it back to yourself. That's the thought process involved, and I was fortunate to be into these types of mental attitudes at an early part of my life and to be able to incorporate them into my game. When the skyhook is working, the hook and I are one. I've been flattered to hear that Bill Russell once called it the most beautiful thing in sports.

The skyhook has definitely been a factor in my longevity as well. I've avoided the beating I would have taken if I'd gone inside all the time and worked directly under the boards. The area under the hoop is serious, serious territory; there's very little levity there. It's where most people end up bleeding.

When the shot is really working, it tends to make opposing centers quite angry, sometimes to the point where they're funny without intending to be. Rick Mahorn really got into it one night. I'd scored a lot of points, but the game was out of reach for us, and near the end Rick turned to me and said, "No, you can't shoot the hook anymore." And the next time the Lakers came down the court, Rick positioned himself way up on my left side. I immediately turned the other way and made a lay-up. "Yeah, that's right, Kareem," Mahorn shouted at me. "But forget the hook—that's out!"

Tuesday, February 14

In practice yesterday, I hyperextended my elbow. I was reaching over Mark McNamara for the ball and got my hand on it just as Mark was pulling it away. It really hurt so I stopped playing and immediately had it iced down. When this happened back in November, the elbow swelled up the next day. But this time I was luckier. The elbow was so mobile, in fact, that I scored a season-high twenty-one points tonight. It wasn't enough to stop the Detroit Pistons, though. They beat us, 111–103, the second time they've beaten us this year. We played hard, and when we play a game like that, even though we lose, we bring that attitude and energy to the next game. That means we're getting better.

Playing against Bill Laimbeer is really something. Aggressive play is the name of the game in the NBA—nobody's out there conducting tours for you—but what makes everybody angry about Laimbeer is that he tends to clobber you and you don't see it coming. He'll knock you silly and say he was going for the ball when the ball was nowhere in the vicinity. When a player can't do anything except hurt you, that's when people say it's enough.

There was one time when Robert Parish was playing behind Laimbeer. The ball was bouncing out to where Laimbeer definitely didn't have a chance to get it, so he just reached back and hit Robert right across his face with his forearm and said, "Oh, I was going for the ball." Parish turned around and slapped Laimbeer about three times on the face, bent him over backward. Nobody said anything. It was one of the few times when there was a really judicious no-call on the part of the officials. So Laimbeer tries to get away with stuff, but he doesn't necessarily try to hurt people. He's a tough player in my mind, but not a "dirty" one.

Monday, February 20

Back in Sacramento, where we had one of our worst games of the season last month. But tonight was different, and for more reasons than one. Not only did we win 100–97, but the man who put the game on ice was David Rivers. He was fouled with four seconds left and the Lakers up 98–97. Sacramento called two time-outs to try to rattle him, but David just smiled and sank the shots. After all, this is a guy who had gone twenty-eight for thirty-one from the line up to now.

Several of the guys on the bench are quiet types. Jeff Lamp is that way, but that doesn't stop him from having a positive outlook and, as a very talented athlete, giving his all on the court. And David is one of the quietest people I've met. I think playing with the world champions has made him even more taciturn. He sat next to me during the flight out to training camp in Hawaii and didn't say a single word to me.

But make no mistake about the fact that David is a bona-fide basketball player. He has exceptional ball-handling skills and I've enjoyed watching him do his workout before practice. It's a seminar for anyone who wants to learn how to handle the ball, because David does most of his drills with two balls going simultaneously. Those who are into right- and left-brain dominance know how difficult that is. In basketball, however, those skills are essential for anyone who is responsible for handling the ball.

Putting pressure on ball handlers is one way to change the momentum of the game, but trying to put pressure on David can be a frustrating experience. He uses a herky-jerky motion and, with no weak hand, can go right or left easily. The only times I see him pressured into a mistake is when a pair of defenders hem him in and lean on him. But as the season has progressed, he has learned to cope with situations by improving his ability to get the ball to the open man.

David was a great player at Notre Dame, leading the team in scoring and named MVP all four of his seasons. While there, he had a near-fatal automobile accident. Involved in a head-on collision, he went headfirst through a van windshield and was ripped nearly in two. He should be dead, but after three hours of surgery all he has is a fifteen-inch scar that crosses his stomach from hip to hip.

But David's put all that behind him and approached his pro career with a great work ethic and a lot of talent. At six feet, he is able to use the strength of the little man—speed—to great advantage on the court. The only players I've seen with the type of vision he possesses, the ability to know where all the men are on the court, are Magic and Isiah Thomas. So David has a promising future in the NBA.

Sunday, February 26

In the past week we've had one of our worst defeats in many years—then turned around and won a big game at home. The low was way down. But the high was more important. We are moving in the right direction.

On Wednesday night, we stunk in Salt Lake City for the second time this season, the last time having been when they beat us easily in the Salt Palace on Christmas Day. But Wednesday night was awful. After scoring only thirty-two points in the first half, we got blown out, 105–79. Mark Eaton blocked four shots to take second place behind me on the NBA all-time list and our 34.8 field goal percentage was the lowest of the season. The defeat was perhaps our worst in fifteen years. A loss like that is hard for me to explain. We were doing great and then we simply stopped applying ourselves. We're at .500, 14-14, on the road, and 35-17 overall, eight games off last year's record.

Then, tonight, we played another tough opponent, the Phoenix Suns, and scored a 134–122 victory. The Suns, having won seven of their last eight games, came in one and a half games behind us in the Pacific Division. They're the most improved team in the NBA, the first club in seven years to give us a race in our division. They'd beaten us in Phoenix at the beginning of the month, and another victory would have put them only half a game out, as opposed to the two and a half back they are now. We've put some space between us. Magic's return to the lineup—he came back for our Friday-night win over Sacramento—was obviously important; he scored twenty-five and had nineteen assists. Just as important, though, was our state of mind. The pregame attitude was purposeful; we had a serious job to get done—let's do it. And we did.

Mark West, the Suns' center, is a resilient guy. There have been two separate occasions when I've accidentally socked him in the head, hard. I immediately said, "Hey, I'm sorry." The first time, he didn't even acknowledge me. The second time I said, "Hey, Mark, listen, man, I wasn't trying to hit you in the head."

He just looked at me and said, "Don't worry about it." He is one physically tough individual.

Monday, March 6

We are on our last big road trip of the season—five cities coast-to-coast in eight days. We started in Houston yesterday. It was our third nationally televised game, and the third one we've lost, this time by an 88–83 score. They got physical with us and clogged up the middle and we weren't patient enough against that kind of defense. We managed

only thirty-seven points in the second half and got outrebounded fifty-
five to thirty-eight; we just didn't play a very good game.

Then we left immediately for Atlanta and had plane trouble. First
we sat on the ground in Houston for two hours, and then we circled
Atlanta for another hour due to weather problems. Finally we were sent
to Jacksonville, 354 miles to the south, where we spent an hour re-
fueling and I pitched quarters in the terminal with some of the guys
before we took off again. Now I know what the crew of the *Flying
Dutchman* must have felt like. We were originally scheduled to get into
Atlanta at 10:15 P.M., but the reality was we didn't walk into our hotel
rooms until 3:15 A.M. And practice was scheduled for noon. The mood
on the plane was definitely ugly.

Tuesday, March 7

Our first game with Atlanta this season and, with the help of A.C.
Green, who muscled his way to thirteen rebounds and fifteen points
against the very physical Hawks, we came away with a 106–97 victory.
It was our fortieth win of the year and felt especially good coming after
the Houston game, which had left us rather somber. Getting a tough
one from a good team on the road is always sweet.

One of the things I enjoy about playing Atlanta is getting a chance
to catch up with Cazzie Russell, who's an assistant coach with the
Hawks. When I visited the University of Michigan as a high school
senior, it was Cazzie who took me out to dinner, and we've been friends
ever since. He has a great sense of humor. When he was the sixth man
on the great Knicks team in 1970, he called himself "Nestlé's Instant
Offense" because they'd put him in when Bill Bradley wasn't shooting
well. And when they took Stu Lantz, now Chick Hearn's assistant, to
a plane in a wheelchair after a minor back injury, Cazzie's the one who
began calling him "Stuside," after Raymond Burr in *Ironside*. When
I first came to the Lakers for the 1975–76 season, Stu, Cazzie, and I
all played together. We finished dead last.

Though there isn't the rivalry between us there used to be, playing
against Moses Malone is still a challenge. He's both very physical and
very smart as a player. One of the toughest rebounders in the league,
he never stops coming at you.

In 1983, when Moses was with the 76ers, they blew us out of the finals in four straight games, and he was just relentless. After that I felt I had to appraise what I was doing wrong, so I went to Pete Newell, a genuine savant of the game who at the time ran a summer program that helped pros correct flaws in their performance. I took him some videotape of the play-off games and asked him to critique my perform-ance against Moses. What Pete noticed was that I was holding my hands at my sides and, just before a rebound, Moses would lean against me and pin one of my arms. This would knock me off balance for a split second, which was enough to let him get the rebound. Moses makes his living doing things like that, and he's the reason Akeem Olajuwon plays the way he does; they played pickup games a lot when Moses was in Houston and Akeem in college. Newell showed me that I had to keep my hands and arms up higher and use my butt to knock people's weight off me so that I didn't get thrown off balance myself. The advice worked, and my play against Moses improved.

Wednesday, March 8

It is the first season of play for the Miami Heat. In fact, at 8–49 before tonight, they still have an outside shot at breaking the NBA record for worst season, which the 76ers hold at 9-73. We pushed the Heat to 8-50 with an easy 127–87 cruise. The reserves got a lot of play; Tony Campbell was able to tie his season high with nineteen points and Mark McNamara got a season-high thirteen rebounds. Everybody got into it. We didn't have to conspire but we made sure we beat them real good.

Tony and Mark are quite different, and I connect to each of them differently. On the team Tony is known as Top Cat, and I can't think of a more appropriate name for him. Top Cat is a cartoon character with extraordinary abilities to save situations that have been given up for lost, and that fits Tony to a T.

T.C. is one of those multitalented athletes who could have played a number of sports. He has the speed, strength, and hands to be a tight end in the NFL, and he can play the outfield with the best of them—he also has a history of hitting the long ball to the power alleys. He told me that he had to choose one sport, so he made it basketball. T.C. is ambidextrous and he puts that ability to great use in the game. One never knows which direction he will take as he approaches the basket, and that puts a lot of pressure on the defense. During the summer of

1988, he led the L.A. Summer League in scoring. And when I saw in the paper that a Tonie Campbell won an Olympic medal in hurdling, I thought for a minute that it might have been Top Cat. There's nothing that's too much for him to handle athletically.

For me, it's also a pleasure to be with him off the court because he's the first player from the New York metropolitan area I've played with in some time. He's from Teaneck, New Jersey, but his family has a bakery on 125th Street, Wimp's Bakery, so we always have a few laughs about how the boys "uptown" would react to a given situation. He explained to me that Kool Moe Dee's song "Wild Wild West," real popular with the Forum crowd last year, is about the western edge of Harlem, my old stomping grounds. It just feels good to have a teammate who can relate to 125th Street and understand what it means when 1-2-5 is mentioned.

As for Mark, he's the only native Californian on the Lakers, and that is a source of pride for him. He has a hearing problem, caused by calcium deposits in his ears from surfing so much. When they make announcements on the plane, you have to yell it in his ear before he understands. That's when I started to call him Marco Quasimodo, or sometimes Ears of Stone.

Mark's somewhat of a journeyman, having been traded a few times and played in Italy. He's a linguist who studies French and Italian in his spare time, and I'm constantly checking out what he says to see if any insults or put-downs are lurking in his asides. Jeff Lamp knows some Italian as well, so they sometimes conspire for a few jokes at the expense of the non-Italians around, but Mark's sense of humor is so evident that no hard feelings ever result. I enjoy his presence because he's upbeat and can see the irony of whatever situation we're in. When you're stranded in an airport somewhere, that's a great asset.

Mark's got a degree in environmental economics from Berkeley, and of all my teammates, he's the most well read. We've had discussions about a variety of subjects that would startle those who harbor stereotypical notions about athletes. As a Berkeley grad, he never misses a chance to put down the Bruins of UCLA, but since UCLA beat Cal for twenty-five straight years in basketball, from 1962 to 1987, I have plenty of ammunition for my side of the debate.

Mark has also given me some insight into the mind-set of the average American. It's obvious that professional basketball is dominated by black players and, aside from an occasional statement of that fact, not much is said about it. But Mark gets feedback from fans that would never make the paper, and he's depressed and sometimes offended by what he hears. Things like "It sure is good to see some white guys in the league," "You should be playing in front of So-and-So," and "Why don't they give you guys some time?"

These comments make Mark start to doubt himself because he doesn't know if he is playing because he is a skilled athlete or because he is a white athlete; there have been times when he has known for sure that his presence on a team was due to attempts at racial balancing.

The thing Mark resents most about the racism in our society is how it poisons the climate of real friendship. Because he's seen the subtle forms of exclusion and the double standards that are applied to blacks and other minorities, Mark understands why a lot of blacks have "attitudes," that chip on the shoulder that shows up when black people suspect foul play. I have been suspicious of racist motives myself when none were working against me, but you never know, and that makes it hard to relax and let people of like minds come together and enjoy each other. Suspicion kills the impulse to live and let live, and we all suffer.

This season, Mark has played the role of backup center, coming off the bench behind Mychal Thompson, who's playing his third season with us.

Mychal is one of the very few athletes from the Bahamas to have done well in America. His agility and size, six feet, ten inches, are a requisite for playing the front line in the NBA. Jerry West's trade for him from San Antonio in 1987 was a brilliant move that guaranteed us the bench strength we needed to go all the way. To get him we gave up Frank Brickowski, who had been a first-rate front-line player.

Shortly after Mychal joined us, unfortunately, it became all too evident that he was an athlete as gifted in hype as he was in basketball. He was easily and often given to exaggerated claims of his abilities in a wide range of areas off-court, claims like: I've got the prettiest feet on the team; I'm the best-read guy on the team; I've fought twelve-foot sharks when fishing; I'm going to be the prime minister of the Bahamas; and I can outbox anybody in the NBA.

By the end of his first year with us, we had the chance to effectively challenge that last statement, at least. Byron had wanted to test Mychal's boxing skills, so I bought a pair of boxing gloves and brought them with me to the season's final team meeting, the day after winning the '87 championship against Boston in L.A. I was the last to arrive in the locker room at the Forum that morning and noticed that amidst all the continuing euphoria over our victory, Mychal was unusually subdued.

I broke out the gloves, but as I did so Byron told me, "We won't be needing those, Cap." Disappointed, I looked closely at Mychal, who was holding his lip gingerly and not speaking to anyone. It turned out that they had already tried some bare-knuckle sparring, which had ended rather quickly when Byron busted Mychal's lip.

"He scratched me with his nails," Mychal said.

We all knew, of course, that Byron has no nails to speak of.

Friday, March 10

The last time I was in North Carolina was to go to James Worthy's wedding in Winston-Salem. That was in 1984, his second year on the team. Our mutual roots in North Carolina have added to the closeness that James and I feel—my mother is from Anson County, not far from where James was born. James is also a jazz fan, and he has turned me on to new sounds and shared opinions with me on the music scene. So I was determined to go to his wedding—I wanted to be with him when he walked the last mile. James and Angela were college sweethearts when he played for North Carolina and she was a Tar Heel cheerleader. It's a classic tale of love and romance.

James's father came to the hotel yesterday afternoon to pick us up and take us to dinner at his house, which is in Gastonia, about thirty miles away. James's parents are devoted fans who catch every game their son plays on a satellite dish. We had turkey and greens with giblet gravy and mashed potatoes and corn. It was really good, and we all had a terrific time. James is a major hero in Gastonia. The local paper ran four articles on him on the front page today, including a huge picture of James's mother standing at the door inviting us in for dinner.

James has grown into being one of the best in the league at the position of "small" forward. I use quotes because anyone who is six feet nine is not really small. Bill Russell was six-ten when he played center, and he dominated the game; that's one indication of how far the sport has evolved. When James came to the team, Jamaal Wilkes was starting and doing a great job at that position. But James just overtook him and made it very hard for someone Silk's size (six-six, 190 pounds) to play the front line. The future of the small forward position belongs to guys like James and Charles Barkley. Players like Silk and Julius Erving had to try to play at off-guard. Some made it, some didn't.

As far as skills go, James has all he needs to be a perfect small forward: great speed up and down the court, great hands, and the instinct to pursue his goal through all obstacles. And he's willing to work with the team; he doesn't get into any of this "Give it to me" nonsense. His contribution to the Lakers has been awesome, and he has been a steady, reliable performer, especially at money time. His games in the play-offs, his league record of 60 percent from the floor during the second season, are testimony to that.

James is a quiet player—he just gets the job done. You hardly ever see the effort, just the results. He comes from a tight-knit, religious family, and when he finishes playing I think he might go home to North Carolina.

Among the Lakers, James is known as "Clever." He and our former teammate Mike McGee were going to the same barber and when he cut James's hair the barber said he looked real clever. So Mike started calling him that and it stuck, partly because it also describes the way he plays. He has so much physical ability, and then he fools you at the end. He'll fake the lay-up so he can get you up in the air and then either go under you or step away and shoot the jumper. He has a very clever game.

My most enduring memory of James will be of the way he finishes a fast break. He reminds me of a large bird, like an eagle or a big seabird, trying to get it together to take off. The steps are almost awkward, gawky, as he gets up to speed and then the last stretch turns into a soaring glide that makes your mouth fall open as he floats in for a lay-up, a graceful soar that leaves the defense earthbound, staring helplessly as the ball is dropped into the hoop. That play is always going to be part of the game and James will always be remembered for his unique style of delivery. Thank you, James.

Tonight was both my first and last night playing in Charlotte. We won easily, 123–90, and I liked what I saw. People here are just crazy about basketball—they'll give you a standing ovation if you dive on the floor for a loose ball. That's why in a city with a population of only 338,000, they can sell out the league's largest arena, the new 23,000-plus-seat Charlotte Coliseum, almost every night. They make southern hospitality seem like a very real thing.

Friday, March 17

The Forum at last. We have nothing but one-game road trips for the five weeks left in the season. Nobody in our conference has been through what we've been through in terms of travel, and now those dues that we paid early in the season are finally going to pay off.

We came home feeling strong. The road-trip record was 4-1, after besting Golden State 126–115 on Sunday. Riley told us we should get into our play-off–drive mode. He said our new goal should be the best record in the league so we can get the home-court advantage. Now that we've gotten a little momentum, we can see that as a good possibility.

We had a close call with Dallas tonight, winning 106–103. The team looked decimated to me. James Donaldson ruptured a tendon in his knee a week ago and is lost to the Mavericks for the rest of the season. But this game was nothing compared to the one against Houston on Monday. I had one of my best nights of the year, tying a season high with twenty-one points and setting one with thirteen rebounds, but as a team we shot only 38.9 percent from the floor and once were down by as much as fourteen points. But, with the Forum crowd standing and screaming in encouragement, we scored eight straight points late in the game and tied it 96–96 with forty-nine seconds left. Then, with but a single second left on the clock, A.C. Green hit a free throw that won it for us. It was a great, emotional win for us, one we got on sheer determination.

I read today that Norm Nixon has retired. He's had a rough road since the Lakers traded him to the Clippers in 1983. When he left, Bob McAdoo just flat out said to him, "You'll never be heard of again," and that's about what happened. Norm himself told me he had some difficulty in his new situation because he'd gotten so used to playing with the Lakers. When double-teamed, I would always hit him with a really good pass that came up into his hands right where he could shoot the ball. Then he started playing with Benoit Benjamin and Terry Cummings and it didn't work. He'd have to run the ball down. By the time he was in a position to shoot it, somebody would be in his face. His game really suffered.

Norman was a very talented athlete who had startling quickness, a deadly jump shot, and great ball-handling ability, right- or left-handed.

We were tough to beat when we had Norman because if our opponents tried to stop Magic in the backcourt, Norman had all the skills to run the fast break in Magic's place, with Silk in the wings. With that combination in the early eighties, we were a great running team. Nobody could keep up with us. A few weeks ago, when I first heard that Norman was thinking of leaving the game, I gave him a call and told him, "Whatever you do, you've had a great career."

Tuesday, March 21

Suddenly, we've lost two home games in a row, only the second time that's happened this season. So much for our chances of having the league's best record. Tonight the loss was 104–103 to the Chicago Bulls, with Michael Jordan getting the game-winning free throws with forty-eight seconds left and tying his career mark with sixteen assists. When you see him jump in the air and do all the stuff he does, it is awesome. And he's shown a lot of class off the court as well. All the attention he gets around the league could really go to his head and distort his life, but he's done a very good job of handling it so far.

The Atlanta loss on Sunday was in some ways harder to take, because Hawks guard Doc Rivers hit a jump shot from the top of the key at the buzzer to beat us 113–111. I was disappointed, but I knew we hadn't played well enough to win it. We shot the ball poorly from the free-throw line and gave them twenty-two lay-ups, and you're not going to win when you play like that. I was disgusted with my own play because of turnovers and stuff. For some reason I just wasn't there.

Before these last two games, I think the team's attitude was We're not playing especially well, but we're so good that we can still win. We may be slumping a bit, but we've got the schedule in our favor now and we're really going to make a run at having the best record in the league. After all, there's only a month left, and we're leading the conference.

Then, all of a sudden, we lost two in a row and everybody just said, "Whoa." We realized—again—that it's a fact of life in the NBA that to win you can't just be good, you have to play better than the other guys. Years ago, there was more disparity in the league—you didn't always have to be as much on top of your game. If you were good, you could get by with less than your best effort and beat a lot of clubs. Now everybody has the potential, and everybody is gunning for us all the time. If we're not playing well, then we're going to lose games. We're at the point where we need to play consistently. We haven't done that this season. There are tough teams out there—Phoenix is right behind us, and there is Portland and Seattle to worry about. Still, I remain confident that we have a realistic chance to make it to the finals.

Friday, March 24

For maybe the millionth time, Wilt Chamberlain got on my case today. Doug Krikorian did a column on Wilt's thoughts, which consisted mainly of putting me down. Krikorian asked him about my final season and Chamberlain replied, "When you can't say something nice about somebody, then you shouldn't say anything." But then he proceeded to belittle my abilities and my longevity. Wilt can't get any publicity for what he's doing, so he's trying to get publicity for what I'm *not* doing. The whole thing's just a childish, egotistical play for attention, and the media guys always give him a stroke because it will sell some papers for them.

Wilt and I go way back. When I was in high school, there were only two men I could be like, Wilt or Bill Russell. I kept a scrapbook of photos of both of them in action. Wilt lived in New York then, and I sought out his company. I'd run down the block just to say hello. But as I grew older, I strongly disagreed with some of the positions he took, like supporting Richard Nixon for president and denigrating black women in his autobiography. But I've never really disliked Wilt, and I've always respected him professionally for what he achieved. He was one of the best centers to have ever played the game. I've decided to take this opportunity to respond to all the aspersions he's cast on me over the years.

An Open Letter to Wilt Chumperlame

It's been several years now, Wilt, that you have been criticizing my career with your friends in the press. I know you're hard up for media attention, so I'm not really surprised when your critical quotes surface in the paper. Since this pattern of behavior does not seem to have any end in sight, I feel that I might as well have my say about the situation.

I now have quite a bit more time to deal with your childish outbursts, so what the heck.

It would seem that someone who achieved as much as you did would be satisfied with his career. After all, some of the things you did in your time were quite admirable and have given us an enduring set of records for the books. You were an exceptional athlete who helped redefine the role of center. Under the basket you were so dominant they had to widen the lane by four feet to deal with you, and no individual has yet broken your 100-point record for a single game. You made the 1967 Philadelphia 76ers, at 68-13, and the 1972 Lakers, at 69-13 with a 33-game winning streak, probably the most overwhelming single-season winners the league has ever known. So why all the jealousy and envy? And why direct them at me?

In trying to figure this out, I started to look for what you would be jealous of, and that's when the picture started to become clear. Many remember how frustrated you were when your team couldn't win the NCAA tournament. Unfavorable comparisons were made between you and Bill Russell, who led the University of San Francisco to consecutive titles. Why, people asked, couldn't Wilt lead his team to the top? Your talent and abilities were so great that everyone assumed the NCAA was all yours. But after a terrific triple-overtime game, Kansas lost. You complained about the officiating, your teammates, and other things, and then quit, leaving college early to tour with the Globetrotters and make your fortune. That seemed to set a pattern for you. After any tough test in which you didn't do well, you blamed those around you and quit. People who knew sports would wonder why someone with your talents could not provide the leadership to get to the top. An answer was never forthcoming.

Your professional career was marked by the same kind of pattern. Bill Russell and the Boston Celtics gave you a yearly lesson in real competitive competence and teamwork. All you could say was that your teammates stunk and that you had done all you could, and besides, the refs never gave you a break. Poor Wilt. You got all these rebounds and scored all these points and you were stuck with worthless teammates. What a shame! You had definitely outclassed the other centers in the league. But it doesn't surprise many people, considering that none of them were seven feet tall or agile enough to give you much competition—a twelve-foot three-second lane was also a big help to you while you were establishing your scoring records. You did very well against that type of competition unless you went against the Celts, which usually ended in frustration and loss.

In 1967, your team finally broke through, and in a real big way. That 76er team established records that are still standing today. But the following year, things got tough. The Sixers lost and, predictable as ever, you quit. You came out to L.A. and got with a dream team. No lack of talent there, with Jerry West and Elgin Baylor. The only lack that team had was leadership at the center position. Bill and the Celts took one from you in '69 and the Knicks followed suit in '70. People are still trying to figure out where you disappeared to in that series. All that was necessary for a Laker victory was one win against a team whose injured starting center, Willis Reed, could not move. But Willis could still come out to compete and inspire his teammates. Yes, the Knicks won with Dave Stallworth, six-seven and 200 pounds, and Nate Bowman, six-ten and 215, playing most of the game at center. In that game you were a nonentity.

The same teams played for the world championship in 1973, and that time the Knicks didn't have any *center! Jerry Lucas, six-eight and 230, played high-post center that year. He was always considered a forward but he had enough guts and smarts to outplay you consistently. Yes, Wilt, we know you got umpteen rebounds per game, but no one really cares about those stats. The only significant stat is the New York Knicks' world championship. I guess that was the final straw for you because, true to form, you quit after that season and haven't been seen on the court since.*

Of course, you come out every so often to take a cheap shot at me, and in those statements one can find the roots of your animosity. Somewhere, you must think that I personally was trying to embarrass you. This was never the case. I only took advantage of your shortcomings, which you still are probably not aware of. When you were entertaining pipe dreams about fighting Muhammad Ali, he set the record straight on your attributes, saying to me, "Wilt can't talk, he's ugly, and he can't move!" Which says it all. So when I dropped those fifty points on you at the Forum, or held you scoreless at the Forum, it was not a personal attack. I was just taking advantage of your weak defensive skills to try to help my team win. By not admitting to any faults, it has been impossible for you to see how your play was missing necessary ingredients. You've criticized people like George Mikan and Danny Manning in truly ridiculous ways, saying that your stats are so great compared to theirs. One thing they can point to is their leadership at crucial times. They are winners. George Mikan is the man who had the pride and determination to show that big men could be great athletes. All of us big men should thank him for that. I know I do. But I digress.

During the sixth game of the world championship series in 1988, you

*stated, "Kareem should have retired five years ago." I can now see why
you said that. If I had quit at the time you suggested, it would have been
right after a disappointing loss to the 76ers. And it would have been
typical of one of your retreats. But I decided that I had more to give, the
Lakers had more championships to win, and I had no intention of
quitting, even after another disappointing loss to the Celtics in '84. I
believed in myself and in the Lakers and stuck with it. From that point,
we went on to win three out of four world championships between '85
and '88. I was able to be the MVP in the '85 world championship and
to give the Lakers solid play in the center for the '87 and '88 back-to-
back titles. This is what you wanted me to miss, Wilt. And it's easy to
see why. The two teams you played on that won world championships,
in '67 and '72, never repeated. They never showed the consistency that
the Lakers of the eighties have shown. And you didn't want me to be
part of that.*

*Given your jealousy, I can understand that. It's too bad you didn't stay
for the end of the game in '88, though. You would have been able to
see me win the game at the free-throw line with a few seconds left. On
the other hand, that probably would have reminded you of your own
ineptness at the free-throw line.*

*It's probably better you left. You've never seemed to understand that
in a team sport what the team accomplishes means more than what any
individual does. The Lakers asked me to stay because they knew I could
contribute to more championships. It's like the B-52 bomber in the
strategic air defense of this country. Yes, it's an aging plane that could
not ever compare performance stats with the B-1A, but it does a great
job as part of the team that defends the U.S. of A., and it does its job
very well.*

*So, now that I have left, one thing will be part of my legacy: People
will remember that I worked with my teammates and helped us win. You
will be remembered as a whining crybaby and a quitter, stats and all.*

*Yours truly,
Kareem Abdul-Jabbar*

Tuesday, March 28

We cannot shake Phoenix, no matter what we do. Sunday night at the
Forum I thought we'd put them behind us. Magic hit a fifteen-foot

jump shot at the buzzer to beat the Suns 118–116 and leave them four games out. Still, it's nerve-racking to have to wait to the buzzer to put one away.

Tonight, in Phoenix, the Suns got their revenge. They blew us out, 127–104, meaning they won all three home games with us this season. They are once again three games out, and the division race is the closest it's been in seven years. No Western Conference team has yet been able to beat Phoenix at Phoenix, but that was no consolation to Riley. He raged against us, talked about competitiveness and pride and million-dollar salaries.

Tuesday, April 4

At last, it's April. Three weeks left. The games all seem bigger now because it's near the end. We're no longer trying to catch Detroit for the league's best record; winning in the West is all we are focused on now. We've won three out of five world championships without the home-court advantage, and we can do it again if we're sharp.

Physically, I'm feeling all right. My knees hurt after games, but that's a sign that I'm playing hard. Mentally, it feels like the end of my senior year in high school, like "Jeez, why do we still have to go to class?" I've definitely got senioritis.

An unexpected call came in today from Sandy Saemann and Don Wasley of L.A. Gear; I started working with them last season. They told me a Houston film festival had given us an award for a commercial we'd done together in the fall, the one with me and the kid in the locker room. I was pleased because that kind of success outside the world of basketball is where I want to head.

Tonight was our fiftieth victory, the tenth year in a row we've achieved that milestone. We beat Seattle 115–97, largely courtesy of A.C. Green. He scored a career-high thirty-three points and collected ten rebounds for good measure, which is not surprising since he's led the team in that category for the past two seasons.

A.C. has made a name for himself as a hard and determined worker whose play has improved every year since he's been here. His success displaced another hardworking player, Kurt Rambis, who had been a

Laker for seven years. Last season, A.C. was the only Laker to have appeared in all eighty-two games and over the last three years he's missed only three games. Not only does he rebound relentlessly and effectively, but he has the one great quality that helps the Lakers win consistently—speed up and down the court. However, A.C. was pretty tentative offensively his first year and missed passes, the kind of short, quick ones that require soft hands and quick reactions to catch. He'd fumble the ball out of bounds, bounce it off his foot. That's when we began calling him Hands of Stone, like Roberto Durán.

At his first training camp with us, A.C. was subjected to the hazing that all rookies must endure. He was told to sing his school song, fight song, rap song, any song at all, and all he could think up was a gospel tune. This struck everybody as rather too serious and not in the spirit of the moment, and, more or less, caused us to view A.C. as a very straight-laced type who probably felt the Lakers lived their lives fast and loose, with questionable moral standards. Accordingly, as much promise as he showed on the court, we didn't think he would be much fun to be around.

Gradually we realized that A.C. is a highly moral and religious person who takes the guidelines of his religion seriously and tries to live by them. At one point, I tried to talk to him about his attitudes and tried to coax him into being a little more tolerant of some of the guys who didn't have the benefit of his kind of home life and religious training. It didn't happen right away, but imperceptibly, he grew closer to us as people. We learned to tolerate him and share with him, and he with us. Once he lightened up a little bit, everything was fine.

What has surprised us most over the years is that A.C. is a world-class practical joker. He started a couple of "games" the Lakers play, including "the thumb game," where you use your fingers to pluck another player's thumb and cause as much pain as possible. Another one of A.C.'s ploys is "the lip game," which involves finding a player who is unaware that his mouth is open and rubbing your palm on his exposed lower lip. A.C. has some others, but these were the most odious. We got used to them all, and to his hair style (greased to the bone), and he has become family to us all to the point where we call him Junior, his household name. Also, although he never quite shook his "Hands of Stone" handle, his game on the court improved to the point where he was a key in our back-to-back success. It has been a pleasure working with you, Junior.

Thursday, April 6

The weather has been extreme. It was 106 degrees in Los Angeles today, the hottest April day on record. Over the last two days, Los Angeles has been the hottest city in the world, hotter than Cairo or New Delhi, hotter in spots than the Sahara or the Australian outback. I can feel the summer almost here, but it's a different feeling this time around. This summer can go on for a long time, can last as long as I want it to last.

Ramadan begins tomorrow, and I hope to read as much of the Koran as I can in the next month. Ramadan is the holy month of Islam, a special time when we reflect upon the whole faith. It starts and ends with the crescent moon, and with Venus closest to the crescent at the end of thirty days. Islam's calendar is lunar, so the month of Ramadan shifts eleven days every lunar year; it doesn't always fall in spring as it is now, or as it did last year.

Ramadan is significant because it was during this time of year that the Koran, the sacred book of Islam, was first revealed to Muhammad. The book has been divided into thirty parts called *jeuses,* so one can read a section every day until the end of the month, which signifies the completion of Allah's message to humankind.

Last spring, I was able to read the entire Koran this way, even though Ramadan overlapped with the play-offs, as it will again this year. I thought the daily reading was going to be difficult, maybe even distracting, but it turned out to be of great help to me in preparing my mind for play-off competition. I particularly like the passages called "The Poets," "The Moon," "The Ants," "The Troops," and "The Clans." And I hope to get to them all in the coming weeks.

Saturday, April 8

Tonight's farewell at Oakland was definitely one of the more moving, because the man in charge was Nate Thurmond. I've known Nate, who now works in community relations for the Warriors, since I was fifteen.

He and Al Attles, who was also at the ceremony, always had meaningful things to talk to me about when they were pros and I was in high school. They told me positive things to do and focus on. Nate always was, and still is, a dapper dresser, a vision of male elegance, and I like to think that I acquired something of my sense of style from him.

When I entered the league, I considered Nate my toughest competitor, especially when you realize he always played within the rules, that he did not beat me to death and consider it good defense the way so many other guys did. He played for the Warriors for eleven years, and was selected to the All-Star team for six of those. Agile and aggressive, he was a great jumper, and though he never weighed much more than 220 pounds, he could make all the plays defensively. So, tonight, to have him call me the greatest big man to ever step on the basketball floor meant a great deal. And to have a friend, somebody you really know and have known for a long time, come out there and say stuff like that—that's really meaningful.

The game was a letdown. We lost 122–116.

Wednesday, April 12

The most important thing for the Lakers now is concentration. We had an important win tonight against San Antonio, 107–100. Just a few more victories and Phoenix won't be able to catch us. The Spurs have a very talented team and are especially tough at home. Tonight's game was like war. That's the whole thing about being the world champs and trying to repeat. Everybody wants to beat you, especially now. A win against the champs can make the season for a team. They can say, Well, we beat the Lakers and we're going to get it together for next year.

Riley played the bench a lot tonight, but not Orlando. Orlando has been struggling with his game for most of the season. Tonight was the fourth time in the last five games that he wasn't played. We know he's down; he's told us that he is. But I'm confident he'll work his way through this.

Play-offs loom. I'm going to start working out with the six-pound medicine ball when we get back to L.A. I use it to strengthen my hands and arms in the motion of my shot, taking it and throwing it up on the backboard and playing with it. It's good because it's specific to what I have to do, and it's time to be at my best.

Sunday, April 16

My thoughts are on Jackie Robinson today, my birthday. I was born in Harlem the day after Jackie's first major league game across the river in Brooklyn's Ebbets Field. It was forty-two years ago that I was born and that Jackie Robinson, in 1947, at age twenty-eight, crossed baseball's color line. I have always considered it a gift that I slipped into the world just at that moment.

All the courage and competitiveness of Jackie Robinson affects me to this day. If I patterned my life after anyone, it was him, not because he was the first black baseball player in the majors but because he was a hero. Though he always appeared quiet and contained, inside he was fiercely concentrated and competitive; you could feel it coming off of him. He never gave in to outward displays of passion or anger, and there was plenty of reason for both. He went through hell in his rookie year as a Dodger. It was said that nothing earlier had matched such racial viciousness. Even among his teammates, there were players who wanted him and players who definitely didn't. My father says he took their guff, their opponents' guff, and the public's guff, and he never complained, just kept moving uphill. He was out there like a sore thumb, nowhere to hide. Racial remarks were hurled from the stands. There were death threats and hate mail. Duke Snider, who started with the Dodgers the same day as Jack, said in Maury Allen's *Jackie Robinson: A Life Remembered,* "The pressure on Jackie was enormous, overwhelming, unbearable at times. I don't know how he held up." The Duke, at age twenty, was one of the players who stood by him.

When I first became aware of Jackie as a kid, I didn't know anything about all this. I didn't even know that he was the first black in the majors or, for that matter, realize that everyone else on the Dodger team was white. All I knew was that Jack was out there, it was Jack against the world, and he was going to win. He took no prisoners. Pitchers like Sal Maglie would throw at him, and he would then bunt down the first-base line and try to spike the guy as he fielded the ball. Jack was serious. And the competitive intensity he had—that I understood. I just didn't understand, in the beginning, why it was the way it was.

In Jackie's rookie season, the Brooklyn Dodgers won their first pennant in six years, and they went on to win five more as well as their one World Series championship with him before he retired in 1956. He was an incredible athlete, savvy, cunning, daring. Someone once said that Jackie ran the bases like a teenager with a switchblade, and he did. The way he was always stealing bases, cat-quick, menacing, put the whole game into turmoil. If they walked him, it was like a triple because he would steal second and third. He would get the pitcher crazy, and everybody else. What got to me later was reading remarks by some of Jack's former teammates, like pitcher Don Drysdale, one of the Dodger greats, who was a rookie when Jack was at the end of his career. Jackie was constantly on the young Drysdale about always going at it until the rookie wanted to kill somebody.

Don said, "Jackie would offer little tidbits of advice from the bench or come up to me on the mound and say, 'Throw hard, don't let up, challenge the batters.' He instilled a lot of competitive fire in my soul."

Don Newcombe, who played with Jackie for seven years, said, "I had a tendency to lose my concentration. Jack would come to the mound and get all over me. Call me every name you could think of. I'd get pretty mad at him and take it out on the hitters. I owe everything I have, everything I have made in my life through baseball, to Jackie Robinson."

I remember my mother would come alive when Jackie Robinson came to bat. She used to resent the fact that I liked Willie Mays, who came into the league four years after Jackie. I thought Willie was superhuman, even though he played for the Giants. But you couldn't get too excited about Willie around my mother. She would look at you and say something like "Why is his cap always falling off?" And it didn't mean anything if I suggested, "Because he's running so fast."

Feelings for Jackie Robinson ran deep. Everybody in Harlem loved him. It was a very personal thing, like it had been with Joe Louis, who had already been the heavyweight champion of the world for ten years when Jackie came along. Jackie Robinson and Joe Louis were champs. They had class and they were beating the white folks at their own game. They could compete within the rules laid down. It made all black people feel they could compete. It gave them a whole different idea about their own self-worth. It was all about black hope and pride.

Joe Louis fought his last title fight just a few years after I was born, so I never saw him box. But I knew about him. Boxing and baseball got a lot of attention in my home and, crazy about Joe Louis, my father did a little boxing himself in high school, then afterward in upstate New York while in the Civilian Conservation Corps, and later in the army. He had some good teachers, including one of Ray Robinson's trainers. I remember Sugar Ray used to drive through our neighborhood on his way to his mother's house across the bridge in the Bronx. That was in the 1950s, when he was still thrilling fight fans around the world. Guys would be out on the sidewalk yelling, "Here he comes." Most times it was "There he goes." Sugar Ray Robinson, Hank Armstrong, Kid Chocolate, and Joe Louis were familiar names when I was growing up.

On a warm June night in West Virginia, Jerry West remembers listening on the radio to Joe Louis's second title bout with Billy Conn in New York. Jerry would have been about eight years old then, living in Chelyan, West Virginia, a tiny town with no post office that was tucked in a valley between mountains. The radio reception was sporadic at best. Conn was leading on points when the radio went out, and Jerry fell asleep, not learning until morning that Joe had retained his title, knocking out Conn in the eighth round. Jerry told me that Joe Louis and Sugar Ray Robinson were his heroes then—a white kid living in the hills of Appalachia, a future Hall of Famer in the game of basketball, having his dreams and ambitions kindled by two black fighters from up North. The qualities of these men transcended race and, preceding Sugar Ray, Joe Louis was really the first black athlete in any sport to cross racial lines into the hearts of black and white alike.

Jack Johnson had come twenty-five years before Joe Louis, but Johnson's defiant style outside the ring had made him a controversial figure, a hero desperately needed but tarnished. In 1908, Jack Johnson had become the first black heavyweight champion of the world. This was the history-making event that incited the cry that went out for "the great white hope," the white boxer who could defeat him. It was a profound moment for blacks everywhere. But if Jack Johnson provoked white reaction by his excellence inside the ring, the racial antagonism was exacerbated by his practice of flaunting his numerous associations with white women. After a typical night of beating a white guy in the ring, Jack Johnson would be seen later that same evening driving around downtown in a flashy convertible with three white hookers and his bass fiddle, all loud and crazy. They were like night and day, he and Joe Louis. Joe Louis had white women in his life, but he kept it private. As far as his behavior away from the ring was concerned, Joe Louis wasn't a threat to white folks. He was a threat *in* the ring, but by the time he came along people could tolerate that.

Jackie Robinson worshiped Joe Louis and believed that, because of Joe in boxing, his own way in baseball had been made easier. By the end of Jackie's second season in the majors, he had become an athlete of equal standing to Joe Louis. Later, Martin Luther King would pay Jackie the compliment that Jackie had paid Joe Louis, saying that no one would ever know how easy it was for him because of Jackie Robinson.

All of this about Jackie got filled in over the years. What I got from him directly, the most important legacy for me personally, I just absorbed through watching him. He never spoke to me about his type of competitive play, and nobody could have told me about it or described it to me. I just took in Jackie Robinson through observation. To always be doing what he could do to win—that's what I got from Jackie Robinson. It wasn't a conscious thing; he taught me by his example.

My last memory of seeing Jackie Robinson play was in the summer of 1956, when I was nine. My father had taken me to a game at Ebbets Field. During some unremembered inning in the game, I was distracted or daydreaming, and suddenly the bleachers erupted; Jackie was stealing second base. My eyes were on him in microseconds, but I was able to catch only the last part of the slide. It made me realize I had to pay more attention in the ballpark. I have that lasting image, though, of Jackie Robinson stealing second base in the middle of the afternoon in a cloud of dust.

Friday, April 21

Finally, tonight, on the next-to-last game of the season, we clinched the division title with a 121–114 win against Portland. It was our eighth consecutive Pacific Division title. The Blazers needed a victory for a play-off berth as well, so they played really tough, and Clyde Drexler got forty-three points, the most our defense has given up to a single player all year. Magic was busy too: His ten assists made him only the second player in the NBA to reach eight thousand in his career. The other, of course, was Oscar.

Only a week ago we lost to the Clippers 119–107. That defeat was like a wake-up call for the team. Since coming back from that last big road trip in March, we'd rarely won convincingly and we hadn't put together any kind of winning streak. That loss—to a weak team—made us realize that all the superfluous parts of the season were really over. I've said it before: We haven't played consistently this season, and we need to. This week we've found our rhythm. After the Clipper game, we beat Miami, Denver, Sacramento, and now Portland. Four in a row.

Because we've been pushed so hard by Phoenix, we felt we had accomplished something in taking the title. So the guys went out to celebrate, and they saw Jeff Lamp, Jazzy Jeff, entertaining a young lady. They saw him through a window sitting in a restaurant, with candlelight and wine and a guy playing the violin. It was quite a show, they said.

Jazzy's having a hard time with this one. Because Jazzy is real quiet, never gets apprehended, doesn't like having his business known, so there aren't that many openings. Now, every time the subject of ladies comes up, everybody will have something to say. To be in the middle of it, to have four or five teammates yelling "Jazzy" through the window, that's like the worst you can get. And that's what happened.

Sunday, April 23

The last day, the last regular-season game of my career, and the last ceremony. I left the house around 10 A.M. One of my neighbors in the canyon, Joan Knickmeyer, had purple-and-gold banners and ribbons flying from her fence, as usual. When things were rough for me early in the season, she would include a message as well, something like "That's it, Cap!"

The sellout crowd at the Forum arrived early. Lou Adler and Jack Nicholson were both there, courtside. Jack was really decked out in a black top hat and tails, black shoes, purple socks, a faded yellow T-shirt with a sketch of me silk-screened on in purple, and with a purple satin hanky in his pocket, a Laker ticket stuck into his hatband, and a black bow tie around his neck.

Amir was on hand early too. He had decided he wanted to sing the national anthem, and as I waited for the ceremony to start, the only performance anxiety I had was for him. It's a tough song for anyone—it really tests your range—and I wondered if he had the chops to pull it off. After all, he is only eight years old. But nobody put him up to it. In fact, he kind of demanded that he be allowed to do it after he learned that my other son, Kareem, had been asked and said, "No way!" Amir's class has been practicing the anthem at school this year so he was up on it and thought he could do it. He did a dry run at an assembly on Friday, and when it didn't seem to bother him to sing in front of everybody, the teacher said, "Go for it."

The ceremony started at about 11:45. First my parents, Cora and Al, were introduced, then my four kids. Then Chick Hearn, who was emcee, said, "Now, take your gloves off. Let's hear it. Here is Kareem Abdul-Jabbar!" The fans applauded and cheered for three long minutes with shouts of "Kareem, Kareem, Kareem." Chick kept trying to interrupt: "Kareem thanks you, his parents thank you, his children thank you." Finally, in desperation, he said, "Remember, everybody, that we've got a play-off game Thursday."

At last, Amir got to sing the anthem. He did a great job, but I was so nervous for him I forgot that I was supposed to be standing, and stayed in this giant rocking chair on the court that they had put me in. It was easily the most emotional of the anthems sung this year.

Hearn read a congratulatory telegram from President Bush. Then he brought out Riley, who introduced a musical tribute to me that all my teammates sang as they rocked me in my chair. I tried to keep from feeling silly. There was tremendous goodwill, but I couldn't help wondering if the guys weren't going to come at me with a pie in the face. But what they were really doing was hiding from me my present from the team, a brand-new white Rolls-Royce. Magic gave me the keys and said, "Since you've been carrying *us* on your back for all these years, we decided to get you something that would carry *you*."

I was stunned. The car, they told me later, cost about $175,000. Some of the guys put up more than $10,000 apiece. It's very radical for the players to come up with that kind of gift. I don't believe it has ever happened before. I was hoping for something good, but they really beat the band. I hugged everybody. Magic said that the car was about appreciating the success they've been able to be a part of because of what I've given the team. "I know that I always wanted to be like Kareem Abdul-Jabbar," he said. "You set the standard for basketball by your example . . . but I think more than that you've taught us a lot away from the game . . . and from those guys sitting over there and for myself we'd just like to say thank you. . . . So before I start crying, I've got to turn this over because, unfortunately, we still have a game to play."

There was no way I could really thank them. I wish I could put the Rolls on my mantelpiece. I don't even know if I'll feel comfortable driving it. It's something I would just like to keep. It wasn't just a car. It was a gift from their hearts.

Other presents and awards followed. The city of Inglewood renamed the street next to the Forum "Kareem Court," and Jerry Buss said he was going to build a championship tennis court on my land in Hawaii. Then Hearn turned the mike over to me. It had already been a half an hour since the ceremony began, but the fans clapped on and on, vigorous, intense, thunderous, roaring on, coming in waves, applause without end, it seemed, continually renewing itself.

I started to speak. "This is going to be very tough on me," I began. "If I forget anybody I ask for your forgiveness. I have to give praise and thanks to Allah the Almighty because without him and his presence I wouldn't be here at all. Second, I want to thank these folks right here, my mom and my dad. When your dad is a cop and your mom believes in what's right, they set exacting standards for you, and I've tried to live up to them. They did it with a lot of love and a lot of patience. Thank you, Mom. Thank you, Dad.

"I want to thank these four little people over here because my relationship with them is not what it could have been because I had to come out here on this court. They've never responded with anything other than love and appreciation. And I love you, guys, and it's wonderful to have you here.

"As you go through the path of life, you meet people, people who have an influence on you, people who turn you the right way at the right time, and I've been very fortunate to know a number of people like that. I'm thinking about one of my teachers in grade school, Sister Hannah—she was beautiful; my grade school coach, Farrell Hopkins; my high school coach, Jack Donahue; and then I came out to a place called Los Angeles and hooked up with a man called John Wooden. He taught me a whole lot about becoming a man, which had nothing to do with basketball. It had to do with living your life as an intelligent human being, which was something very important to him, something he tried to impart to us. . . . Thank you, Coach Wooden. Finally, I got to come back out here to play in this building, and that has been a wonderful experience because I got an opportunity to share that with you people. It's been a long time. It's been fourteen years now. Of course, at first, I didn't appreciate how much you people were behind us. There were a few ups and downs . . . but you guys have grown with the game, you've learned about it. They used to say funny things about you, about how you leave early and don't stay through the game. Well, you don't leave early. You stay through the game and enjoy it. We've grown together and learned to appreciate each other and appreciate this great game that we play. And I just want to say thank you, fans. You've been wonderful."

Then I addressed the coaches. "Thank you," I said, "for your leadership and the fact that you cared about us, and the fact that you've tried to make this as human as possible. We try to keep up an inhuman schedule in the NBA. You guys have tried to make it as good as you can."

Finally, I turned to the players. "The last people I want to thank are the guys that I work with. It's been quite some time now. Mike Cooper and I go back the furthest. He's been here eleven years. He's going to be the old-timer next year. This could be a very difficult life if it were not for the people you work with, these gentlemen over here. You guys and the other teammates I've played with in the NBA—that's the main reason I've stayed. I certainly could not have had a professional life if I did not work with people of your caliber who care and who are my friends and not just out here on the floor."

As I started to thank the guys upstairs, "the guys named Jerry," my voice went hoarse. "I've run out of words," I said. "I'm losing my voice. I want to say I love you all."

Though it seemed anticlimactic, we had a game to play against the Seattle SuperSonics, who had a seven-game winning streak coming in. When the Lakers came out on the court, our guys were all wearing goggles and the Laker girls put on white T-shirts with "33" on the back and "We'll miss you, Kareem" on the front. And despite all that, we won the game 121–117, our fifth straight. My last points came on a dunk off a Magic pass with 2:14 left to play. So when I walked off the floor for the last time, with 1:42 left, it was with 38,387 career points.

One more surprise. While I was doing the postgame interviews, the team took a pair of scissors and shredded my clothes, and had pictures taken to show me exactly how they did it. I had to go home in my sweats. But if somebody gives you a Rolls-Royce, I guess they can tear your clothes up if they want to.

It was, all in all, a great day.

IV

Second Season: The Home Stretch

Unwinding on the hill behind my house, the sun still up and warm, a sea fog just beginning to roll over the hills from the west, I'm listening to Joe Henderson and watching the birds in the canyon and thinking about the days ahead. The partridges are fat and sassy and look like serious dinner for the hawks, and the hummingbirds, who live so fast they have to go comatose at night, have been having their aerial courtships, the males making their rapid vertical dives to the females. All of the spring trees have flowered in the canyon, so there's a perfume in the air, and the big sycamores have their leaves again.

I'm feeling restored, light, as though a weight has been lifted off. The regular season is completed now. The retirement activities are over. And all the extraneous elements have been removed. Life has been pared down to the essentials, and all I've got to do is play basketball. For myself and for the team, the play-offs have been just over the horizon for the last month, and, although we didn't say it then, even to ourselves, we couldn't wait for the regular season to end and the postseason to begin. In spite of the ups and downs, we finished out the season strong, winning all of our last five games and taking the best record in the Western Conference for the eighth straight time. And with all the beating we took on the road in the winter, we are the only team besides Detroit to have ended the season with a winning road record. We are going into the play-offs healthy and in good shape.

Back in training camp, we talked about what a wonderful thing it would be to win three in a row and to send me out with a world championship. It sounded like a nice bookend for the eighties. A lot of work still lay ahead of us at that point, but now we're at the end of that road, and the conclusion of the story is about to be written. The decisive moments are here.

We anticipate a tough series of rounds—we expect it to be as difficult to get out of the West this year as it was last—but I believe we have the potential to go all the way again. We have all the ingredients: We have the talent, we have the experience, and we know what sacrifices have to be made to win a world title. You can't have any letdowns, you can't forget your game plan, and you have to perform at a very high level. You have to be a perfectionist about your own play, and that's one of the strengths of a serious veteran team. In the postseason there's no money on the table to speak of; at that point, you're playing for pride. As long as we keep that feeling within ourselves now, we'll be tough to beat. We want to finish off the decade properly.

In some ways, the play-offs are easier than the regular season. You don't have to travel all over the place. There is time for preparation and adjustments, and you can concentrate on your opponent, really hone in and study their tendencies. You know exactly what they're doing, and whatever shot you have to take to beat them, you have it. Sure, you're tired from a long winter, but this second season is about championships; the rest is really prologue. Now the game changes. Once you're in the play-offs, you're basically starting over. Everything the team did before only gets you this far. And what we did to get here is great, but what we're after now is history: three titles in a row.

But if we don't win three, I'll be able to accept it. I've never been obsessed with a championship and I've never started a season or a play-off series with exaggerated expectations. Of course, this year it won't be like, "Hey, we'll win it next year." That's not part of the equation anymore. This is the last time the eighties Lakers will be together as a team.

I've played 222 play-off games, more than two and a half seasons' worth. Now I'm at the end of a long road, a twenty-year road, and I'm going to take my last walk on the play-off stage.

The team is prepared mentally for what has to be done—we know more about play-offs than anyone else—plus we're going in as underdogs, which is always nice. No one really thinks we have a serious shot at a back-to-back-to-back, especially with how tough the three Western Conference rounds look to be and with Detroit having the home-court advantage if we both get to the finals. It's been a rough year all around the league, with the Celtics needing the full eighty-two games to clinch a play-off spot (Bird never was able to come back), and the Mavericks, who were one game away from the finals last year, not even making it into the first round this time.

But as I said, the regular season doesn't mean all that much now. You have to win, obviously, but of the twenty-five teams in the NBA, sixteen are *guaranteed* a play-off berth. When I started in the league, the play-offs were shorter and you had to finish first or second in your division to get into them. Now, the league has expanded the play-offs into a second season that they can promote to people who aren't particularly into basketball. The networks are paying a lot of money to put the play-offs on the air, and the NBA operates on money. They've diminished the regular season, turned it into a job, and the fans who really appreciate the game are being cheated, because, with all the travel we do, they're seldom seeing us at our best. That's a part of the game I don't like. Is the top team the one that has the best record after eighty-two games, or the one that survives the play-offs?

I've seen more changes in the game than anyone else simply because I've been around so long. There are rookies in the NBA who've watched me play since the very first time they saw pro basketball on TV. Truman was president when I was born, and these guys relate to him like Abe Lincoln. Some of my teammates—Byron and James, for instance—were in grade school when I entered the league, A.C. hadn't even started kindergarten, and there are a lot of coaches in the NBA whom I used to play against. Usually I don't feel out of place, but sometimes, when I see some of my former professional buddies who haven't played in ten or fifteen years, I really feel the gap, because they look so much older, like they were never a part of the NBA at all. Age is a matter of temperament and circumstance. You can't afford to feel old, say, when you're facing the play-offs.

Make concessions to age, and age will take over. Up to now, I have made no concessions to age. Conditioning has always been a part of my career—a grueling part, most of the time—but one that I think has been critical to my longevity. I think about that a lot now as I look back on what has kept me going.

My first encounter with a serious training program was at UCLA. Every day we were pushed to the limits. After practice, I would be too tired to read or write, so I would eat dinner, go to sleep, and then do my assignments. Thank goodness we had weekends off. Within three weeks, though, I was able to survive the whole day without a nap.

John Wooden did not believe that weight training would help a basketball player to any great degree, so he always emphasized cardio-vascular conditioning to complement our fast-break approach. And since intense lifting will cause anyone to lose his shooting touch due to the sudden increase in upper-body strength, I passed on weights at that time.

I was very fortunate to discover the importance of stretching during this period. My interest in the martial arts began while I was in grade school, and I finally got the opportunity to study aikido between my sophomore and junior years at UCLA. The stretching they do is not that advanced but it does cover the basics for your legs, emphasizing the groin and hamstrings.

On my return to UCLA that fall of my junior year, I was introduced to Bruce Lee, and that marked a new phase in my physical preparation.

He was interested in being the best, number one, and for him that meant being in top condition and having the most thorough approach to being an efficient and effective fighter. The stretches he used were more in line with current ideas about stretching, namely no quick, repetitive stretches. Every stretch was static and held for a longer count. Bruce also pushed me to try weight lifting, but because of John Wooden's feelings on that subject, I didn't try to add that to my program. It was not until after my first year as a professional, again at Bruce's suggestion, that I took up weight training. It certainly made an immediate difference. The following season was our championship year in Milwaukee, and my strength and endurance were certainly key to my success then.

The reaction to my stretching program at my first training camp in Milwaukee was something. The photographers took pictures of me as I stretched, and the photos ran everywhere. I was the only person in the league at that time who was attempting a stretching program. The only other guys who stretched like that on a regular basis were male dancers, and they were not exactly viewed as a macho bunch. So I got a few stares, but I continued on that path. And by the time I was ready to leave Milwaukee, I had started to train year-round.

Yoga was something else that had interested me since before UCLA. Henry Albert, a fellow student at Power Memorial and a runner on the cross-country team, had a book on yoga breathing. I noticed it in class one day, asked to borrow it, and found some good breathing exercises and meditation techniques that I have used ever since.

In college, I studied the history of India and chanced upon a copy of *Autobiography of a Yogi* by Pramahansa Yogananda, a book that opened my mind and spirit to the benefits of yoga, and enabled me to adapt those lessons to conditioning my body. When some friends suggested I try a hatha yoga class taught by Nawana Davis, I did and was very impressed.

A few years later, my friend Brenda Venus referred me to Nawana's teacher, Bikram Choudhury, and he was the final link in my yoga discipline. I know that I never would have lasted as long as I did in the NBA if it were not for Bikram's instruction. He has a total approach to fitness, and his style of hatha yoga has been streamlined and adjusted for the modern world. And as world weight-lifting champion at 118 pounds in 1963 and an Olympian in 1964, he also knows the demands that world-class sporting competition puts on an individual.

Yoga promotes good mind/body coordination, and it kept me from injuring my muscles by ensuring that I maintained my flexibility. In addition, I learned that Bikram was instructed by Yogananda's brother and is now president of the Self-Realization Fellowship, which was started by Yogananda to promote self-realization and brotherhood through yoga. So by studying with him I have come full circle.

Strength training was the next aspect of total conditioning that I incorporated into my regime. I reintroduced it to my program in the summer of 1975, right after I was traded to Los Angeles. Initially, I used Nautilus equipment because of the way it worked you through the whole range of motion. That enabled me to maintain my flexibility, something that was obviously a key for me.

But by the early 1980s, the size of NBA players was increasing, and that forced certain players out of their positions or made them adjust their games. Centers now can be over seven-five and weigh close to 300 pounds. By 1985, at seven-two and 255 pounds, I had become your average-size center.

After an early exit from the 1986 play-offs while being bumped around underneath by a noticeably muscular young man named Olajuwon, I decided to try the other style of strength training, free weights. My friend Taaj Jaharah gave me a program that was exactly what I needed to build muscle and strength. I stuck to it that summer while still doing some stretching and intensive cardiovascular work, swimming, and jumping rope. The results were dramatic. I gained 13 pounds of muscle, going up to 268. My body-fat content went from 13 percent to 8 percent. The added weight took a few inches off my vertical leap, but the strength and mass enabled me to hold my ground.

More than that, certain of my physical characteristics had really changed. My center of gravity had probably been closer to my sternum than my hips, which is really a problem when you're seven feet tall. But after I'd finished my training program, I'd gained a lot of muscle through the middle of my body. It was the one area that I had never worked on in my entire athletic career, and it was strange suddenly having the strength there, and being able then to hold my ground under the basket.

Training camp and exhibition games in the 1986–87 season went well for me, but I was intensely interested in how things would go under the basket during the regular year with that newly acquired bulk and strength. And when we played Boston and I faced Robert Parish, a player who'd always used a subtle bump against me, I knew that I had done the right thing. At crucial times of the game I would get the ball and back Robert in toward the hoop. He would respond by bumping me off balance with his lower body à la Moses Malone. But this time the bumps did not have the desired effect—I just absorbed them and held my ground or returned the bump at the moment of impact, which knocked Robert backward and a little off balance. I could then shoot the ball comfortably.

After that game I had a chance to chat with John Havlicek. His first words were "I know that's you, Kareem, but you have a new body." John always would stop and visit when he had a chance because I was the only player left in the league who had played against him. As I told him my story about not having sand kicked in my face anymore, he just smiled his usual amused smile and wished me well for the season. And as the season went on, all the guys that had successfully pushed me around under the hoop—Moses, Rick Mahorn, James Donaldson, Alton Lister, Jack Sikma—found out that the equation had changed. I did not see a dramatic increase in rebound statistics, but there were many times that I knew my newfound strength helped me keep a great rebounder from getting to a key rebound, and that was very satisfying. I even got a key rebound over Moses in the All-Star game in Seattle that year, roughing him up in the process. After the game, he complained in the press. I was thoroughly tickled by that development because it had been the other way around for quite some time.

Diet is the final aspect of training that is crucial for the professional athlete. Here my problems were minimal because I was always considered to be too thin anyway. But diet is also key to *maintaining* a well-conditioned body. I changed my eating habits for the better in 1966, when I decided I wanted to be a Muslim and, among other things, eliminated pork from my diet. In the ensuing years, I stopped consuming large quantities of sugar also. These simple habits, coupled with my training program, have made it possible for me to last as long as I have. Magic Johnson's mother is a Seventh-Day Adventist, and she strictly follows dietary rules that encourage fresh, homemade cooking and forbid pork. I'm positive this dietary regimen has enabled Magic to be nutritionally healthy, which in turn has given him the foundation to be a world-class athlete. So that's the physical basis of my longevity: conditioning, yoga, diet, and the mental attitude these engender.

When you finish first in your division, as the Lakers did, your first-round opponent is the team with the worst regular-season record in the conference, which this year turns out to be the team that also had the worst record of all sixteen teams that qualified, the Portland Trail Blazers. So, though we expect to win the first round, if we're to be successful we have to forget that we've beaten them five in a row this year. Clyde Drexler's gotten a lot more involved in the offense, and he and Terry Porter have great speed, making the Blazers a team who run for a living. They figure to be tough. Back in the preseason, at least one magazine picked Portland to pass us in the Pacific Division. Riley warns us to take nothing for granted.

Thursday, April 27

The first game at the Forum went according to form tonight, with a 128–108 victory. Magic led us with thirty points and sixteen assists, but the win was an example of the team unified. All the starters scored in double figures, and that's the sure way to win games. If you look at the Celtics in the sixties, that was their trademark. The high scorer would have nineteen points and they'd have something like six guys in double figures.

I also felt some satisfaction because I'd been working with assistant coach Bill Bertka on big-man drills. With Mark McNamara as my practice partner, I worked on maintaining position, on getting used to the pushing and shoving, the more physical game some centers like Portland's Kevin Duckworth play. Duckworth is one of those strong, quick guys. He shoots the ball really well inside, in medium-range jump shots, and he's been an offensive force for them. But I was effective against him tonight, getting him to foul out with but five points and five rebounds.

Wednesday, May 3

Round one is history. We swept the series 3–0. After a relatively simple 113–105 victory at the Forum on Sunday afternoon, we flew up to Portland and clinched tonight's game by almost the same score, 116–108. The Blazers did have the lead for almost thirteen minutes, most of the second quarter, and part of the third—the first time they'd been ahead in the whole series—but I don't think even they expected it to last.

I played nearly thirty minutes and scored twenty-two points, a season high for me. It was a flash of the panther—we were called the Panthers at Power Memorial—still sleek and limber.

Clyde Drexler came up to say good-bye when we were walking off the court. I just told him, "Hey, man, continued good luck. You're a hell of an athlete and I hope you continue to have a great career." He wished me success and said he felt if he could get anywhere close to where I'd gotten, he'd be proud of that. It was a really nice exchange, and from the heart.

Another team completed a sweep tonight, but it wasn't the one we expected. The Utah Jazz, the team a lot of people thought would offer us our stiffest competition, instead got swept in three games by the Golden State Warriors with their midget team. Golden State ended the regular season with six consecutive losses, but the Jazz got caught looking past their opponents and got sideswiped. It reminds me of Mark Antony, whose big boats were attacked by a swarm of little boats as he turned in the midst of battle to follow Cleopatra—overcome in the moment of distraction. That's something we as veterans have come to understand not to do. We take each round seriously; we don't look ahead. We learned that lesson against Houston in 1981.

Golden State, I think, was just too fast for the Jazz. They had Manute Bol playing at half court and shooting three-pointers, so all of a sudden Mark Eaton couldn't stand under the hoop. And once that happened, the Jazz were an entirely different team. And down at the other end, Manute can do what Mark does—he blocked something ridiculous like thirteen shots in three games. So the Jazz got the shoe put on the other foot.

This is only the Warriors' second play-off appearance in twelve years; their improvement from a dismal 20-62 last season is the fourth best in league history. We thought Utah and Phoenix would face each other in round two and hopefully tire each other out. Now we don't know what'll happen.

We don't know ourselves yet who we'll play in the second round, whether it'll be Houston or Seattle. It'll be tough either way for me, because both Olajuwon and Alton Lister are really physical. You can't have a preference anyway, though, because no matter who it is, you have to be at your tip-top. You can't take a relaxed attitude toward your preparation—you have to get ready to play your best.

We learned tonight that it will be Seattle in the next round. We were 4-2 against them during the regular year, with both losses at Seattle and two of the three home victories by a total of only four points. They finished the season strong, with an 8-2 run, and after beating Houston they'll be primed for meeting us.

The Sonics are one of the most aggressive, physical teams in the league. They dive for loose balls, go for every rebound, compete for everything. They lead the league in fouls and offensive rebounds, are second to Detroit in overall boards, and in Dale Ellis they've got the number two scorer in the league.

The Sonics try to annoy you to death, but if they didn't foul us, we'd start running by them. It's not dirty play, not like hitting you in the head when you don't see it coming, but it's their philosophy of the game. They foul you to slow things up, to keep you from shooting lay-ups and make sure you earn every basket. When you're playing a team like that, you just have to make your free throws.

We had the kind of tough first game we expected on Sunday, but we came out on top, 113–102, helped a lot by James's twenty-eight points and twelve rebounds. Free throws, as we expected, were the difference: We made thirty-seven of forty-six, while they hit on eighteen of twenty-five. The Sonics led at halftime, as well as after three quarters, and we were up only 94–89 when Michael Cooper made a spectacular block, one of the best of his career. Sedale Threatt had driven past Magic for what looked to be an easy lay-up, but Coop came out of nowhere for a heroic rejection that led to a Laker basket. It was timed perfectly, a well-executed play, and it was really inspired.

The second game, tonight, was not as close, more like a blowout, the final score coming in at 130–108. Seattle spent the first two contests trying to take Magic out of the game, but since Magic is more than happy to pass, that was no problem. Eight Lakers were in double figures tonight, including Orlando, who had maybe his best game of the season.

And, for no reason anyone could really figure out, in the third quarter the Forum crowd spontaneously erupted in sustained applause that lasted several minutes. I'd never really seen anything like it. It was deafening; they wouldn't be stopped. They even drowned out the Laker girls. It's as though the crowd has been waiting all year to explode like that. They love to see us winning.

Friday, May 12

It's been sunny in Seattle since we arrived early yesterday afternoon, among the few clear and almost cloudless days this city enjoys. From my room you can see snow on the tops of the Olympic Mountains to the west, and, to the south, on Mount Rainier as well. It gets dark late here, around nine, as if summer has arrived early.

The Coliseum is one of the three smallest arenas in the league, seating only fourteen thousand. Above the floor hang three NBA banners, one for the world championship in 1978–79, and one each for the Western Conference titles in 1977–78 and 1978–79.

The Sonics finally gave us the battle we've been expecting in tonight's third game. In a close, intense contest, we played really hard and really smart and came out ahead 91–86. And this despite shooting 46.4 percent and not having a field goal for the last seven minutes and thirty-eight seconds of the game. But Seattle only shot 36.9 percent and we made ten straight free throws in the last 3:19, including the last four by Michael Cooper, to come out on top. We nearly blew it in the fourth quarter. The crowd went crazy as the point spread narrowed. The Sonics were within one point at 1:21, and then our free throws started to matter. With thirty seconds to go, we were up by five, and that's how the game ended. We're playing together as a team the way we should be, and that's the key.

Sunday, May 14

Another sweep.

Hard as that is to believe, it's even harder to believe that we even made it close today, much less won. Seattle was up 32–12 at the end of the first quarter and then scored the first nine points of the second period to take a twenty-nine-point lead. At that point, a loss may have seemed a foregone conclusion. But not to us. In what was probably the biggest comeback in play-off history, we won 97–95, a harrowing, nerve-fraying game. I don't ever remember a comeback like this one.

This game wasn't as dire for us as for the Sonics—we weren't facing elimination—but still we came back. With eight minutes to go in the second quarter with us down by twenty-seven, Riley got an intentional technical. He remarked to Jake O'Donnell that we weren't getting a whole lot of calls. But even though Jake is an excellent official, he's something of a prima donna, and just saying that to him is enough to make him crazy. Sometimes he makes a point of showing you he's not going to give you the benefit of the doubt, just to emphasize that he has the power and you don't. O'Donnell's prima-donna qualities come from being a good official, from twenty years of officiating in the league. But I'll endure his excesses, because when it really matters, he's always fair.

That technical was a signal to us: It helped us realize that we were out there by ourselves, and the refs weren't going to give us any calls. So it was "Don't take any prisoners—just play as hard as you can and don't care about fouling because they're going to call a foul anyway." We felt we could get our heads up out of the mud playing them hard, as opposed to playing the score and accepting the defeat. And that worked in our favor.

Magic said to us during a time-out, "Let's just try to get it down to fifteen." Everybody knows you can lose a ten-point lead in a quarter. By halftime we had closed the gap to eleven, and during the third quarter we continued to eat away at their lead. It was like gnawing through steel. Experience told us, "You don't give up. You can make it back from that kind of a deficit." At the fourth-quarter mark we were down by eight, and you could hear the crowd chanting, "L.A. sucks." But it turned out to be Seattle that didn't have enough gas.

Then, with 7:39 to go in the game, I got called for two obscure violations or turnovers by O'Donnell, one for "ball handling out of bounds," the other for "end-line violation of backcourt." Bill Bertka yelled out, "For Christ's sake, Jake, give him a break," and began to run out on the court to protest. Then, suddenly, he just collapsed onto one knee.

Bertka never lost consciousness, but he didn't look too good. Doc Kerlan gave him some nitro just in case it was his heart, while O'Donnell gave him a double technical and ejected him from the game. He was helped to the locker room and we didn't see him again until after the game. It turned out to be just a fainting spell, probably brought on by the warm, stuffy air inside the arena, but it was unnerving for a while.

This year has been a really rough one on the coaches, on *all* the coaches around the league. Jerry Reynolds collapsed on the court in December, Bernie Bickerstaff was hospitalized for a bleeding ulcer in March, Jack Ramsay and Frank Layden resigned, Gene Shue and Mike Schuler were fired, Doug Collins's job looks on the line, rumblings are afoot that John MacLeod won't last too long in Dallas, and Rick Pitino is talking about going back into college coaching. Maybe he's seen what's coming and doesn't want to wait around for his hair to turn gray.

The first lead we got in the game, 82–81, came with a bit more than six minutes left on a pair of free throws by Orlando. The game was tense all the rest of the way, with A.C. making our last three points on free throws within the last nine seconds. What a game! Musashi would call it "crossing at the straits."

We savored the comeback a little in the back of the bus on the way to the airport—it was great for our confidence as a team. The sun was still out as we took off over Puget Sound and the mountains, and it was light almost the whole way home, though dusk settled in and darkness fell once we began descending through the clouds to L.A.

We're 7-0 in the play-offs, 12-0 if you go back to the end of the regular season. We haven't lost a game in a month. We advance to round three and, once again, wait to see who our next opponent will be. Phoenix is expected. The Suns have a 3–1 lead against Golden State in the second round and will play the fifth game on their own home court on Tuesday. We may know then.

For me, the light at the end of the tunnel now is no small circle—it's more the size of a refrigerator. I'm making arrangements for the house in Hawaii to be ready. I feel surprisingly relaxed about playing. It's the rest of my life I'm excited about.

Saturday, May 20

The Pistons got a surprise yesterday: They'll be playing the Chicago Bulls, not the New York Knicks, in the Eastern Conference finals. Our opponent in the Western finals has turned out to be Phoenix, as anticipated, and we kept on our roll, beating them tonight 127–119 in the Forum. Counting this one, fourteen games is the most I can possibly play now.

The Suns are an interesting team, and their improvement from last season to this is the third best in league history. They have trouble winning in the Forum, but then we have almost as much difficulty on their court, losing there three times this season. They're a young team, though; they even make A.C. look old. They're going to try to outhustle us, getting loose balls, second shots, things that take an effort, things that you get from being hungry and trying 100 percent in every instance.

Kevin Johnson, their excellent point guard, had twenty-seven points and eighteen assists tonight. Sportswriter Jim Murray said he has the bored look of a guy painting a fence while he's on the court, but I don't see him being bored, just involved in serious concentration. He's only twenty-three years old and has had only two years in the league, but, with great penetration and passing ability, he takes charge of their offense like a veteran.

It was our bench that made the difference today. Magic fouled out, the first time he's done that since 1981, and Cooper had to run the offense. And Orlando had his best game since joining the team, with thirteen points, seven boards, three assists, two blocked shots, and an important steal late in the game. He's finally gotten it into his mind that it's more than just scoring, and he's begun to play all-around basketball for us. He really became a Laker tonight. I'm happy for Orlando. He's being recognized and appreciated. That's going to help him for the rest of his life. He can believe in his own work.

Tuesday, May 23

Only two more wins to the finals. We beat Phoenix 101–95 tonight in
the second game, holding them to under 100 for the first time in the
play-offs. Magic, who was named MVP for the regular season yesterday, got his award at halftime, but a lot of the kudos today went to
Byron Scott, who was high man with thirty points and racked up six
steals as well.

But our defense was really the key here. We just shut them down.
Anytime you can hold a team that's been averaging 122 points a game
to 95, you're doing really well. We had them doing stuff they didn't
want to do, getting them away from their strengths.

One of the things we figured out was that we had to pick up Kevin
Johnson earlier, stop him and turn him and hopefully make him give
up the ball as soon as he came across half court—just go at him
aggressively, get the ball out of his hands. He's got so much speed that
if you don't do that, he'll run by you. What he wants to do is cruise
across half court, see where everybody has set everything, and then
create his thing and beat you to the hoop.

But Cooper didn't allow him to do that, and he was able to shut
Kevin down for about eight minutes, forcing him into seven turnovers
and only 33 percent shooting in the second half. It got to the point
where he didn't even want the ball—he was letting the other guys bring
it up. And that hurts them. Losing two in a row, of course, hurts them
even more. Now that they have the pressure on them, they can't afford
to lose at home. And that does something to you. If we can win either
Friday or Saturday in Phoenix, it's going to be a short series. We've
got to try to get it now.

Friday, May 26

The Southwest is in a heat wave, with the temperature near or over 100
every day. Interest in the series is pretty feverish as well, with lines
around the block and people camping overnight at the Coliseum to get
tickets for these two games. Tonight we beat Phoenix on their home

court for the first time this season, 110–107, setting a new play-off record with ten victories in a row in the process. We've done everything we had to up to this point. I've done my share, or at least that's how I feel. And as a team, we are working together unselfishly: James was high scorer with twenty-nine points, the sixth time in the past seven games he's done that, and five other Lakers were in double figures. Orlando has made a difference in all three series. A.C. doesn't attract as much crowd reaction, but he gets it done.

This third game was a slugfest, one of the toughest games in the play-offs so far. The Suns were tenacious, coming back from ten points behind to take a three-point lead with one minute to go in the game, but we got eight free throws in that final minute to ice it. Beating Phoenix on their home court maybe has put a dent in their confidence, but even at 3-0 we still have respect for the Suns' ability to come back. They are a young team, quick and aggressive, and they play with confidence verging on cockiness, like the Pistons do.

Sunday, May 28

Another sweep, the third in a row. Maybe we are unstoppable. We didn't take any of these victories for granted, so winning one game after another begins to really add up in terms of achievement. Maybe we *are* hotter than the desert. We've set an NBA record by sweeping the first three rounds, and today's win gives us our longest winning streak of the season. We're 18-0, counting the last five games of the regular season.

This afternoon we came out on top, 122–117, with half a dozen clutch free throws near the end. More classic teamwork: Orlando had his Laker play-off high of fourteen points, Byron a career play-off high of thirty-five points, and Magic's twenty assists gives him fifty-seven for the four games against the Suns, an NBA record. Everything's clicking; we're tough to beat when everybody's delivering. The bottom line is that the play-off Suns were similar to the regular-season Suns, but they didn't realize they'd be playing the play-off Lakers, a tougher bunch than the regular-season crew.

It's an hour flight home, west with the sun across the desert. We came in over the Forum and landed around seven, long before sunset, with a feeling that there was plenty of time left. It's almost been too easy. So far we haven't looked past our opponents, and we've met every challenge. We didn't expect to sweep anybody—it just worked out that way. Now there's just one series left. I'm traveling with a color postcard of the beautiful Hawaii coastline where my property is. To have that promise of paradise with me becomes increasingly important as the days go on.

Tuesday, May 30

There's a peaking aspect now, a sense that we're building to climax. Like a ball of yarn, or a snowball, the play-offs gradually acquire more reporters, more pressure, more tension, as they move along. As you make your way from one round to the next, you're emboldened, but at the same time the stakes are getting higher. Now we're nearing the crescendo. And as I went into the play-offs not knowing which round might be my last, I go into the finals not knowing what night will be my last.

I also don't know who our opponent will be, whether it will be the Chicago Bulls, the closest thing to a one-man team the play-offs have ever seen, or the Detroit Pistons, who evened their series at 2–2 yesterday. That means they will go to at least six games with the Bulls, so the earliest the finals can start is a week from today. Riley has decided to do what he's done last year and the year before—take us up to Santa Barbara for a mini–training camp at Westmount College.

We leave tomorrow for a 2 P.M. practice in Westmount's gym. We stay just south of Santa Barbara proper at the Biltmore in Montecito, an enclave for the very rich that is filled with groves of eucalyptus, palm, and cypress trees. It's a first-rate place, and Riley thinks he's doing the team a favor by getting us up there and away from distractions. But I don't feel there are any distractions at home; on the contrary, it's where I'm most comfortable. For me, being away from home is the distraction; it's a sacrifice to be up there.

The practices in Santa Barbara were hard, very hard, with a scrimmage yesterday more physical than our games will be; the refs called few fouls, probably on Riley's orders. I feel in great shape coming home, but I've never thought things like this were the wisest idea for the team. As a championship group, we're pushed to such a high level by all our opponents on every night that we're going to be more susceptible to injury anyhow. And we've been at that level for a long time—not only this three-year stretch in the finals, but the four years from 1982 through 1985. So it's really seven of the past eight years. That's quite a long line of professional achievement.

We found out tonight what I had always assumed, that Detroit is going to be our opponent in the finals. For the second year in a row, we're the two teams left standing at the end of the season. And until they beat the Celtics last year, the Pistons had never been in a finals before, and that victory in fact made them the only Eastern Conference team other than Boston or Philadelphia to make it to the championship round in the 1980s.

The Pistons took us to seven games last year, and in fact almost won it in six. They were up 3–2 in the series and, with sixty seconds left in Game 6, we trailed 102–99. But Byron Scott hit a twelve-footer, Isiah Thomas missed from deep in the left corner on the other end, and, with fourteen seconds left, Bill Laimbeer was called for his sixth foul for bumping me. Laimbeer was always pushing me underneath, but this time he went a little higher over my waist than usual and that caught the ref's attention.

The Pistons took a time-out; they wanted me to think about it. But I've never had a problem with free throws. I generally do a good job of deflecting the pressure. What I try to do is block out the crowd, block out the situation, and just concentrate on making the shot. All my years of experience, all the times when I'd been able to stay detached and dispassionate, really served me well at that one moment. And it is actually easier sometimes to have all that pressure, because it can make you concentrate, and when you concentrate you can do extraordinary things.

I went to the line, bounced the ball a few times, and hoped good things would happen. When the first one went down, it meant we had a chance to win it. I just shot the second one, and gave us what turned out to be the final margin of victory, 103–102. Making those two was pretty special to me. Like Sandy Amoros's catch off Yogi Berra that saved the 1955 World Series for the Dodgers, those free throws are going to be remembered.

A previous finals experience with the same team always helps a club, even if they don't win, and the Pistons no doubt came out of last year understanding what it takes to win and setting their sights accordingly. Compared to last year, though, our side is healthy and our bench is outstanding in scoring, rebounds, and blocked shots. We've got balance, and we're tough to beat when everyone's delivering.

The press is playing up the Pistons' Bad Boys image, Motown versus Showtown, Beauty versus the Beast. They are tough defensively and no play-off opponent has broken 100 against them so far. There is a swagger to the Pistons, but the image has little or no effect on us. They are almost as cocky as the Celtics, but they don't have the experience behind them. They're newcomers. We do have different styles, but the contrast isn't as marked as it's played up to be. We would prefer to run and they would like to slow us down and force us into a half-court offense, and if they get to play their game, and dominate, they'll win. They're going to play me physical, but it's up to the refs to deal with that. It's not like the Pistons are out there trying to trip you up or anything; you just play the game a certain way. And I respect them as competitors.

Sunday, June 4

We left for Detroit today, late afternoon after a practice at Loyola, but the plane was an hour and a half late in taking off. We'll be in Detroit for the first two games, and the team is feeling positive and happy.

We're going to be staying at the same place we did last year, a Guest Quarters hotel. The entire seventh floor is set aside for the team, the coaches, and staff; no wives or girlfriends allowed, and a twenty-four-hour security guard is posted at a desk outside the elevator just to make sure we're not disturbed. There are VCRs in every room, and all you have to do is call over to a video store and they deliver. Under the circumstances, it is as homelike as you can get, so it'll be nice returning there.

We landed in Detroit at one in the morning, slipping into town in the middle of the night, and it was two-thirty by the time we got to the hotel up north of the city. Just before the team got off the bus, suddenly, out of the darkness, Magic began to yell, almost like he was reciting a chant: "It's the Laker show. I'm ready. This is the *real* bad boys. I'm ready to tear some limbs off. I can't even sleep at night. It's the Laker show again." Even though we're all used to Magic, there was something spooky about that early-morning outburst. We went to sleep with his incantation still in our ears. And the eerie feeling turned out to be accurate. We were in the middle of a rebounding drill this afternoon at the Palace, the Pistons' new arena, when suddenly I saw Byron go down. He was jumping just as David Rivers was trying to get to the ball, and that awkward positioning caused the fall. He went down and stayed down, rolling in pain on the floor. You could tell it was something serious. After a while, Gary helped him stand up and he limped out of the gym and onto the bus. It was surreal, hard to believe.

We didn't get the official diagnosis until Doc Kerlan arrived around 11 P.M. but since I was in the same drill, I'd heard Byron's tendon pop and I knew he'd torn a hamstring. It's not the kind of thing you can mask with a painkiller; you could actually harm it further and accelerate it into a career-ending injury.

In the summer, all I do is hamstring work; when I was hurt at the beginning of the year, my hamstrings tested stronger than my quads, and that's one of the reasons I've never been injured badly. The thing with hamstrings is that even after they've healed, they bother you. You have to stop everything and heal all the way. So for me it's a question of how long Byron is going to be out. I'm afraid it'll be the whole series.

After practice was over, Riley said, "We're not going to let this affect us," but on the bus back to the hotel, we were numb, in shock. Everybody knew it was serious, but no one would talk about it. Emotions are paradoxical things for professional athletes: On the one hand, you have to be in control of your feelings, but on the other, you have to have more than your share of emotion and competitive desire to be successful.

Jerry West, who's superstitious, must be really upset by this. Gary thinks he might have jinxed us. He was talking about the health of the team just a few minutes before Byron went down. And Doc Kerlan is also blaming himself. He thinks he jinxed us by putting on his 1985 championship ring, which he rarely wears, before leaving for Detroit.

We spent the whole week gearing up for the Pistons, and now with Byron out we'll have to reevaluate. I didn't try to talk to Byron privately. What can you say? He's given everything he could; and he got hurt trying to make us successful. The loss of Byron could cost us twenty points a game. To have come this far, with everything going our way . . . it is as if fate has scowled on us.

Tuesday, June 6

With Byron's injury the whole chemistry of the team and the tenor of the play-offs has changed 180 degrees, like a liquid in a test tube going from clear to cloudy in an instant. Tonight, in Game 1, we had our first postseason loss, 109–97. James, who had shot over 60 percent in the play-offs, missed his initial five attempts, even throwing an air ball on his first shot, but that was just symptomatic of a malaise that affected the whole team. I didn't sleep well last night and I got my fourth foul early in the third quarter, so I barely played in the second half. Magic had no shots in the third quarter. It was that kind of a night.

The problem is there is no time to adjust, psychologically, to losing Byron. You're playing, all the pieces are in place, and then suddenly one piece drops out. It's a domino effect that throws everything else out of sync, but there's nothing you can do about it. We just weren't able to get into the competition the way we wanted to. A play-off streak doesn't guarantee anything. You can lose that capacity for success at any minute.

After the game, Orlando got on the bus right after I did. He turned around and said to me, "Cap, I'd forgotten this feeling."

We have to regroup. I know we can play better; I know the team can play better. We have to understand how to apply ourselves. We lost one game last year at the beginning of the finals. It's a long way from being over. We have to find a way.

Thursday, June 8

A heavy rain fell this morning, lasting nearly an hour. The sky was dark and there were thunderstorms on the way back to the hotel from shootaround. Is the rain cooling off the Michigan heat? Is it a postscript to the lightning that struck us on Monday? Or a gloomy precursor of another defeat tonight?

We didn't want to go home without a split; we wanted to take away Detroit's home-court advantage, and we knew that only two teams have gone on to win the finals after being down 2–0. The Pistons, for their part, didn't want to repeat last year's pattern, where they won the first game and lost the second. So there were pressures on both sides.

The crowd was intense, even more so than in Game 1, "Beat L.A." a constant chant. With Cooper replacing Byron, as he did in the first game, we started out strong, more like the team we'd been for the first three rounds. We took an early 9–2 lead and were up by six at the half. The Pistons got their first tie, at 75–75, with 4:39 left in the third quarter, and at that precise moment Magic pulled up lame, holding the back of his left leg. I knew it was serious, because Magic won't stop playing just because he's hurt. Gary went out to him, but Magic pushed him away. Coop then went over and Magic said, "Keep the leadership, keep the fire going." Gary walked Magic off the floor toward the locker room, not the bench. It turned out to be his left hamstring, the same one he'd injured back in February, the same one that got Byron. While Magic was in the dressing room being diagnosed, the emotion was wrenching. The Palace crowd went crazy.

At first we responded with a 17–9 spurt to take a 92–84 lead, but we lost it in an abysmal fourth quarter. We managed to hit on only two of fourteen shots and scored only thirteen points, tying a record for the worst quarter in NBA play-off history. We still had a chance at the end—James was on the line with two seconds left and two shots. If he'd made both, we would have tied. But he made only one, which left us behind 106–105. Then Isiah made two free throws with one second left, making the final score 108–105. It was the first time a team had gotten over 100 points against Detroit in this season's play-offs, but that's hardly any consolation.

For a second game in a championship series, the tension tonight felt unprecedented, the equivalent of a seventh game. Every possession was a battle for life because both sides felt that the team that won this one had an excellent chance of winning the series. If we'd won it, it would have turned the whole series around, really done a psychological number on them. And then, while we were in the act of doing it, Magic went down. Coop did a great job of holding the team together, and he got a personal play-off high of nineteen points, but it wasn't enough.

Magic was the last player on the bus after the game; it got very quiet as he stepped on. One of his sisters had brought his mother's usual bags and boxes of fried chicken, sweet-potato pie, cakes, and stuff onto the bus, and that lightened the mood a little. But we were hurting. What were the odds of Byron and Magic getting injured in exactly the same part of the body at the same time? The irony of the situation is that the injuries are basically routine; it's the timing that makes them so devastating. After the first one, we didn't think anything else would happen, but we found out differently. It's like lightning striking twice in the same spot. With Magic going out—and I know it's for good— fate has scowled on us a second time. As Coop said, "Things just didn't work out here in Detroit." At least we're going home.

Sunday, June 11

When we approached L.A. from the air on Friday, the city was blanketed in a presummer coastal fog. It was gray, even wintry, because the air-conditioning in the plane was so cold. When we got to the terminal, Magic and Byron left with Gary to go directly for treatment.

Al picked me up. "Well, you played as hard as you could, son," he said. I was just happy to be home. And happy to be able to rest in my own bed.

Going into Game 3 today, everybody said, *No* team has ever gone on to win the finals after being down 3–0. Either we won this time, or it was over.

Magic led the team out on the floor from the locker room as usual, and he led the team in warm-ups. I was surprised when he did that, but I knew he was just trying to give us as much as he could, even if all he could give was inspiration. He was showing his heart. He played a little less than five minutes in the game, but it was obvious he couldn't cut it. He'd be risking his career if he played more, but we miss him.

It's as if you had a great sports car and a great driver and all of a sudden you had to look to a guy that's been driving a bus to drive the car. It's pretty tough.

Still, we had a shot at pulling this one out. We had the ball with nine seconds remaining, down 113–110, but David Rivers had the ball stolen as he was taking a shot with six seconds left, Laimbeer added one more free throw, and we lost 114–110. As I was walking out of the locker room after the game, my father handed me a stat sheet: twenty-four points, thirteen rebounds, my best game of the season. But that didn't seem to matter. We did everything we could today—Coop played the whole forty-eight minutes. But we couldn't contain their guards: Isiah Thomas had twenty-six points and Joe Dumars thirty-one, including seventeen straight in a twenty-one-point third quarter. I don't know if we can play any better, but we're going to have to try. We're fighting for our lives now. It's hard to be optimistic, but we're determined.

Monday, June 12

After practice at the Forum this morning, I saw Earl (the Pearl) Monroe, who was doing some interviewing. "All we can do is go through it," I told him. "A great effort requires great attitude. I plan to go out and do my best. Everything else will take care of itself. I know the next game may be my last one, but I have to concentrate on the business at hand."

The same lessons I had learned with Coach Donahue in high school, with John Wooden at UCLA—they all come into play now, at the end.

Tuesday, June 13

When I came down the stairs to leave for the game today, I found a glass bowl of gardenias floating in water with a note from Quincy Jones. An appreciated touch. And Joan Knickmeyer was standing in front of her house, which, besides the usual purple-and-gold stuff, had signs saying "Rock 'em Cap" and "Happy Skyhooks." I stopped to say hello and she told me that for Thursday's fifth game—and she was confident there *would* be a fifth game—she'd have to be out of town, but that I shouldn't take her absence as a bad omen.

I felt we were close to the end of this particular story. Just like in life, you participate in the outcome, but you don't control it. Yet at the same time I knew we could beat the Pistons. We just had to give our best effort and hope something good happened.

Jack Nicholson was at the game, naturally. He'd flown in by helicopter from location in Valencia for *Two Jakes*, the sequel to *Chinatown* he's making now. On the blackboard in the team locker room the messages were: Play guards hard. Don't let them get open. Every time you get the chance, take the ball to the hole. Good advice. I hope we can take it. At Byron's stall there were lots of letters from fans. At Magic's stall, there were yellow roses on the shelf.

We started out strong, and were leading by two, 78–76, at the end of the third quarter, having been up by *sixteen* midway through the second. But we couldn't keep it up. We collapsed in the final quarter, even though every fiber in the team, and in the crowd, was straining to win. That's what you've been trained for, even at the eleventh hour. Especially at the eleventh hour.

When it was over, the Pistons were on top 105–97. James had forty points, a career professional high and almost half our total. But one of their reserves, James Edwards, scored thirteen points in the final quarter and really hurt us. Joe Dumars was high scorer for the Pistons, as he was for two of the other games, and got the series MVP. But ref Earl Strom came into our locker room and gave me the game ball. He probably remembers the other time we lost four straight in the finals, to Philadelphia in 1983. This one is harder to take, though, because this time we were going for writing our names in the sky.

It was a strange mixture for me, losing the series and saying good-bye, celebration in the midst of defeat. I'm disappointed—we worked very hard to get here—but that's life, and we have to live with it. Even though central parts were missing from our machine, we didn't lie down and die—we stood up and fought. We ended on a note of disappointment, but not a note of failure, and that's important. Through our achievements in the eighties, we have secured our position in the upper pantheon with other sports dynasties. When I walked off the court for the last time, with nineteen seconds left, I hugged the guys and just listened to the crowd. They chanted, "Kareem, Kareem, Kareem," until the buzzer sounded. I just tried to take it all in.

Magic's mother, Christine, came into the locker room afterward, and told us, "You're still the champs to me." I saw her trying to get through the layers of reporters surrounding my locker, trying to say something to me, but she couldn't get through. I'm sorry we didn't have the chance to go after the title with our best team. If we'd had her son, I'm positive we would have beaten Detroit, even without Byron.

From a certain perspective, the outcome of this series makes an odd kind of ending for a career such as mine. The proper epic conclusion would seem to have been another world championship, a triple crown the only fitting way to go. But I'm reminded of the story of Cyrano de Bergerac, an incomparable swordsman who would have been expected to go out in a sword fight with fifty men, but who instead died suddenly when a piece of timber fell from a roof gable and hit him on the head. Choosing our own fate is not an option open to us.

I took Amir home and then came home by myself. There were a few calls from friends. Everybody was okay. Considering the circumstances, they all seemed to enjoy what we were able to give. In the hours after the loss, I had already accepted it.

Monday, June 14

We went to the Forum this morning to clean out our lockers, get our play-off money, and say good-bye for the summer. The floor was dark. It was only 11 A.M., but for the first time this year the Forum lights were out. Everybody wanted a piece of my uniform, including Riley. So I gave it to them. And then I left.

V

Epilogue

I have been at my place in Hawaii for more than two weeks now. The campaign has finally let go of my consciousness, and I'm just trying to let it sink in that my career, as well as the season, is now over. I plan to rest for as long as it takes to restore myself from the 5:30 A.M. wake-up calls, the ones you get so you can catch the next plane to the next city and the next game.

This was a tough year, but a great year. We were eliminated through no fault of our own at the very end—and we almost did it. I'm proud that the team gave its best, that I gave my best. The defeat won't haunt me; nothing will. There are no "if onlys" as I retire. The experience is complete. I have no regrets about not leaving earlier, and I have done everything I wanted to do in this profession. My career has paralleled a very exciting time in the sport. I've played basketball with some of the greatest players in the history of the game. And, including college, I've been a part of nine championship teams. There's nothing I've missed.

I think I've basically played for an idea, which is how close I could come to being at my best. I put some hard work into that, I had the good fortune to have been given talent, and I was also lucky enough not to have gotten hurt.

I had no major injuries that could have knocked me out of the game before I was ready to leave. None of that came my way. And I'm retiring virtually unmarked.

I always knew that this would have to end. There comes a time to give things up, to let things go. It's been fun fighting off the inevitable for as long as I have; I feel I've pushed it to the limit. But now it's time to let one life end and see what happens in my new life as a regular citizen. The sport goes on. People will find new heroes. And I'm flattered they'll be compared with me. That's something I can enjoy for the rest of my life, as I will the memory of my last time around the league and the late-autumn sunshine I received from the fans. In my twenty years of playing, I always felt appreciated by my teammates, but I never fully knew until this year how the people felt about me and what I've done in my career. The tour of cities was a distraction from play, as was the increased glare of attention it drew toward me, but it was worth the price because of the chance it gave to the fans and me to leave nothing unsaid. The disappointment of the final series will not detract from that, and never could.

I've brought over some posters of the team that I promised to friends here in Hawaii. When I look at the poster now—at James, Byron, Magic, Coop—I'm filled with a sense of pride in what we achieved. Some of my teammates' faces remind me of our professional status, while others make me smile and think of the fun and craziness we were able to enjoy. I won't be able to taste those moments again, but they will not be forgotten.

Thanks for the good times, Lakers.

You were the tops.

Appendix:
Lifetime Statistics

Kareem Abdul-Jabbar
(formerly known as Lew Alcindor)

Born April 16, 1947, New York, New York
Height: 7'2" Weight: 267
High School—Power Memorial, New York, New York
College—University of California at Los Angeles
Drafted by Milwaukee on first round, first pick, 1969
Traded to Los Angeles, June 16, 1975

HIGH SCHOOL

- Member of three CHSAA city championship teams, Power Memorial (Catholic High School Athletic Association of New York).
- All-American, three years.

UCLA RECORD

Year	G	FGA	FGM	Pct.	FTA	FTM	Pct.	Reb.	Pts.	Avg.
65–66*	21	432	295	.683	179	106	.592	452	696	33.1
66–67	30	519	346	.667	274	178	.650	466	870	29.0
67–68	28	480	294	.613	237	146	.616	461	734	26.2
68–69	30	477	303	.635	188	115	.612	440	721	24.0
Varsity Totals	88	1,476	943	.639	699	439	.628	1,367	2,325	26.4

*College freshman participant

- Member of three consecutive NCAA championship teams: 1967, 1968, 1969.

- NCAA Tournament Most Outstanding Player, 1967, 1968, 1969 (only college player in the history of the Final Four to have received this award three times).

NBA REGULAR-SEASON RECORD

Season—Team	G	Min.	FGA	FGM	Pct.	FTA	FTM	Pct.	Reb.	Ast.	PF	BS	Pts.	Avg.
69–70—Milwaukee	82	3534	1810	938	.518	743	485	.653	1190	337	283	—	2361	28.8
70–71—Milwaukee	82	3288	1843	1063	.577	681	470	.690	1311	272	264	—	2596	31.7
71–72—Milwaukee	81	3583	2019	1159	.574	732	504	.689	1346	370	235	—	2822	34.8
72–73—Milwaukee	76	3254	1772	982	.554	460	328	.713	1224	379	208	—	2292	30.2
73–74—Milwaukee	81	3548	1759	948	.539	420	295	.702	1178	386	238	283	2191	27.0
74–75—Milwaukee	65	2747	1584	812	.513	426	325	.763	912	264	205	212	1949	30.0
75–76—Los Angeles	82	3379	1728	914	.529	636	447	.703	1383	413	292	338	2275	27.7
76–77—Los Angeles	82	3016	1533	888	.579	536	376	.701	1090	319	262	261	2152	26.2
77–78—Los Angeles	62	2265	1205	663	.550	350	274	.783	801	269	182	185	1600	25.8
78–79—Los Angeles	80	3157	1347	777	.577	474	349	.736	1025	431	230	316	1903	23.8
79–80—Los Angeles	82	3143	1383	835	.604	476	364	.765	886	371	216	280	2034	24.8
80–81—Los Angeles	80	2976	1457	836	.574	552	423	.766	821	272	244	228	2095	26.2
81–82—Los Angeles	76	2677	1301	753	.579	442	312	.706	659	225	224	207	1818	23.9
82–83—Los Angeles	79	2554	1228	722	.588	371	278	.749	592	200	220	170	1722	21.8
83–84—Los Angeles	80	2622	1238	716	.578	394	285	.723	587	211	211	143	1717	21.5
84–85—Los Angeles	79	2630	1207	723	.599	395	289	.732	622	249	238	162	1735	22.0
85–86—Los Angeles	79	2629	1338	755	.564	439	336	.765	478	280	248	130	1846	23.4
86–87—Los Angeles	78	2441	993	560	.564	343	245	.714	523	203	245	97	1366	17.5
87–88—Los Angeles	80	2308	903	480	.532	269	205	.762	478	135	216	92	1165	14.6
88–89—Los Angeles	74	1695	659	313	.475	165	122	.739	334	74	196	85	748	10.1
Totals	1,560	57,446	28,307	15,837	.559	9,304	6,712	.721	17,440	5,660	4,657	189	38,387	24.6

- Member of six NBA world-championship teams: 1971, 1980, 1982, 1985, 1987, 1988.
- Most Valuable Player, 1971, 1972, 1974, 1976, 1977, 1980 (only player in the history of the NBA to have received this award six times).
- Holds NBA records for scoring, games played, minutes played, field goals made, field goals attempted, blocked shots, and personal fouls.
- Holds NBA record for most seasons played (twenty).
- NBA Rookie of the Year, 1970.
- Holds NBA All-Star-game records for scoring, games played, minutes played, field goals attempted, field goals made, and personal fouls. Named to All-Star team nineteen times.

NBA PLAY-OFF RECORD

Season—Team	G	Min.	FGA	FGM	Pct.	FTA	FTM	Pct.	Reb.	Ast.	PF	BS	Pts.	Avg.
69–70—Milwaukee	10	435	245	139	.567	101	74	.733	168	41	25	—	352	35.2
70–71—Milwaukee	14	577	295	152	.515	101	68	.673	238	35	45	—	372	26.6
71–72—Milwaukee	11	510	318	139	.437	54	38	.704	200	56	35	—	316	28.7
72–73—Milwaukee	6	276	138	59	.428	35	19	.543	97	17	26	—	137	22.8
73–74—Milwaukee	16	758	402	224	.557	91	67	.736	253	78	41	39	515	32.2
76–77—Los Angeles	11	467	242	147	.607	120	87	.725	195	45	42	38	381	34.6
77–78—Los Angeles	3	134	73	38	.521	9	5	.556	41	11	14	12	81	27.0
78–79—Los Angeles	8	367	152	88	.579	62	52	.839	101	38	26	33	228	28.5
79–80—Los Angeles	15	618	346	198	.572	105	83	.790	181	46	51	58	479	31.9
80–81—Los Angeles	3	134	65	30	.462	28	20	.714	50	12	14	8	80	26.7
81–82—Los Angeles	14	493	221	115	.520	87	55	.632	119	51	45	45	285	20.4
82–83—Los Angeles	15	588	287	163	.568	106	80	.755	115	42	61	55	406	27.1
83–84—Los Angeles	21	767	371	206	.555	120	90	.750	173	79	71	45	502	23.9
84–85—Los Angeles	19	610	300	168	.560	103	80	.777	154	76	67	36	416	21.9
85–86—Los Angeles	14	489	282	157	.557	61	48	.787	83	49	54	24	362	25.9
86–87—Los Angeles	18	559	234	124	.530	122	97	.795	123	36	56	35	345	19.2
87–88—Los Angeles	24	718	304	141	.464	71	56	.789	131	36	81	37	338	14.1
88–89—Los Angeles	15	351	147	68	.463	43	31	.721	59	19	43	11	167	11.1
Totals	237	8,851	4,422	2,356	.533	1,419	1,050	.740	2,481	767	797	476	5,762	24.3

- Holds NBA play-off records for scoring, games played, minutes played, field goals made, field goals attempted, blocked shots, and personal fouls.
- Holds NBA play-off record for most seasons played (eighteen).
- Play-off Most Valuable Player, 1971, 1985.

ACKNOWLEDGMENTS

My gratitude to the many whose knowledge, memories, time gener-ously given, and good wishes contributed to the creation of this book: my parents, Cora and Al Alcindor, Malek Abdul-Mansour, Lou Adler, Leonard Armato, Bill Bertka, Michael Cooper, Richard Crystal, Rudy Garcidueñas, Chick Hearn, Farrell Hopkins, Taaj Jaharah, Earvin Johnson, Tania Jolly, Rafee Kamaal, Robert Kerlan, M.D., Mitch Kup-chak, Stu Lantz, Mary Lou Liebich, Linda Lombardo, Steve Lom-bardo, M.D., Dan McCarthy, Brian McIntyre, Mark McNamara, Lourdes Morales, Randy Pfund, Pat Riley, Josh Rosenfeld and his staff, Claire Rothman, Byron Scott, Susan Stratton, Lawrence Tanter, Jerry West, and James Worthy.

My special appreciation to Lorin Pullman and Gary Vitti for assist-ance given over and above the call of duty throughout the season.

Mignon is indebted to all those above and also to Charlotte Sheedy for her guidance from beginning to end; Dennis Danziger for his creative spark and for being there at the writing's start; Esther Newberg for first spotting the project; Ellen Ellison, who said the right words at the right time; Sue Moore for her love; to dear friends and family for their patience and page-listening; Susan Hopkins and Crystal Brian for tape transcriptions and more; the NBA research staff; and to Mitch Chortkoff, Doug Cress, and Don Greenberg for wit and warmth in the press room and on the road from October to June.

We both wish to thank Kenneth Turan, whose assistance down the stretch enabled us to meet our deadline; Amy Edelman, our copy editor, whose refining touch improved every page; and Peter Osnos, our editor, whose tenacity and enthusiasm for this book were instrumental in making it a reality.

MIGNON MCCARTHY is the co-author of Jane Fonda's *Women Coming of Age,* an international best-seller. She was educated at the University of California at San Diego, where she graduated Phi Beta Kappa, and at Stanford University, where she earned an advanced degree in literature. She lives in Santa Monica, California.

38,387 POINTS SCORED, 1,560 GAMES, 20 SEASONS, 19 ALL-STAR APPEARANCES, 6 MVP AWARDS

ALL ON 1 VIDEOCASSETTE

"KAREEM: REFLECTIONS FROM INSIDE" is a career retrospective told by Abdul-Jabbar himself. THIS VIDEO FEATURES:

- Kareem's 3 decades of basketball
- POWER MEMORIAL HIGH SCHOOL
- UCLA
- THE MILWAUKEE BUCKS
- THE LOS ANGELES LAKERS
- Appearances by many of Kareem's teammates, coaches and others.
- The personal side of Kareem which has rarely been revealed.

THE ULTIMATE COLLECTOR'S ITEM FOR ANY BASKETBALL FAN! GET YOUR COPY NOW!

$24⁹⁸